Buying a House in

Spain

Dan Boothby

Distributed in the USA by
The Globe Pequot Press, Guilford, Connecticut

Published by Vacation Work, 9 Park End Street, Oxford
www.vacationwork.co.uk

BUYING A HOUSE IN SPAIN
by Dan Boothby

First edition 2003

ISBN 1-85458-299-2

Publicity by Roger Musker

Cover Design by Miller Craig
& Cocking Design Partnership

Illustrations by Mick Siddens

Typeset by Brendan Cole

Printed and bound in Italy by Legoprint SpA, Trento

Contents

PART I
VIVA ESPAÑA!

PART II
LOCATION, LOCATION...

PART III
THE PURCHASING PROCEDURE

PART IV
WHAT HAPPENS NEXT

PREFACE

According to the Council of Mortgage Lenders (www.cml.org.uk), owners of second and holiday homes travel abroad approximately six times a year and tend to be in their mid-40s to late-50s. However, the profile of second home buyers is getting younger and demand for housing abroad is increasing year on year, with levels of house price inflation reaching record levels. A buoyant property market at home means that many of those who may have only got themselves on to the property ladder in the past five years already have enough equity to consider buying a place abroad. As for the future, the budget flight boom has, as a side effect, increased the number of students at school who have chosen to take Spanish as a language option to the detriment of French, and these students will inevitably want to visit Spain and try out their language skills. Our children are also prospective Spanish property owners.

People from all over the world have bought property in Spain; in addition to the British many property owners have come from Scandinavia and the northern European countries, but there are also a number of North Americans living in Spain. They may have been travelling around Europe, working in the UK, or taken an internship in Spain, fallen in love with the country and its vibrant people and decided to make their home there. Once you've bought a property in Spain you will belong to a truly cosmopolitan set.

It is reckoned that around 50,000 second homes are bought every year by the British. According to research undertaken in 2002 by the market research company, Mori (Market & Opinion Research International), 39% of Britons would emigrate 'if they had the chance'. The Foreign and Commonwealth Office estimates that there are 14.2 million British nationals living abroad – the majority residing in Canada and Australia. Approximately 500,000 live in Spain, the fourth largest number of expats, after South Africa.

One in every eleven UK pensions is now paid to someone living abroad. Soaring property prices at home and worrying announcements by the government and pension companies have led many to seek other ways to invest their savings or to fund their retirement. And of course there is the fine weather that Spain offers; the Costa del Sol has a celebrated 3,000 sun hours a year. Even further north on the Costa Brava there is 2,500 sun hours a year and the average temperature is a pleasant 16° Celcius. By comparison the annual average temperature in the warmest place in the UK – the Scilly Isles, off the coast of Cornwall – has a mean temperature of only 11.5° Celcius.

There are several reasons for the flood of foreigners looking to buy property in the Iberian Peninsula – a good exchange rate on the Euro and the ease and cheapness of air travel has much to do with the deluge, but for decades now people have been looking for ways to escape to an affordable life in the sun. Many have made their dreams a reality: some have hit hard times and wondered why they ever left their homeland, their friends and family, but many more have found that they've never had it so good, sitting on their balcony, listening to the gentle chirrup of the cicadas and gazing out to sea with a glass of Rioja.

Dan Boothby
Mallorca, March 2003

ACKNOWLEDGEMENTS

The author would like to thank Lindy Walsh, J. Stuart Anderson, Stewart & Jeanne Males, Jane Bettany, and Vanessa, Dave & Daisy Roberts for information, hospitality and help during the researching and writing of this book. Thanks also to Canning House, London; Trinity College, Carmarthen; and all at Vacation Work, the Tower and Ffynone.

Special thanks to Mick Siddens for the illustrations of Spanish houses.

Photographs of houses in Camposol and Ciudad Quesada courtesy of Propertunities

Part I

VIVA ESPAÑA!

LIVING IN SPAIN

RESIDENCE & ENTRY

Living in Spain

CHAPTER SUMMARY

- Every year, Spain plays host to a staggering 40 million or more visitors. The annual revenue it earns from tourism is over $30 billion. The tourist trade employs 1.2 million workers and contributes over 11% to the country's GNP.
- An estimated 300,000 Britons have made their homes in Spain and many have set up businesses.
- In winter and summer, expats and short-term residents continue to be a familiar feature of life along the stretch of the Mediterranean coast from the Costa del Sol to the Costa Brava and the Balearic Islands.
- Spain's birth rate is just 1.16 children per woman of childbearing age. This is well below the 2.1 birth rate needed for a generation to replace itself, and is the lowest in the world.
- Spain's most famous wine is sherry, both dry and sweet, and it used to flavour entrées and desserts as well as being served as an aperitif.
- **Languages**. Besides Spanish (Castilian) there are three other distinct languages spoken: Basque, Gallego (Galician) and Catalan.
- **Politics.** Spain was a dictatorship under General Franco until 1975.
  - Spain can best be described as a federalist monarchy having democratically elected parliaments in the autonomous regions, and a monarch, King Juan Carlos as the nation's representative.
- **Education**. More than 70% of young people stay on at school until the age of eighteen, while 40% receive professional training.
  - International schools tend to be regarded as the best alternative by expats considering the long-term

education of their children.
- **Press**. Glossy magazines such as 'Hello!' are known as the *Prensa de Corazón* (Press of the Heart) and are among the most popular magazines in Spain.
- **Health**. Anyone who claims sickness or invalidity benefit in the UK and is moving out to Spain permanently is entitled to continue claiming this benefit once in Spain.
- **Police.** There are three main police forces in Spain: the *Guardia Civil*, the *Policía Nacional* and the Policía Municipal.
- **Names**. In Spain, women do not take the surname of their husband when they marry. Instead, the maiden name of the mother is added to the surname of the couple's offspring.
- **Madrid.** The central site for the capital was chosen for strategic reasons in the seventeenth century.
  - All distances in Spain are measured from the centre of the capital.

INTRODUCTION

Spain has been popular as a holiday destination since the first charter flights of the 1950s opened up the Mediterranean Costas (from north to south: the Costa Brava; the Costa Dorada; the Costa del Azahar; the Costa Blanca; and the Costa del Sol) to foreign visitors. Every year, Spain plays host to a staggering 40 million or more visitors, the numerical equivalent of the indigenous population. The annual revenue it earns from tourism is over $30 billion. The tourist trade employs 1.2 million workers and contributes over 11% to the country's gross national product.

The onset of mass tourism inevitably led on to an expatriate property-buying boom, which began in the 1960s and has been continuing ever since. Places like Jávea and Altea, whose climate has been declared amongst the healthiest in the world by no less a body than the World Health Organisation, represent the extreme of expatriate saturation – at least a quarter of the residents of those towns are estimated to be Brits. Other areas are catching up fast and the Costa del Sol – stretching from Málaga to Gibraltar – has a firmly established reputation as a centre of expat life and Marbella is considered by many to be the most up-market resort on the Costa del Sol and is still popular with the European jet set – it is the Spanish equivalent of the Cóte d'Azur in France.

An estimated 300,000 Britons have made their homes in Spain and many have set up businesses catering for their fellow countrymen and women or have found employment in the tourist industry or with British, American and Spanish firms. Many others take their holidays in time-share accommodation and a current vogue for elderly Britons is to spend the winter months in a Spanish resort and so avoiding the heating bills and gloomy cold weather back home. About 400,000 elderly or retired Britons spend the so-called 'swallow season' in Spain each year. Over 200,000 of them own property there. If you are planning to retire to Spain you won't be alone. An estimated 750,000 Britons have bought retirement homes there with the most popular destination for retirees being Majorca. At 65 years of age you will receive the benefits of a retired residency – free private medical care and tax breaks. If you want to get a forecast of your pension income and state entitlement ask the DSS for a BR19.

There are social as well as economic consequences of this wave of seasonal emigration. Some expatriates complain of isolation and poorer quality hospital treatment and social services than they are used to back home. However, the British Consulate-General in Madrid reports that there are relatively few problems, considering the size of the community. Expats tend to live in harmony with their Spanish neighbours, who have a live-and-let-live attitude and no deep-seated antagonism towards the Brits. UK residents say they prefer the warm weather (the climate of the Spanish *costas* in particular remains the principal attraction for many Britons in Spain) and many move to Spain after enjoying many of their holidays there, or for a change of lifestyle, or simply for the cheap cigarette and alcohol. Spain (along with Portugal and the South of France) is now the European equivalent of the American 'sun-belt', with a clientele of mainly British and Dutch people.

Living in Spain is a breath of fresh air – Stuart Anderson
Nothing is really missed, apart from the closer proximity of friends and family. The best thing about living in Spain is the sense of freedom and the fact that nobody appears the least bit interested in social status – former jobs, the school you attended, the number/kind of cars you own, etc. A breath of fresh air!

Younger residents rave about the Spanish way of life and cite the relaxed social mores as their reason for choosing to live there. Festivals, fiestas and a singular *joie de vivre* are part of the Spanish way of doing things, and many expats quickly rediscover that life isn't only about career, the gym, checking one's investments and keeping up with the Jones's. Cafés, bars and restaurants are plentiful and their menus cheap; food and drink are enjoyed and understood in a country that still retains strong rural and agricultural roots. Outside the cities, traditions still play an important part in local daily life. Everywhere, in towns and villages, the evening starts with a leisurely stroll (the *paseo*) through the main streets, everyone checking out everyone else. Many Spaniards take a siesta; and lunches, even during the working week, are long and languid. In the towns and cities, and along the coast, nightlife begins late and continues into the early hours.

Spain has of late been undergoing a series of radical reforms – both political and economic – bringing it from a dyed-in-the-wool 36-year-old dictatorship, which lagged far behind the rest of Western Europe (with the exception of neighbouring Portugal) to an increasingly liberal and open society where democracy has been firmly established. Spain was classed as a developing nation by the United Nations as recently as 1964; yet today it is the world's ninth industrial power. Nowadays, Spain takes its modernity for granted. Government used to be highly centralised but power has been devolved to the regions, most notably in the Basque Country, Catalonia and the Canary Islands.

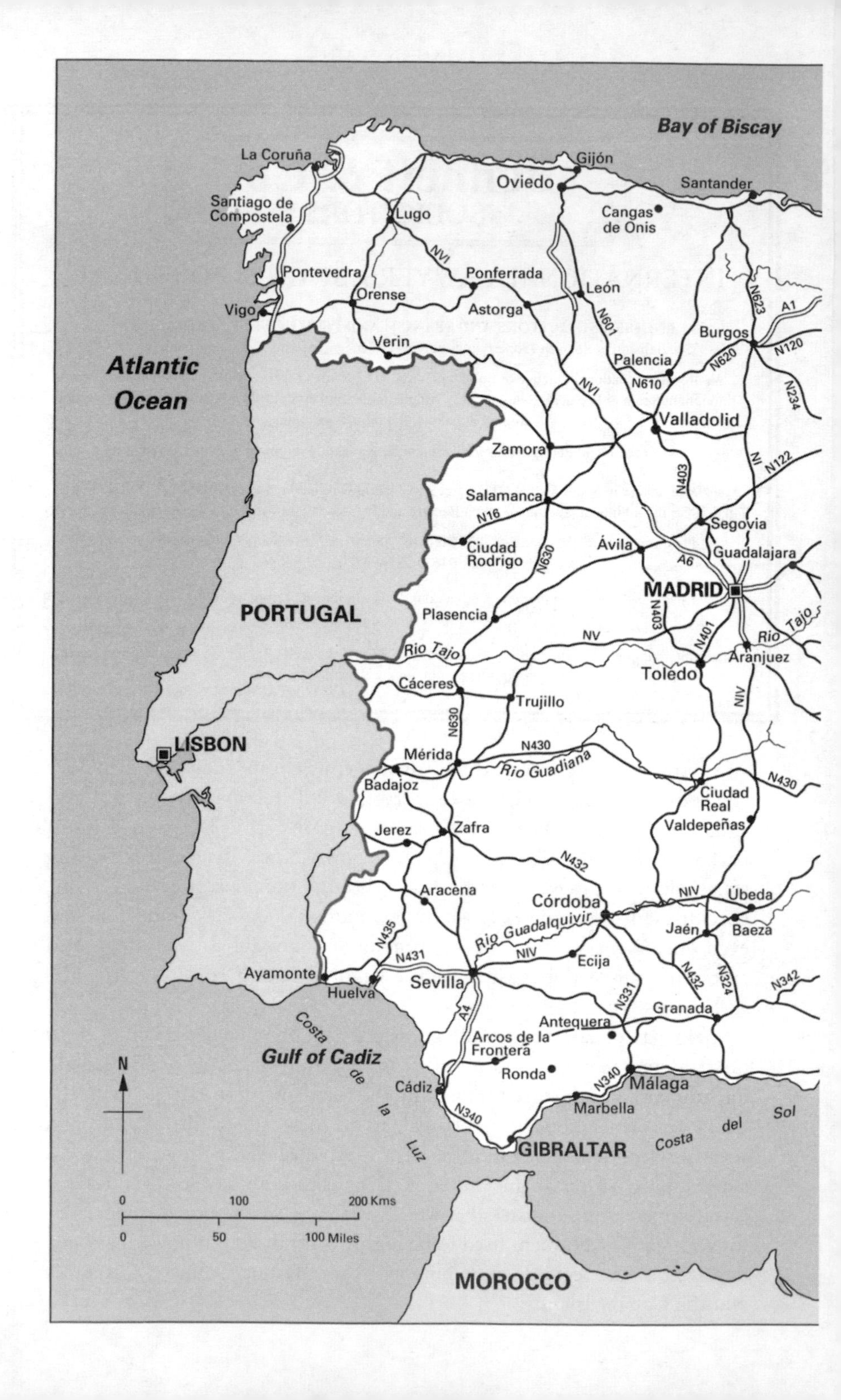

Bay of Biscay
Atlantic Ocean
La Coruña
Gijón
Oviedo
Santander
Santiago de Compostela
Lugo
Cangas de Onis
NVI
Pontevedra
Ponferrada
León
Orense
Astorga
Vigo
N601
N623
A1
Burgos
Verin
N120
Palencia
N620
NVI
N610
N234
Valladolid
Zamora
NI
N122
N403
Salamanca
N16
Segovia
Ciudad Rodrigo
Ávila
Guadalajara
N630
A6
MADRID
PORTUGAL
N403
Plasencia
N401
Rio Tajo
NV
Rio Tajo
Aranjuez
Toledo
Cáceres
Trujillo
NIV
N630
LISBON
N430
Mérida
Rio Guadiana
N430
Badajoz
Ciudad Real
Valdepeñas
Jerez
Zafra
N432
Aracena
NIV
Úbeda
Córdoba
Rio Guadalquivir
Jaén
Baeza
N435
N431
NIV
Ecija
N432
N324
N342
Ayamonte
Sevilla
Huelva
N331
Granada
Costa de la Luz
A4
Antequera
Arcos de la Frontera
Gulf of Cadiz
Ronda
N340
Málaga
Cádiz
Marbella
N340
Costa del Sol
GIBRALTAR
N
0
100
200 Kms
0
50
100 Miles
MOROCCO

Major Towns & Cities of Spain
FRANCE
ANDORRA
San Sebastián
Bilbao
Vitoria
Pamplona
Canfranc
Jaca
Logrono
Uncastillo
Huesca
Rio Ebro
A68
Soria
Zaragoza
Lleida
Montblanc
A7
Barcelona
N330
NII
Alcaniz
Tortosa
Tarragona
Portbou
Figueres
Cadaqués
Girona
Lloret de Mar
Costa Brava
Costa Dorada
Teruel
A7
Cuenca
Castellón de la Plana
NIII
Valencia
Costa del Azahar
Albacete
Gandia
Denia
N322
N301
Costa Blanca
Alicante
Murcia
Lorca
N340
Cartagena
Mojácar
Almeria
Balearic Islands
Menorca
Ciudadela
Mahon
Mallorca
Alcudia
Arta
Palma
Manacor
Ibiza
San Antonio Abad
Ibiza
Fernando
Formentera
Mediterranean Sea
La Palma
Santa Cruz de la Palma
Tenerife
Santa Cruz de Tenerife
Gomera
Hierro
Las Palmas
Gran Canaria
Lanzarote
Arrecife
Puerto del Rosario
Fuerte-Ventura
The Canary Islands

The Spanish people are welcoming and most have rejected the isolationist attitudes of the past. Historically, Spain's history has always been one of the world's great powers, and its present position within the EU (which it joined in 1986) has helped to define its increasingly cosmopolitan outlook. Events such as the 1992 Olympic Games, held in Barcelona, and Expo'92 in Seville, and its contemporary writers, artists, actors and film-makers have brought Spain to international attention. These are some of the cultural reasons that may also prompt Britons and others to consider moving there.

Other recent economic developments such as joining the European Monetary Union, followed by the adoption of the euro as its currency in 2002 and the ongoing programme of privatisation have brought a new wave of workers skilled in areas like finance, consultancy, electronics, information technology and industrial design which have little to do with the service sector and tourism. Spain's economy is booming, inflation is low as is the public sector deficit.

As Spain changes, so the kinds of workers and expatriates who move there are changing. In winter and summer, expats and short-term residents continue to be a familiar feature of life along the stretch of the Mediterranean coast from the Costa del Sol to the Costa Brava and the Balearic Islands (Mallorca, Menorca and Ibiza). Elsewhere, Madrid boasts a large Spanish-speaking expat population of professionals, as do Barcelona and, to a lesser extent, Valencia and Seville.

Pros and Cons of Moving to Spain

One distinct advantage of moving to Spain is that over the last few decades the procedures involved in buying and selling property have become well documented, with many agencies in the UK and elsewhere specialising in removals and conveyancing. Nowadays it can be easy for the prospective property buyer to avoid the pitfalls simply by consulting one of the reputable relocation agencies or specialists. There are a number of books covering living and working in Spain besides this one and there are websites that can give you an outline of the procedures involved in buying property in Spain. However, books and websites are not a substitute for professional advice. Laws and procedures can change fairly frequently in Spain as everywhere else in the world and only a specialist lawyer will be able to advise you of how things are done at the exact time when you are buying your property. According to the Honorary British Vice-Consul in Benidorm, the most common problems cited by prospective expats in Spain are associated with 'the language barrier and property purchases'. A useful and practical book is *Long Stays in Spain* by Peter Davey (published by David & Charles in the UK, and in the United States by Hippocrene Books Inc), and there are a number of others dealing with living, working and buying property in Spain.

If you are considering moving to Spain permanently and looking to find employment there things are pretty good for the EU citizen. The completion of the transitional period of EU membership and the removal of barriers to employment across the EU (including self-employment) mean that visitors from Britain and other EU states do not need a work permit, although a residence card (*tarjeta de residencia*) will still be required. North Americans considering the move will have to satisfy a wide range of criteria, which means in practice that getting a job will be much more difficult for them. There are still many rules and regulations that EU citizens should be aware of – everything from equivalence of qualifications and regulation regarding the setting up of a business, to tax laws and other requirements which are different to those at home.

Contrary to popular belief there are no particular income tax advantages in moving to Spain, as the tax rates are roughly comparable; the personal income tax threshold is around the UK level (about €7,800); and the 48% top tax rate is significantly higher than that in Britain or the USA.

Those contemplating buying a place on the Spanish coast will find that the sun shines reliably year round, while prospective residents of Madrid will discover that winters there can be much colder than in the UK due to the continental climate. If you are looking to buy in the south of Spain, being geographically nearer to the African continent has one major disadvantage: red dust and sand sucked up from the Sahara Desert by seasonal winds is often dumped along the coastline and hills of southern Spain – a recurring, rather irritating but not too serious phenomenon for several weeks or months during the winter. Expats with gardens may grow nostalgic for the verdant lawns and flowerbeds they have left behind as the battle to keep lawns green, and flowers and vegetables healthy, in the harsher climate is a tough one that is often lost.

Culturally, every country has its advantages and disadvantages and Spain is no exception to this rule. The presence of so many expats from the colder northern European countries of Britain, Holland, Germany and the countries of Scandinavia in Spain may be a good thing or otherwise according to your point of view. It may seem superficially easier to adapt to a new way of life surrounded by English-speaking neighbours; but rather more difficult when you come into contact with the wider Spanish community. Many Britons choose to continue living a more or less familiar

(British) way of life but the true enjoyment of living in another country comes from discovering the local people, their culture, the way they live and in truly adapting to your new environment. This assimilation into a new culture can only really be done by living outside an admittedly cosy coterie of English-speaking friends. You may choose purposefully to find a place to live away from the *costas* and the centres of expat existence, where foreigners are scarcer and a more undiluted Spain still exists. Lastly, there is still an association in many Spanish minds of the English with hooligans and this can lead to something of a cultural apartheid – this way of things is most evident on the *costas* where the two-week all-night lager binges take place, reinforcing the stereotype. The following is a summary of the main pros and cons of living in Spain:

PROS & CONS

PROS

- Property prices are generally lower than in the UK or USA except in the most popular areas, e.g. the Costa del Sol.
- There are well-established procedures for buying and selling property.
- Residence and work procedures are relatively straightforward for EU citizens.
- Spain is an incredibly diverse country with a fascinating history and a vibrant culture.
- The large expat population means good employment opportunities and prospects for qualified staff to cater for their needs, e.g. in medicine, hospitality, law, property, finance etc.
- Major cities and the most popular resorts aside, you can still live relatively cheaply in Spain (as many retired Britons and 'part-time' residents can testify).
- Communications are good and air travel is inexpensive.
- The country is welcoming to foreign visitors and residents.
- The economy is still booming and prospects for the future are good.

CONS

- Some property may not be up to the standard that you are used to at home.
- Property prices are high in the major cities and along the more popular coastlines.
- Older residents may find it difficult to adapt to a new way of

life.

- Social services and utilities may not be up to British or US standards.
- There is strong competition for jobs at the unskilled level and it may be difficult to find long-term work outside tourism.
- Crime rates are quite high on the *costas* and in some of the major cities such as Barcelona, Seville and Madrid.
- Language can be a barrier when dealing with officialdom and looking for, and finding, work.
- Tax rates at the top level are high.

POLITICAL AND ECONOMIC STRUCTURE

History

The key to Spain's recent political development lies in its rich and varied history. For those who are interested in finding out more *A Horizon Concise History of Spain* by Melveena McKendrick (published by Cassell) outlines the main events of Spain's past, from early times until just before Franco's demise in the early 70s. There are many books available on every aspect of Spanish culture and history and anyone seriously considering the possibility of buying either a permanent or a second home in Spain would do well to *gen up* on Spain. The *Spanish Tourist Office's* brochure line (☎ 09063 640 630) provides some excellent brochures on the different regions and history of Spain and also publishes an information sheet, *Books about Spain*, which includes general and regional guides, city guides and books on specialist subjects and the Spanish language.

Spain's past (and present) has been shaped by many factors including its imperialist expansion during the sixteenth and seventeenth centuries and the fascist dictatorship of General Francisco Franco Bahamonde (1892-1975). Further back in history, the five hundred years' rule of southern Spain from AD 718 by the Moors left it with a legacy of Islamic art and architecture in such cities as Granada, Córdoba and Seville unique in Western Europe and which influenced Spanish traditions in music and literature.

It took the Christians thirty-six years to complete a military reconquest of Spain in the thirteenth century (although the Moors retained their stronghold of Granada until the fifteenth century). Outside of the Iberian peninsula there was a period of colonial expansion: the colonising of vast territories in Latin America and Asia, while in the more recent past, a bitterly fought Civil War and the right-wing military dictatorship of General Franco coloured the Spanish experience of the twentieth century.

Franco's death in 1975 ended a period of stagnation and oppression, although for some Franco embodied a 'restored' and united Spain. It is only as recently as 1996, with the election of the government of José María Aznar, that Spain can be said to have entered a period of true democracy, with both the elected government and the main opposition party having experience of democratic rule.

Economy

Spain was exhausted by the Civil War of 1936-39 – a conflict that sprang from a matter of an internal military rebellion against the elected government turning into an international affair. Volunteers including writers such as George Orwell and Laurie Lee, and of course Ernest Hemingway, travelled to Spain from all over the world to help fight against the fascists. Half a million lives and a brutal war later the army seized power and Spain's economy was in a state of ruin worse than that of her neighbours in the aftermath of the Second World War six years later.

The post-war era was a lean one for all the European nations who struggled to rebuild their devastated economies, but the main protagonists of World War II at least benefited from financial aid under the Marshall Plan. Spain had remained neutral and even provided active aid to the Axis Powers in return for their support for Franco's dictatorship. For these reasons, Spain was penalised by a UN economic blockade that lasted until 1950. The extreme hardships of the post-war years came to be known as *los años de hambre* ('the years of hunger'), when cats and dogs disappeared from the streets and it was said that only handouts from Perón's Argentina kept the country from total starvation. Economic isolation combined with disastrous economic management had a devastating effect on living standards in Spain throughout the fifties. A Stabilisation Plan then brought some benefits and Spain finally began to creep back into the twentieth century in the 1960s.

In the latter years of Franco's dictatorship there were some signs of economic progress, particularly between 1961 and 1973 – the so-called *años de desarrollo* (or 'years of development') when the economy was growing at the rate of 7% annually – second only to that of Japan. International companies including Chrysler, John Deere and Ciba-Geigy set up operations in Spain and tourism became a huge earner for the country. An estimated 1,700,000 Spaniards left their homes to work abroad and their earnings, sent back to swell their bank accounts at home, contributed to their country's economic expansion (a situation paralleled today in the third world and some of the transition economies of Eastern Europe).

Increased prosperity also had an effect on the movement of population within Spain. Traditionally, there had always been migrant workers from the poorer regions like Andalucía moving around the country following the harvests. However, with economic expansion, the disparity in living standards between the cities and rural areas caused many craftsmen and artisans to seek their fortunes in the cities. The resulting depopulation of the countryside, in particular of the *meseta* (central Spain), caused an extreme imbalance in Spain – between the wealth and high population of the cities and the desolation and poverty of the countryside.

The Current Situation. By 1975, five of the nineteen provinces (Madrid, Barcelona, Valencia, Biscay, and Oviedo) were producing nearly half the country's industrial output; concentrating the wealth of the country in the North and East. Today, the position is much the same, except that Navarre (also in the North) has taken over from Oviedo as a centre of industrial development. Owing to the more recent liberalisation of the Spanish economy (compared with other Western European nations) there is still a relatively uncompetitive industrial sector and the workings of business continue to be hampered by labour laws left over from Franco's era. Old-fashioned industries such as the northern coalmines seem not only unviable but also permanently inviolable, even under a right-wing administration that has privatised many other companies. The tradition of political patronage is also a factor that continues to hamper economic growth and development.

Today, British companies such as BP, Cadbury Schweppes, CGNU, ICI, Lloyds TSB Bank, Plessey and Unilever all have operations in Spain, and there is a British presence across a wide area of industries and business activities. Few Spanish companies are well known outside Spain; perhaps Seat (the Spanish branch of Fiat) was the nearest thing to an internationally owned company, but it was bought by Volkswagen (although the Seat *marque* has been retained). Spain's economic growth continued at 5% annually up to 1990 but then varied during the next decade between 2% and 5% and is currently about 2.5%. It is likely to grow again and has potential to be one of the fastest growing economies in Europe.

Government

During the years of his dictatorship, Franco held the disparate elements of Spanish politics together through a coalition, and enforced rigid centralised government. As well as being a fascist Franco was also a monarchist, and after making himself head of state with the power to appoint his successor he began to groom Prince Juan Carlos to take over the reins of power after his own death. In spite of this grooming by Franco, it remained a generally held belief that the young Juan Carlos would not be a capable figurehead and that the political future of Spain post-Franco would be an uncertain one.

It also became obvious during the last months of the dictatorship that certain areas of Spain where the populace had their own language and culture and who had experienced a measure of autonomy under the Republic (such as the Basques, Catalans and Galicians) were looking to regain their autonomy from Spain. Additionally, there was a widespread fear that the kind of monarchy envisaged by Franco was unlikely to be any more liberal than his dictatorship. Regions which had formerly not been looking to gain self-rule also became wary of what the future held; and the prospect of a loose federation of states (derived in part from the pattern of the old mediaeval kingdoms) caused a mounting *fiebre autonómican* (autonomy fever) throughout Spain.

After Franco's death in 1975, King Juan Carlos transferred power to a democratically elected parliament. In consequence Spain has become what can best be described as a federal-monarchy, which the Spaniards call an *estado de las autonomías*. The king pays taxes in keeping with his constitutional role and has powers strictly limited to the promulgation of laws and decrees, the calling of elections and referenda, and the appointment of prime ministers and ministers. However, it is said that he wields considerable personal influence on politics, and he is also the Commander-in-Chief of the armed forces.

The Constitution. In 1978, the Spanish constitution was drawn up, largely at the behest of King Juan Carlos. The most important task of the constitution was to allow the devolution of power to the regions, which entitled them to have their own governments, parliaments, regional assemblies and supreme legal authorities. This radical transition to a democratic and devolved system of government, carried out more slowly in some regions than others, formed the present-day seventeen Autonomous Communities of Spain, each having their own flag, capital city and president. Catalonia, the Basque Country, Galicia and Andalucía were the first of the regions to become Autonomous Communities. The central parliament, or *Cortes*, retains overall control of such matters as foreign policy and defence. Spain is a mosaic of parliaments and regional identities, and local politics still arouses far more of an interest from Spaniards than the machinations of politicians at a national level.

Political History. The first Prime Minister of Spain, Carlos Arias Navarro – a political appointee chosen by Franco – lasted in office barely six months. He was replaced by Adolfo Suárez, the man chosen by King Juan Carlos as the best person to transform Spain from a dictatorship to a democracy. Suárez was responsible for many political reforms including the creation of a two-tier parliament, (the *Cortes*), comprising of a lower house, an upper house, the Congress and the Senate.

During this early period in Spain's democratisation a plethora of political parties were formed to contest the 1979 elections. Suárez resigned shortly after the elections for a variety of reasons arising mainly from the government's proposed liberalisation of various laws. He was honoured with a dukedom by King Juan Carlos in recognition of his achievements in setting up the new democracy.

In 1981, between the dissolution of the Suárez government and the creation of the next, reactionary elements of the army, alarmed by what they saw as political turmoil and the end of Spanish unity, attempted a coup d'état. Brandishing a pistol, Antonio Tejero Molina, a lieutenant-colonel in the Civil Guard, led his men into the lower house of Parliament and proceeded to hold the entire Congress hostage for twenty-four hours. However, when King Juan Carlos, who still commanded the loyalty of the monarchist army, announced that the attempted coup did not have his backing, Tejero, who was isolated from the more senior officers who had orchestrated the coup attempt, became demoralised and surrendered to the police.

A long period of rule by the 'moderate' socialist party, the PSOE (*Partido Socialista Obrero Español*) followed. Its leader Felipe González, originally a lawyer from Seville, presided over the renewal of the Spanish economy and society and a slow process of privatisation and economic reform. It brought riches to some, but at the cost of high unemployment, and discontent among federalists as well as among nationalists in Catalonia and the Basque Country who sought full independence.

The election of 1996 saw in a government led by the Popular Party of José María Aznar. General elections are held every four years and there are plans afoot for reform of Spain's complex and decentralised constitution. In March 2000, José María Aznar's Popular Party was re-elected and became the first party of the right to gain an absolute majority in parliament since democracy was restored in 1977.

Political Parties

The history of Spanish politics has a Byzantine complexity. During the thirties, the main elements of the fascist régime headed by Franco included his own *Falange* (fascist) party, the church and the monarchists fused into an unusual coalition. The many political parties within these elements were known collectively as the *Falange Española Tradicionalista y de las Juntas de Ofensiva Nacional-Sindicalista*, or *FET de las JONS*, and also known as the *Movimiento Nacional.*

The *Falange* progressively became the most dominant element of the movement and the coalition itself was the only legal political entity allowed under the dictatorship. Illegal opposition parties without political power could only seek influence through street demonstrations, which were invariably banned or broken up by the police. However, barely a year after Franco's death political parties were legalised – the Socialists in February 1977, the Communists in April 1977. Along with these reforms came the legalisation of trade unions and the right to strike. The *Movimiento* was abolished and the new constitution was drawn up in 1978 through all-party consultation.

The new political parties organised themselves for the 1979 election which was won by Suárez and his coalition the UCD (*Unión de Centro Democrática*). The UCD combined vestiges of Francoism with elements of liberalism and in the election of 1982 the UCD not only lost, but did so spectacularly – its 168 deputies being reduced to 13 and its 119 senators to four. The ascendant party was the PSOE (*Partido Socialista Obrero Español*) led by Felipe González, which gave the socialists an overall majority in parliament for the first time. The PSOE has its origins in the Spanish Socialist Workers' Party, started in 1879 and the oldest political party in Spain, and which held the balance of power from 1982 until 1996.

The current government party is the centre-right PP (*Partido Popular*), formerly known as the *Alianza Popular*, which has a mandate for privatisation and some economic and constitutional reforms. Television viewers in Spain can get an insight into some of the many political shenanigans from a programme called *Noticias de Guiñol* – the Spanish equivalent of the late lamented British TV series *Spitting Image* – which includes a puppet of Prime Minister Aznar whose catchphrase *España va bien* ironically echoes the mood of the country. To paraphrase a former British Prime Minister, Spain has never had it so good.

GEOGRAPHICAL INFORMATION

Mainland and Offshore Spain

Spain occupies 85% of the great landmass that forms the south-western extremity of Europe, the Iberian Peninsula, covering a total of 194,885 square miles/504,750 sq. km. Including the Balearic and Canary Islands, Spain is the third-largest European nation after Ukraine and France, and in its average altitude second only to Switzerland. The Pyrenees form a natural barrier between Spain and France to the northeast while Portugal lies to the west. The province of Galicia in the northwest of the country has an Atlantic coast, and northern Spain is demarcated by the Bay of Biscay. The south and east of the country has Mediterranean frontage, and a mere ten miles (16 km) of sea (known as the Strait of Gibraltar) separates Spain from Africa where Spain holds sovereignty over the two tiny enclaves of Melilla and Ceuta in Morocco. The Balearics, which comprise the four main islands of Mallorca, Ibiza, Menorca and Formentera, lie off Spain's northeast coast and occupy 1,936 sq. miles/5,014 sq. km. The Canary Islands, of which seven are inhabited, are situated about sixty miles (97 km) off the west coast of North Africa and occupy 2,808 square miles/7,273 sq. km. The population of the Canary Islands is Spanish and the variety of climate and landscape of each island, as well as the long sandy beaches, have made islands like Tenerife and Gran Canaria familiar to tourists from all over Europe.

THE NINETEEN AUTONOMOUS REGIONS OF SPAIN AND THEIR PROVINCES

ANDALUCÍA – Almería, Cádiz, Córdoba, Granada, Huelva, Jaén, Málaga and Sevilla (Seville)
ARAGÓN – Huesca, Zaragoza (Saragossa), Teruel
ASTURIAS – Oviedo
CANTABRIA – Santander
CASTILLA-LA MANCHA – Albacete, Cuenca, Ciudad Real, Guadalajara, Toledo
CASTILLA Y LÉON – Avila, Burgos, León, Palencia, Salamanca, Segovia, Soria, Valladolid, Zamora
CATALONIA (CATALUÑA) – Barcelona, Girona, Lléida (Lerida), Tarragona
COMUNIDAD DE MADRID – Madrid
EXTREMADURA – Badajoz, Cáceres
GALICIA – A Coruña, Lugo, Orense, Pontevedra
ISLAS BALEARES (BALEARIC ISLANDS) – Palma
ISLAS CANARIAS (CANARY ISLANDS) – Las Palmas de Gran Canaria, Santa Cruz de Tenerife
LA RIOJA – Logroño
MURCIA – Murcia
NAVARRA (NAVARRE) – Pamplona
PAIS VASCO (BASQUE COUNTRY) – Bilbao, Donostia-San Sebastian, Vizcaya-Gasteiz
VALENCIA – Alicante, Castellon, Valencia
CEUTA
MELILLA

Population

While the populations of several countries of the European Union – notably Italy, France and Germany – have been falling over the decades, the population of Spain was slowly increasing up until 1998. More recently, however, the Spanish birth rate has fallen dramatically as Spanish women work longer hours, face mounting childcare costs and so decide to delay having children until after their 30th birthday. Spain's birth rate is now reported to be so low that some estimate that on present trends the population could fall by nearly ten million over the next 50 years. From being a nation synonymous with large families, and despite the Catholic Church's hostility to contraception, Spain has seen its birth rate fall to just 1.16 children per woman of childbearing age. This is well below the 2.1 birth rate needed for a generation to replace itself, and is the lowest in the world.

The current population of Spain is around 40 million with an average density of 77 inhabitants per square kilometre. However, there is wide disparity in the population density – the Basque country and Madrid province together comprise only 3.02% of the total area of Spain, yet around 16% of the population live in these regions. If you put together the provinces of Extremadura, Castile/La Mancha, Castile/León, Aragon and Navarre which, put together, represent over half of the Spanish land mass, their total populations would still not exceed the combined population of the Basque Country and Madrid. This population imbalance and the wide variations in prosperity between the regions results from decades of internal and external migrations from rural to industrialised areas. The largest conurbations are Madrid, Barcelona, Bilbao and Valencia.

Climatic Zones

Spain is a country of climatic extremes. In the north-west of the country (Galicia) the climate is as wet and the landscape as correspondingly verdant as parts of Wales or Ireland while in the south much of the province of Almería is so arid that westerns have been filmed in the scrub there. The nearly sub-tropical climate of Almería means it has become a centre for market gardening (especially tomato growing) and there are areas where vast polytunnels can be seen glinting under the ever present sun. Another sunny area not yet totally spoiled by tourism is the Costa de la Luz (Coast of Light), which runs from Huelva near the Portuguese border to Cape Trafalgar overlooking the Strait of Gibraltar.

The town of Seville in Andalucía has the highest temperatures in Spain and regularly reaches 34°C/94°F between July and September. By contrast, Santander, in Cantabria in the north of Spain, has a climate similar to that of England. The vast area of central Spain known as the *meseta* (tableland), though not a precise geographical area, embraces the Castiles La Mancha and León, Extremadura, and the extreme limits of Navarre and Aragon. The inhabitants of the *meseta* are baked by the sun in summer and endure freezing temperatures in winter. The capital Madrid, located slap bang in the centre of Spain, has the lowest winter temperatures in the country and those looking to buy property there should be prepared for the colder conditions that prevail due to the altitude of the city.

Along the Mediterranean coast the climate is far less variable than in the *meseta*, but the *costas* to the northeast of the country may be subject to cold winds, which in the winter bring snow to the Pyrenees and the *meseta*. The mountainous sierra ranges of the Mediterranean hinterland protect the *costas* to some extent from extremes of climate and funnel warm air to them during the summer.

The offshore provinces of Spain – the Balearics and the Canaries – have their own weather patterns. The Balearic Islands usually have warm comfortable summers, tempestuous autumns and colder winters, while the Canaries, situated off the coast of Africa, are in fact nearer to the equator than the Bahamas and their winter climate is correspondingly warm and welcoming to those in search of winter sun. In spite of the relatively long flying time from the UK (around five hours) the popularity of the Canaries as a place to live, especially Gran Canaria, Lanzarote and Tenerife, is continually growing.

AVERAGE MAXIMUM TEMPERATURES

Area	Jan	Apr	Aug	Nov
Cádiz	15°C	21°C	30°C	20°C
Málaga	17°C	21°C	30°C	20°C
Sevilla	15°C	23°C	36°C	20°C
Murcia	12°C	19°C	29°C	20°C
Alicante	16°C	22°C	32°C	21°C
Valencia	15°C	20°C	29°C	19°C
Barcelona	13°C	18°C	28°C	16°C
Santander	12°C	15°C	22°C	15°C
Pontevendra	14°C	18°C	26°C	16°C
Madrid	9°C	18°C	30°C	13°C
Mallorca	14°C	19°C	29°C	18°C
Gran Canaria	21°C	23°C	31°C	24°C

CULTURE SHOCK

Everyone who moves to another country will experience, to a greater or lesser extent, a phenomenon known to psychologists as culture shock. Even moving from England to Wales, or from Texas to California will bring on some form of culture shock, and it is as well to be aware of this and to be prepared for its effects – ranging from elation to disappointment depending on the individual, the environment and the experiences he or she has. You should understand that living abroad has its highs and lows and that such changes are entirely to be expected.

There are several stages in the process of acclimatisation which you can expect to experience, beginning with a 'honeymoon stage' when, in a state of general excitement, you are prepared to accept and enthuse about every aspect of your new environment. The next stage in the process will, however, strike no matter how euphoric your initial impressions of the new country or experience are. Be prepared for a period of crisis and disintegration as you become more aware of differences in values and behaviour. At this time you may experience feelings of intense isolation. Next follows a period of readjustment or reintegration, in which you look for a return to the values and beliefs of your own, native, culture, and you may even reject the new culture, preferring to keep company with those with a similar background to your own – American expats start finding things in common with their British colleagues and so on. You may cling to stereotypes about your own country that you find reassuring and your own prejudices about the country you find yourself in may be reinforced. Nonetheless, at this stage you will begin to find your own space in a new and unfamiliar world and with time and growing self-esteem you will move towards a state of 'autonomy'. From this position, you will find yourself enjoying the positive aspects of the new culture as well as being prepared to forgive the negative ones. The more self-confident and well travelled an individual is, the easier the transition is to living in a new country. Others less flexible or accommodating are likely to eventually return home or move to another country, where the whole cycle will start all over again.

Like any mild disorder, culture shock can be combated with some simple coping strategies. Awareness of the symptoms – which can include physical and psychological effects ranging from headaches and tiredness to sleep problems and irritability – helps, as does good preparation. Prior contact with local people and a good (theoretical) knowledge of the local way of life are immensely useful. It is a good idea to avoid mixing only with expats and other foreigners, and you should try to reduce stress during the crisis stage by keeping fit and healthy. Try keeping a journal, or seeing if you can change or influence those aspects of the new way of life that you find you dislike. Finally, should you decide to return home, be aware that some of the symptoms of culture shock can be repeated in reverse as you reintegrate back into your native environment.

GETTING THERE

By Air

These days getting out to Spain and back is not a problem at all. The massive demand for air travel by the hundreds of thousands of travellers to Spain (and elsewhere) each year has created a boom-time for airlines offering cheap no frills tickets. This stampede of air travellers, lured by the cheap flights, cheap property and guaranteed sun, has put a grave strain on airports, and new runways and airports will need to be built and existing airports extended. In 2001, according to government figures, approximately 10% of the population of the UK flew at least three times a year, with three percent taking more than six flights a year. Trips taken solely for leisure purposes now account for 76 percent of all air travel, and those with second homes abroad are now overtaking the business traveller in number of flights being taken per year.

Almost a third of the millions of international passengers who visit Spain each year travel by air; and of these more than 70% arrive by charter flights. To some destinations like the Canary and Balearic Islands a charter flight may be the only suitable option. The UK and Spain are the only two countries in the world to record such a high percentage of international charter flights; and the relatively cheap tickets are one reason why many Britons choose to live there. There are also low-cost scheduled services to both major cities like Madrid and Barcelona and smaller airports, a trend which looks like continuing with the proliferation of budget airlines following the deregulation of air travel within the EU.

A huge investment plan for Spanish airports has resulted in many improvements and in particular those at Seville and Barcelona airports (a spin-off from the World Exposition and the Olympic Games which were held in those cities). Madrid's Barajos Airport is the centre of domestic traffic (airport information ☎ 913 058 343/4/5/6) and Barcelona is becoming increasingly important (airport ☎ 934 785 032). A regular hourly shuttle service – from 7am to 11pm in Madrid, from 6.45am in Barcelona – operates between these two cities which transports over two million passengers each year. There are also frequent connections between all the main cities in Spain, including flights between Barcelona, Madrid and the Balearic and Canary Islands which, after the shuttle service, are the most frequently used.

It is now possible for those who are self employed to commute between homes in Spain and Britain. It is not unknown for a person with business interests in the UK, but their heart (and home) in Spain, to fly into Luton airport on a Sunday evening and return home to Barcelona on the Friday afternoon. Shopping around for the cheapest fares online, and travelling only with hand luggage (to cut down on customs and the dreaded baggage carousel) makes such a lifestyle a real, and, it has to be said, attractive possibility. By booking flights well in advance the cost of a return flight between the Spain and the UK can be cheaper than a rail ticket from London to Manchester. If such an option sounds attractive you will need to think very carefully about where you locate your business, and find a home in Spain that is close to one of the main airports (where flights are frequent all year round) and main lines of communication. Remember that not all areas of Spain are well connected by either air or land and prices for travel services, and travel to the more obscure areas will be more expensive than in somewhere such as the Costa del Sol. Scanning the travel pages of newspapers like *The Guardian* and *The Independent* as well as the free London magazine *TNT* or your local press is a good way of keeping in touch with the best flight deals, including the many new budget airlines offering amazingly cheap flights to Spain.

The main budget airlines offering flights between Spain and the UK mostly fly from the newer UK airports. There are nine airlines flying from the UK to Spain and it will always pay to shop around as prices fluctuate enormously. A search on the Internet through a company such as E-Bookers (www.ebookers.com) or www.cheapflights.co.uk will throw up all kinds of flight times, prices and routes. A standard fare on one of these budget flights, if booked in advance can be as little as €100 one way. Many of the low cost airlines fly regularly to some of the less frequented destinations in Spain – for example *Ryanair* flies to Jerez and Girona, as well as daily to Murcia airport serving the Costa de la Luz, the Costa Brava, and Costa Calida/Costa Blanca respectively. Prices will often change daily, and it is generally cheaper to fly mid-week (and at unsociable hours) that at weekends. Another useful repository of cheap and last minute flights is to be found on television's Ceefax and Teletext pages, which will often throw up a host of possibilities. Travel agents tend to resent searching through their computer systems to find 'bargains' and you will be better off searching yourself through the Internet and Ceefax. Useful websites that search for the cheapest flights available at any time are www.SkyScanner.net, www.Aerfares.net and www.easyValue.com.

If you are flying to Spain from the USA or Canada you are likely to arrive in Madrid, with perhaps a connection on to Barcelona. Alternatively you will be routed via London. The cheapest option is always to fly via the transport hubs of the world i.e. New York, London, Amsterdam, Frankfurt and then pick up a cheaper flight once you have arrived in Europe.

Main airports and areas served

Madrid: Madrid's Barajas airport acts as a hub for all internal flights within Spain and will be where the transatlantic, intercontinental flights will arrive. There are also services to European, African and Asian destinations.

Barcelona: Barcelona also sees some intercontinental long-haul flights and serves Catalonia, the Costa Brava and the Costa Dorada.

Málaga: Málaga airport is a major airport serving Andalucía as a whole and the Costa del Sol in particular.

Jerez de la Frontera: Close to Cádiz, this small airport serves the Costa de la Luz and parts of Andalucía west of Gibraltar.

Gibraltar: Serves the Costa del Sol, with onward flights and ferries to North Africa.

Almería: Serves the Costa de Almería, the eastern Costa del Sol and Mojácar.

Alicante: Serves the Costa Blanca.

Murcia (San Javier): Close to the Costa Calida, and Costa Blanca South.

Valencia: Serves the Costa Blanca North and the Costa del Azahar.

Girona: Girona airport is a small airport a short distance from the French border. It serves the Costa Brava, the Pyrenees, Catalonia and at a push Andorra.

Reus: A small airport south of Barcelona near Tarragona serves the Costa Dorada.

The Balearic Islands: There are airports in Ibiza, Menorca and Palma de Mallorca.

The Canary Islands: There are airports at Santa Cruz de Tenerife, Las Palmas de Gran Canaria, Lanzarote and Fuerteventura.

In addition there are other small airports such as Santiago de Compostela (serving Galicia), Bilboa (serving Cantabria and the Basque Country). These and others are mainly connected by internal flights only.

Below is a chart of Spain's major airports and the airlines that serve them. Please note that airline services can and do change frequently, and so it would pay to check all the carriers listed when planning a journey in case services have been added or suspended. Indeed, the carriers themselves can change: as this book prepared for press Ryanair bought up the leading budget airline Buzz. It is being rumoured that British Airways would like to become more closely involved with the Spanish national carrier Iberia in which it already has a 10% stake, but current legislation would forbid this.

MAIN AIRPORTS AND THE AIRLINES THAT SERVE THEM

	1 AIR EUROPE	2 BMIBABY	3 BRITISH AIRWAYS	4 EASYJET	5 IBERIA	6 MONARCH SCHEDULED	7 MYTRAVELLITE	8 RYANAIR
ALICANTE		●	●	●	●	●	●	
ALMERÍA						●		
BARCELONA		●	●	●	●		●	
BILBAO			●	●	●			
GIRONA								●
IBIZA		●		●				
LA CORUNA					●			
MADRID	●	●	●	●	●			
MÁLAGA		●	●	●	●	●	●	
MURCIA		●						
PALMA DE MALLORCA	●	●	●	●		●	●	
SANTIAGO					●			
SEVILLA			●		●			
TENERIFE		●	●			●		
VALENCIA		●	●		●			
ZARAGOZA					●			

The Airlines

Air Europe: flies from Gatwick. ☎0870-2401501; flight details from www.air-europa.co.uk

BmiBaby: flies from East Midlands and Cardiff. ☎0870-264-2229; flight details from www.flybmi.com.

British Airways: flies from Birmingham, Heathrow, Gatwick, Manchester and Stansted. ☎ 08457-733 377; flight details from www.britishairways.com

easyJet: flies from Luton, East Midlands, Bristol Gatwick and Liverpool. ☎ 08706-000 000; flight details from www.easyjet.com.

Iberia: flies from Heathrow, Gatwick and Manchester. ☎ 08456-012854; flight details from www.iberiaairlines.co.uk

Monarch Scheduled: flies from Birmingham, Gatwick, Luton and Manchester. ☎ 08700-405040; www.flymonarch.com

MyTravelLite: flies from Birmingham. ☎ 08701-564 564; www.mytravellite.com

Ryanair: flies from London Stansted. ☎ 0871-246 0000; www.ryanair.co.uk.

By Sea

Depending on your budget regarding time and money, travelling by sea to Spain is possible, but tickets aren't cheap and travel time is fairly long. There are ferries running between Portsmouth and Bilboa twice a week, which take about 30 hours one way. Contact P&O European Ferries (www.poportsmouth.com). Ferries operated by Brittany Ferries (www.britannyferries.co.uk) run between Plymouth and Santander twice weekly and take about 24 hours. Ferries connect Morocco with Algeciras, Almería, Málaga, Tarifa and Gibraltar. A car ferry also serves Tenerife and Gran Canaria, leaving Cádiz once a week. The trip takes about 40 hours.

The Balearic Islands can be reached, as well as by air, by ferry services operated mainly by Transmediterranea (www.transmediterranea.es) from Barcelona, Valencia, Denia and Vilanova i la Geltru near Sitges.

By Land

Obviously having your own car while in Spain is very useful and something that many will want to consider. Once across the Channel the fast roads in France can get you to the Spanish border in around 20 hours, but realistically you should reckon on a couple of days' travel overland to reach southern Spain. Remember that if you stick to the motorways in France and Spain you will have to pay a hefty amount in tolls. It is better, therefore, to stick to the main trunk roads and take your time, take in the scenery and acclimatise yourself to the life of 'mañana' waiting ahead of you.

There are a number of cross channel ferries to consider as well as the Channel Tunnel, though the time and money saved by taking, say, a ferry from Portsmouth to St. Malo rather than from Dover to Calais is debatable. Getting into a port further south in France will cut out the Paris traffic but you will have to head through the countryside for a time before picking up the main arterial motorways. All ferry services, and the Eurotunnel, alter their prices depending on the season, the time of travel, the number of passengers, the size of vehicle, etc, etc. Some of the operators offer frequent-user discount schemes and as with the airlines it is worth shopping around to see what service best suits your particular needs.

Spain's rail network is improving year on year and there are now express high-speed Talgo200 services from Madrid to Málaga (and onwards to Fuengirola and Torremolinos); Madrid to Cádiz, Jerez de la Frontera, Huelva and Algeciras on the Costa de la Luz; and Madrid to Valencia. There are high-speed AVE services linking Madrid to Seville via Córdoba; and Madrid to Lleida with a planned extension leading on to Barcelona and Figueres near the Spain/France border. Other lines are planned to link up Córdoba to Málaga; Figueres to Perpignan in France; Madrid to Valledolid; Madrid to Valencia; and Madrid to Lisbon.

COMMUNICATIONS

The availability and reliability of telecommunication systems in Spain vary depending on where you buy property. Obviously, if you are located in or near the larger towns and cities then there should be no problem getting a landline connection, connecting to the Internet, or being able to buy SIM cards and credit for pay-as-you-go mobile phones. In more rural areas, however, getting connected to the Internet and even the installation of a landline may be problematic – and some out-of-the-way properties have to rely on radiophones or mobiles.

Telephone

Telefónica (www.telefonica.es), Spain's equivalent to BT, was privatised in 1998 and although it has lost its monopoly in Spain, it still retains a powerful hold on the telephone service. If you want a landline installed you will have to sign a contract with Telefónica and the company also operates the phone booths dotted around the country. These phone booths take coins, credit cards and phone cards (which can be bought from *estancos*, news stands and post offices and come in denominations of €5, €10 and €15). Many of these phone booths have multilingual digital displays and it is possible to use these booths to make international calls. There are also a number of call centres in Spain, especially in the bigger towns and resort areas, which offer low-cost calls, though you should compare prices before using these and shop around.

Installation of a telephone in a newly-owned property. To get a telephone installed in a new property you will need to go to the local Telefónica office (the address of local offices can be found in the yellow pages – las Páginas Amarillas). Take along your *residencia* or passport and the *escritura* (if you are renting a property take along your rental agreement) as well as some form of proof of address.

Installation charges. If you are renting a property you may be asked to pay a deposit. Charges are currently around €150 for the initial connection fee and approx. €10 + VAT @ 16% per month's landline rental (the standing charge). You can buy or rent a handset. The standing charge will need to be paid bi-monthly whether the property is inhabited or not and you should set up a standing order to cover this. If a telephone is disconnected (twenty days after the last reminder for payment) there is a fairly hefty reconnection charge but the phone should be reconnected within 48 hours, once the charges have been paid. Connections should not take more than a few days to install, though in more isolated areas this may take longer. Those aged over 65 with a low income are eligible for discounts when using Telefónica services.

Changing the name on an existing telephone contract. If you are taking over the account of a previous owner you will need to arrange for the telephone company to close the existing telephone account, and send a final bill to the owners of the property on the day that you take possession of the property (the day you hand over the purchase price to the *notario*). A new account will then be opened in your name from the day you take possession of the property. There is a charge made for this service. It is also important to make sure that there are no arrears to be paid on previous bills sent to the address by the telephone company. If there are, then once you are the registered owner of the property you will be liable to pay them. Note that if you are going to be renting out your property, you should consider how you are going to charge any tenants for the use of the telephone.

Call charges. Call Charges in Spain are no bargain and are higher than those in the UK. Since deregulation in 1998 competing telephone companies have offered alternative services to Telefónica and there is scope for using these other companies' services, especially for long distance and international calls. Retevisión (www.retevision.es), Jazztel (www.jazztel.com), Telforce (www.usewho.com/telforce/), Aló (www.alo.es), and Uni2 (www.uni2.es) all offer alternative services and tariffs to those of Telefónica.

Within Spain, different tariffs are imposed depending on the time a call is made. Peak rate is from 8am-5pm Monday-Friday and 8am-2pm Saturday; a low rate is in operation from 10pm-8am Monday-Friday and 2pm-8am Saturday as well as all day Sunday and during holidays. Different telephone operators also have different tariffs, which are subject to change due to the competition that exists between the companies. Call charges vary depending on whether you are making a local, provincial or inter-provincial call.

International calls can be made direct from private phones in Spain without the need to book a call. The various telephone companies operating in Spain all offer various rates but generally they all offer a cheaper rate between 10pm and 8am Monday-Friday and all day at weekends and on holidays.

Telephone numbers. There are no codes for towns in Spain but each province has a code, which prefixes and is included in the nine-digit telephone number that all subscribers receive. The full nine-digit number must be used whether calling from within Spain or from abroad. Telephone numbers these days are given as three sets of three digits (ie 966-812-841) the area code being the first three digits of the telephone number. The country code for Spain is **34**.

To dial abroad from Spain you will need to dial the international prefix (00) followed by the country code (eg. United Kingdom – 44; USA – 1; Australia – 61; New Zealand – 64; Eire – 353; Canada – 15; South Africa – 27) followed by the prefix of the area code minus the initial 0, followed by the number of the subscriber.

AREA TELEPHONE CODES			
Alicante	96	Madrid	1
Avila	920	Málaga	95
Barcelona	93	Murcia	968
Bilbao	94	Marbella	952
Burgos	947	Oviedo	985
Cádiz	956	Salamanca	923
Castellón	964	Santander	42
Córdoba	957	Seville	954
Granada	958	Toledo	925

Huelva	959	Valencia	96
Jaen	953	Tenerife	922
León	987	Zaragoza	976

Common services telephone numbers are included in the front pages of the telephone directories, which are available by province. There is a charge made for calls to Directory Enquiries. Some of the more commonly used numbers are:

USEFUL TELEPHONE NUMBERS	
Alarm Call	096
International Directory Enquiries	025
International Operator (Europe/North Africa)	1008
International Operator (Rest of the World)	1005
National Directory Enquiries	1003
Policía Local	092
Policía Nacional	091
Speaking Clock	093
Weather Report	906 365 365

Mobile Phones. If you want to use a mobile phone (teléfono móvil) purchased at home during your time in Spain, you will need to check with the service provider what the call rates are when using the phone abroad and whether there is coverage for the service. Spain uses GSM 900/1800 telephones, which are compatible with the rest of Europe, but not with the North American GSM 1900. You may also need to inform your service provider before going abroad to get international access on your handset activated. There may be a charge for this depending on the phone package that you have. Using your mobile phone while abroad is expensive – you will be charged extra for incoming calls and access to your voicemail may also be restricted.

The mobile phone arm of Telefónica is MoviStar (www.movistar.com). There are also a number of other operators in Spain including Airtel-Vodafone (www.vodafone.es) and Amena (www.amena.com). As elsewhere in the world, mobile phone coverage varies from area to area. Some of the more isolated and mountainous areas of the country will have problems with coverage and you should check with the various operators to see which can provide the best coverage for your home area (as well as the best deals).

> Mobile phones are very popular in Spain, and phone outlets and agents are not hard to find in the towns and cities. There are two ways of paying for calls: either by setting up an account with a service provider, or by using pre-pay cards bought from supermercados, estancos, etc. It will be cheaper in the long run to buy a mobile phone from a Spanish operator but whether you want to do this will depend on how long you intend staying in Spain each year.

Further advice on using mobile phones abroad can be found on the Internet at www.gsmworld.com and at www.telecomsadvice.org.uk.

The Internet

There are a number of internet cafés and cybercafés in Spain for you to make use of if you only plan to spend a few weeks a year in the country, but if you are moving to Spain permanently then you will probably want to get connected to the web. If you have a laptop, remember that the power supply may vary from that in your home country and you will need an AC adaptor as well as an adaptor to fit the plug into a Spanish socket. The website www.teleadapt.com provides information about travelling abroad with a laptop.

There are a number of International ISPs (Internet Service Providers) providing internet access in Spain along with Spanish ISPs such as Tiscali (www.tiscali.es), eresMas (www.eresmas.net) and the largest provider, Telefónica (www.telefonica.es). If you want a free Internet connection (no monthly charge; calls at local rates) you will need to connect with one of the ISPs owned by one of the telephone companies. ISPs in Spain don't tend to give out auto install CD-Roms. You either register on line or over the phone giving your details including your NIE or passport number and you will be given all the necessary information to set up a connection yourself. Telephone companies have special discount tariffs for heavy Internet usage called *tarifa plana*, which charge a flat rate irrespective of usage. For evening and weekend usage rates cost typically €20 per month; unlimited 24-hour access costs around €60 per month.

ADSL Broadband is more popular in Spain than in the UK, mainly because it is cheaper to install (approx. €180). Line rental works out about €35 per month for a standard 256k bandwidth.

You will want to get an e-mail address to allow you to stay in contact with friends, relatives and colleagues through the Internet. There are a number of ways to get hold of an e-mail address, and which you use will depend on whether you have your own internet connection or are dependent on using a cybercafé or other public Internet access points. Two of the most convenient, reliable and free e-mail account providers accessible from any computer connected to the Internet are www.hotmail.com and www.yahoo.com. If you go to their websites you can get a free e-mail account by following the simple signing up process. The Internet is rapidly making the necessity of Poste Restante a thing of the past.

Post

Mail delivery in Spain can be somewhat slow and unreliable. Delays are a common occurrence. Post is usually delivered to the door of private residences and business premises or, in an apartment block or urbanización to a central collection point. Parcels and registered mail will need to be collected from the local post office. Stamps can be bought from the *estancos* as well as from post offices (*oficinas de correos*). Post office boxes (*apartado de correos*) can be rented from post offices. Because of the often erratic nature of the Spanish postal delivery service, do not rely on letters or parcels reaching their destination as quickly as they might at home. Important mail that needs to reach its destination swiftly is better sent registered (*certificado*), urgent (*urgente*) or by Express Mail Service (EMS). Courier services operating in Spain include domestic companies such as Seur as well as the international DHL and UPS. The post office operates its own express delivery service (Postal Exprés), which guarantees delivery between 24 hours and three days, depending on the destination, and is cheaper than using the international courier services.

Opening times at the main post offices are from 9am-9pm, Monday to Friday and 9am-2pm on Saturdays. Times may be more limited in smaller, local post offices and longer hours may be kept in the bigger towns and cities.

FOOD AND DRINK

One of the great pulls of Spain, in addition to the cheap cost of property, the sunshine, the warm seas and the low price of alcohol and cigarettes, is, without a shadow of doubt, its cuisine. In terms of both quality and variety few countries in Europe can beat it. It is a country replete with dishes influenced by the climate and the local way of life of each region; the occupation of the Moors, as well as imports from abroad such as the potato, tomato, sweet potato, vanilla, chocolate, many varieties of beans, zucchini, and the pepper. Local specialities are covered in the regional guide in the chapter *Where to Find Your Ideal Home*. More recently, the need to satisfy the palates of tourists have all had a lasting effect on Spanish cuisine, but the liberal use of olive oil remains a traditional feature. Spain's greatest gastronomic legacy may well be tapas – small portions of regional specialties served in restaurants and bars and accompanied by a glass of wine or beer. Spaniards are very fond of garlic and cured ham (*jamon serrano*), and hot and sweet peppers. Spain's most famous wine is sherry, both dry and sweet, and it used to flavour entrées and desserts as well as being served as an aperitif.

> Food in Spain is taken very seriously. Dining is an important ingredient in the country's social lifestyle. A light breakfast may be taken at 8am followed by a mid-morning snack at 11am and tapas at 1pm. Lunch (*la comida*) is the big meal of the day and is generally served between 2pm and 4 pm. A snack may follow at 6pm; then an evening tapas at 8pm. Dinner (*la cena)* is traditionally served late, between 9pm and 11pm. Restaurants are rated by vertical forks (from one to five) on a plaque outside the entrance. Prices must be listed both inside and outside the establishment.

SCHOOLS AND EDUCATION

The decision of how and where to educate your children is something that poses something of a quandary for parents wherever they live. Moving abroad with young children is in some ways easier than moving with teen-agers as younger children are remarkably adept at picking up languages and fitting into new situations. Furthermore, as their education has not yet begun in earnest, the problem of juggling two differing curricula does not exist. Although the Spanish education system is perfectly adequate, it will obviously not follow the same pattern as the British or American one; and this will create difficulties if a child in the middle of a GCSE course is suddenly uprooted to Spain and expected to do well in Spanish examinations. For this reason, many parents choose to send their children to international schools while abroad, and other parents who can afford to, sometimes choose to keep their children at UK boarding schools so as not to disrupt their education. However, it has to be said that the opportunity to mix with Spanish children and to attend a Spanish school is both rare and exciting.

Previously élitist and badly organised, the Spanish education system has undergone a radical transformation in recent years and is now built on a structure that has opened up education to all classes, and to people of all abilities. Responsibility for education in Spain is shared between the state and the seventeen autonomous communities, or regions. Some of these autonomous regions have now assumed full control over education, and it is likely that decentralisation will go further in future.

It is somewhat ironic that a country that for so many years has fallen behind its European neighbours in respect of the provision of education should at the same time possess a deep and inherent respect for academia not found in many other countries.

The spectacular growth of the Spanish educational system over the past few years has resulted in many changes, but there are still the four basic levels of education in Spain: pre-school; primary *(Educación General Básica)* known as *EGB*; secondary; and university.

After secondary education. At the end of compulsory secondary education (*Educación Secundaria Obligatoria* or *ESO*) students are faced with a choice between following a more academic or a more vocational route. The former usually means going on directly to do the *Bachillerato* – otherwise known as the *Bachillerato Unificado Polivalente* or *BUP* – which is a two-year course covering four areas of study: arts; natural and health sciences; humanities and social sciences; and technology. An alternative route is to leave school and go in for the *Profesional de Primero y Segundo Grado* – the two levels of vocational training, with Intermediate and Higher Grades each comprising two years of study. Those leaving school without qualifications would have to go in for an initial year of training called the Social Guarantee Programme (*Garantia Social*), which would act as a foundation course for the Intermediate Grade Training Cycles (*Ciclos Formativos – Grand Medio*) and subsequently the Higher Grade Training Cycles (*Ciclos Formativos – Grado Superior*). The technical training is largely practical while the two or three years of secondary education leading to the baccalaureate is purely academic. Having to make this kind of decision at such a young age is one of the strongest criticisms levied at the Spanish education system. However, the new system has brought levels of literacy more into line with other European countries and nowadays university is no longer seen as a place of study for a privileged minority.

The reformation and improvement of the system after Spain became a democracy has resulted in nearly all children from four or five years-old attending pre-school education. More than 70% of young people stay on at school until the age of eighteen while 40% receive professional training. Today there is a body of over one million students in Spanish universities. Interestingly, the high rate of higher education is principally a result of the number of female students at university, who exceed the number of males in both secondary education and in the first years of university. The ratio of males to females is only less on the professional training courses, where they constitute 45% of the student body.

State and Private Education

School attendance in Spain is compulsory by law between the ages of six and sixteen. Families in state education are expected to pay only for schoolbooks (which are free only in special cases), school supplies, a certain proportion of transportation services and for some voluntary extra-curricular activities. The academic year usually runs from September to June, with vacations at Christmas and Easter. Religious instruction is voluntary.

Both state and private education are available in Spain, although the former accounts for by far the larger percentage of students. However, the fees charged by private schools are usually not monstrously large, as these schools also receive a subsidy from the state. State education is free and is freely available to all children resident in Spain. More details of the Spanish education system (state and private) can be obtained from the *Spanish Embassy Education Office* in London (20 Peel Street, London W8 7PD; ☎ 020-7727 2462; fax 020-7229 4965) or the *Ministerio de Educación, Cultura y Deporte* in Madrid (c/Alcalá 34, 28071 Madrid; ☎ 915 321 300; www.mec.es). At present, a large minority of all non-university education is private, and Catholic education represents approximately 20% of the whole educational system. However, it is more prevalent in school than university education.

The Structure of the Education System

Pre-school. This is divided into two categories: playschool (under 3 years of age); and kindergartens (3-6 years); both age groups attend voluntarily and for free at infant schools (*escuela infantiles*). Private schools charge a fee, which tends to be most expensive in the non-subsidised international schools. Each category has its own specialised teachers. Despite the rapid growth in recent years in the number of state pre-school facilities, anyone considering this type of education for their children will need to do some research as facilities tend to vary greatly from region to region.

The objective of pre-school education is to develop basic personal aptitudes and co-operative social attitudes through games and other non-didactic methods; instruction in reading and writing tends to be left to the primary schools.

Primary. Catering for children from the age of six, primary education is both compulsory by law and free in Spain in the state sector. Those who have completed the last year of primary school receive the *Título de Graduado Escolar* – a prerequisite for secondary education and university. Those who do not receive the *Título* are given the *Certificado de Escolaridad* which can be used for entrance to technical training courses. Thus, at a very young age Spanish schoolchildren are forced into an irreversible decision that will to a large degree determine the course of their future educational training and careers.

Secondary. The *Bachillerato Unificado y Polivalente* (BUP) provides its students with a three-year academic training as a preparation for university. The first and second years are divided equally between the natural sciences, mathematics, languages and the humanities, while a specialisation is made in the third year. The *Título de Bachiller* is awarded at the end of the course if no more than two subjects have been failed in the final examinations, and this certificate may be used to enter the second stage of the technical training course or to attend a one year pre-university course, the *Curso de Orientación Universitaria* (COU). Students who enter for this level must pass all subjects, as COU is an essential preliminary to university. Some students go on to technical training centres rather than entering the COU course.

Technical Training. The *Formación Profesional* comprises two levels, known simply as FP-1 and FP-2, and is free for most students whether they attend a public centre or a private institution financed by the state. The technical training courses have a strong practical emphasis and take students from the age of 14 years old. FP-1 consists of a two year course and is compulsory for those who fail to gain the *Título de Graduado Escolar*. The course provides a general introduction to a specific vocation such as clerical work, electronics, etc. FP-2 is the second level or cycle of technical training and offers specialised vocational training. In the past the ratio of students choosing to take the BUP (more academic) course over the FP was around 2:1, but as vocational training has become more and more precious the balance is changing and the ratio is now closer to 3:2. Additionally, the high percentage of failures and drop-outs, combined with the reluctant acceptance of the certificate in the job market and the class consciousness in the make-up of the student body, have made FP-1 the most problematic and criticised area in the Spanish education system. However, those who continue to FP-2 and successfully complete the course receive the further *Técnico Especialista* certificate, which enjoys a much better reputation in the job market. Usually, students on this course have divided their time between school studies and working in some kind of business concern.

University. The Spanish university system, like many of its European counterparts, dates back to the Middle Ages. Salamanca University, founded in 1218, is the oldest in Spain. Over the last twenty years, the university system has experienced its greatest growth in history, while at the same time advancing towards a self-governing and decentralised system. There are presently 50 or so state universities in Spain and 20 private ones. Most, if not all, of the private universities are tied to the Catholic Church, one of which, the Opus Dei University in Navarre, carries far more influence than its size would warrant – the majority of its intake comprising the sons and daughters of the powerful, wealthy and aristocratic. The Complutense in Madrid, and the Central in Barcelona, are by far the largest Spanish universities – the former comprising nearly 100,000 undergraduates, the latter nearly 80,000. Despite their size, these two universities are generally regarded as being the best in Spain.

To enter a Spanish university, a student must have passed either the educational or vocational levels of secondary education. A university entrance exam must also be taken. There is a clear division between academic and practical courses. Some universities (*Facultades* and *Colegios*) offer five or six year academic courses while the *Escuelas Universitarias* provide shorter, three year, vocational courses (for teachers, nurses, etc). The latter courses are less favourably regarded than the purely academic ones although this trend is changing as the demand for students trained in a specific vocation rises. Currently, many more students undertake purely academic courses than vocational ones, and those with high academic grades will usually choose to enter the former. A high percentage (80%) of all Spanish students who complete secondary education go on to university.

Foreigners who wish to enrol in courses offered by the Spanish education system at university level must sit the *selectividad* examination either at the university where they wish to study or, if they live abroad, at a Spanish Embassy. Before taking this entrance exam, foreign students must have their qualifications (GCSE's, A levels, etc.) officially validated at the *Ministerio de Educación, Cultura y Deporte* in Madrid (c/Alcalá 34, 28071 Madrid; ☎ 915 321 300; www.mec.es). or through the Spanish Embassy in the applicant's native country. Alternatively, almost all Spanish universities offer special courses for foreign students where it isn't necessary to validate foreign qualifications. However, the certificates gained through following this type of course are not recognised within the state education system. Information on both standard Spanish courses and those specifically designed for foreigners may be obtained directly from individual universities. A good knowledge of Spanish will be required by most universities.

International Schools

International schools tend to be regarded as the best alternative by expats considering the long-term education of their children. This is primarily because they offer the qualifications familiar to selection bodies at British and American universities. Spanish law requires all foreign schools to be supported by their embassies and the *National Association of British Schools in Spain* (NABSS, C/Comercio 4, Escalera 2a, Bajo A, 28007 Madrid; ☎915 520 516; www.nabss.org) works with the British Council to ensure that all its member schools are visited regularly by British inspectors, who then report to the Spanish Ministry of Education. On receipt of a satisfactory report, the school is authorised to continue as a foreign centre of education.

A list of international schools in Spain which teach the British or American curriculum, or a combination of Spanish and international systems (such as the French and German curricula) is available from the *European Council of Schools (ECIS)*, 21 Lavant Street, Petersfield, Hants GU32 3EL; ☎ 01730-268244 or 263131; fax 01730-267914; www.ecis.org. The *ECIS Iberian Office* can be contacted at: *ECIS*, C/ Augusto Figueroa 32-34/1°G, 28004 Madrid; ☎ 915 626 722; fax 917 451 310. Alternatively, you may buy their *Directory of International Schools* from www.johncatt.co.uk.

There are a multitude of British and American schools in Spain. As it is easier to transfer back into the British education system from a British school abroad (and to a US school from a US school abroad), it is advisable to send children to a school that offers the curriculum of your country of origin.

Other schools offer a dual system of Spanish- and English-language teaching and curricula which provide the opportunity for children to be equally well qualified to live and work in Spain or in the UK in future life. Such schools are required to allocate at least 20% of the total number of places available to Spanish students. Another option for parents is to enrol children in a school that teaches the UK curriculum but also includes some Spanish studies (taught in English) in the same curriculum.

HEALTH INSURANCE AND HOSPITALS

Many countries, including the fifteen member states of the EEA (European Economic Area) plus Liechtenstein, Iceland and Norway, have reciprocal arrangements with Spain.

The Spanish National Health Service

The Spanish health service combines both public and private healthcare and anyone who makes social security payments or receives a state pension, is unemployed or under the age of 18, is entitled to free medical treatment. Today 98% of the population is covered by the state health system; however, free treatment is only available in certain hospitals, where waiting lists tend to be long. The shortcomings of the healthcare system are evinced by the fact that preventable diseases such as TB, tetanus and diphtheria are still around in Spain. There are not enough hospitals – especially in the poorer areas – and the emphasis of treatment still lies with curative rather than preventative medicine. Social security resources are inefficiently distributed and administered, and it is primarily because of this that various attempts to reform the health service in recent years have failed. Many Spanish residents, nationals and foreigners, take out private health insurance. Spain has a number of resident English-speaking doctors and it is sometimes possible to join local schemes where for a fixed premium (£100 or so) a certain number of free consultations can be taken. These can be very worthwhile.

Anyone below retirement age working in Spain makes a monthly contribution to the Spanish National Health Service (*Instituto Nacional de la Salud – INSALUD*) through social security payments deducted from an employee's gross salary by the employer. The benefits from subscribing to the *Instituto Nacional de la Salud* include free hospital accommodation and medical treatment. As some hospitals only treat private patients, it is as well to know which hospitals in your area provide national health treatment. A list of national health centres and hospitals may be found in your local office of the *Instituto Nacional de la Seguridad Social (INSS)*, or indeed in the local Yellow Pages (*las páginas amarillas*). Lists of English-speaking doctors are available at the local British Embassy or Consulate.

One serious drawback from a retired person's point of view of the medical treatment provided by Spanish social security (Seguridad Social) is that although it provides financial cover for surgery and hospital treatment, it does not include funding for general medical treatment such as trips to the dentist or a GP. Moreover, the Spanish social security system caters particularly poorly for outpatient and after-care treatment and facilities. Social security will only cover about 75% of a patient's treatment costs; thus the patient has to meet 25% of the costs incurred (or budget for payments for private health insurance to cover this). Those who have worked in Spain and paid into a private top-up scheme – as most Spanish nationals and residents do – will have the bulk of this contribution covered.

Using the British NHS

It is essential that all British nationals intending to move to Spain register their change of address with the Overseas Division (Medical Benefits) of the Department for Work and Pensions Benefits Agency before leaving the UK. Paperwork will then need to be completed in order to receive the Spanish national health card (*cartilla*) from the Spanish social services. This card (or a photocopy of it) must be produced whenever medical treatment is needed; and will cover the holder for 100% of medical treatment and 90% of prescription charges. The *cartilla* will also entitle the holder to full benefits in any other EU country. The two systems of National Insurance in the UK and Social Security (*Seguridad Social*) in Spain are transferable insofar as if you return to Britain at any future time payments towards one count towards the other, and vice versa. What happens in detail is explained in various leaflets available from the Pensions and Benefits Overseas Directorate in Newcastle (☎0191-218 7777). The 'Euroadviser' in your local Jobcentre in the UK may also be able to advise. In Spain, further information about social security can be obtained from the *Instituto Nacional de la Seguridad Social (INSS)*, Servicios Centrales, c/Padre Damián, 4-6, 28036 Madrid; ☎915 688 300; www.seg-social.es.

The E111

Reciprocal medical arrangements that exist between the UK and Spain under EU regulations make it possible to obtain mainly free medical treatment for those whose visits to Spain will last for no more than three months at a time. This arrangement may well prove helpful for those going on a property-searching trip to Spain and those who already have holiday homes there. The E111 only covers temporary residence, not the first three months of a permanent residence and applies only to emergency medical treatment. The form *Health Advice for Travellers* contains the application form for the E111 and is available from post offices, or the Department for Work and Pensions Benefits Agency, (Overseas Division Medical Benefits, Tyneview Park, Whitley Road, Newcastle-upon-Tyne NE98 1BA; ☎0191-218 7547; www.doh.gov.uk).

Spanish authorities have simplified the procedures necessary for foreigners to obtain medical treatment while in Spain and now you have only to present your E111, and a photocopy of it, to the ambulance, doctor or practice when treatment is required. The original E111 will be returned after it has been checked, while the photocopy will be retained. Be sure to carry spare copies of the document, as they will be needed if further treatment is required. If you do not have an E111, you will be expected to pay for medical treatment, and it does not cover you for non-emergency treatment, e.g. prescribed medicines and dental treatment. Moreover, the E111 is not a substitute for travel insurance.

An E111 normally has no time limit but is not valid once you have left the UK permanently, or are employed in Spain. It can sometimes be renewed and it is also possible to get an 'open-ended' E111 if you make frequent trips abroad for a period longer than three months. Explanatory leaflet SA29 gives details of social security, healthcare and pension rights within the EU and is obtainable from main post offices and from the Department of Work and Pensions, Overseas Directorate, Tyneview Park, Whitely Road, Benton, Newcastle-upon-Tyne NE98 1BA.

The E101 and E128

The Inland Revenue, National Insurance Contributions Office, International Services in Newcastle issues an E101 to UK nationals working in another EU country to exempt them from paying social security contributions in that country because they are still paying them in their home country. E101 only gives free medical assistance for three months.

The E128 entitles you to medical treatment in another EU country where you are working, or if you are a student. You have to obtain an E101 *before* you can obtain an E128. Retirees need to fill in form E121 from the Department of Work and Pensions.

Sickness and Invalidity Benefit

Anyone who claims sickness or invalidity benefit in the UK and is moving out to Spain permanently is entitled to continue claiming this benefit once in Spain. Strictly speaking, to claim either benefit, you must be physically incapable of **all** work, however, the interpretation of the words 'physically incapable' is frequently stretched just a little beyond literal truth. If the claimant has been paying National Insurance contributions in the UK for two tax years (this period may be less, depending on his or her level of income) then he or she is eligible to claim sickness benefit. After receiving sickness benefit for 28 weeks, you are entitled to invalidity benefit, which is paid at a higher rate. Anyone currently receiving either form of benefit should inform the Department of Work and Pensions (formerly the DSS) that they are moving to Spain. Your forms will then be sent to the DWP International Services department (Newcastle-upon-Tyne NE98 1YC) who will then make sure that a monthly sterling cheque is sent either to your new address or direct into your bank account. All such claimants must submit themselves, on request, to a medical examination either in Spain or Britain.

Child benefit may also be claimed if the child goes abroad for more than eight weeks. Ask for leaflet CH6.

Private Medical Insurance

Although the level of convenience, comfort and attention offered through private insurance schemes is superior to that received by National Health patients, the treatment itself will not necessarily be of a higher quality.

However, a growing number of foreign residents in Spain are opting to remove themselves from the long waiting lists and sometimes chaotic conditions of the Spanish National Health Service to take out private health insurance. Those who only spend a few weeks or months a year in Spain will anyhow require private medical insurance to cover the balance of the cost not covered by the E111 (see above). One of the advantages of UK health insurance schemes is that their policies cover the claimants for treatment incurred anywhere in Europe, not just in Spain itself. With an increasing number of insurance companies offering this kind of cover, it is worth shopping around as cover and costs vary.

Useful Addresses

British United Provident Association (BUPA): Russell House, Russell Mews, Brighton BN1 2NR; ☎ 01273-208181; www.bupa-intl.com. BUPA International offers a range of worldwide schemes for individuals and companies of three or more employees based outside the UK for six or more months.

ExpaCare Insurance Services: First Floor, Columbia Centre, Market Street, Bracknell, Berkshire RG12 1JG; ☎ 01344 381 650; fax 01344 381 690; www.expacare.net. Specialists in expatriate healthcare offering high quality health insurance cover for individuals and their families, including group cover for five or more employees. Cover is available for expats of all nationalities worldwide.

Goodhealth Worldwide Ltd: 5 Lloyds Avenue, London, EC3N 3AE; ☎ 0870 442 7376; fax 0870 442 4377; www.goodhealthworldwide.com, offers private healthcare plans to expats worldwide.

Private Medical Insurance – Spanish Providers. Spanish insurance policies are widely available and have a distinct advantage over those offered in the UK in that payment for medical treatment is made in the form of vouchers. This means that you can use them to pay for services at the time of treatment, rather than having to pay for treatment up front and then claim back costs from an insurance company after the event. However, although the premiums on Spanish insurance policies may appear cheaper and more attractive than those offered by British companies you may well find that a policy is limited to specific local hospitals – not too helpful if you are in urgent need of treatment but nowhere near a hospital on the policy list. Additionally, the small print needs to be read very carefully (perhaps treatment is only refunded if surgery is performed, or outpatient treatment i.e. visits to the local GP and the dentist, is not included in the policy). Other policies may offer limited cover on surgery, medicines and hospital accommodation. If you do decide to get a Spanish policy make sure that you have read the small print and policy in an English translation.

Sanitas (Avda. Ramon y Cajal 4, 29600 Marbella; ☎ 952 774 450; fax 952 775 912; www.isanitas.com) is the leading private healthcare provider in Spain with more than 1.2 million members and 50 years experience in the healthcare sector. Their Sanitas Health Plan is specifically aimed at foreigners living in Spain. The cost of private health insurance varies according to age. For example someone aged 62 is likely to pay the equivalent of £49 per month for a policy, which will include dental treatment and insurance when travelling outside Spain.

SHOPPING

It is worth remembering that although a couple of decades ago the cost of living in Spain was one of the foremost reasons why Brits chose to go and live there, especially in retirement, the situation has now changed. Prices have risen with inflation while salaries have not, and in the most expensive areas of the Balearic Islands e.g. in Mallorca, the cost of living is now higher than in the UK. In mainland Spain the cost of living is approximately the same as in the UK. The open markets still, however, offer bargains and enable one to live economically with an added bonus of getting a flavour of the country – the Rastro Market held in Madrid on Sunday morning is particularly recommended to those looking for Spanish life at its most colourful. Every region of Spain has its locally produced goods: Catalonian textiles are famous around the world; handmade wooden furniture is one of the traditional products of Valencia; all Spanish leather goods are of a high quality and fine rugs and carpets can be found in the markets and shops of the south.

Spain has a long tradition in crafting leather and goods such as shoes, bags, clothes, wallets and purses are generally considered to be good buys.

Pottery and ceramics and Spanish tiles are world famous, and hand-painted pottery from Seville and Granada are a good buy. Lladró porcelain figures are popular but you should only buy from an authorised Lladró outlet (look for the sign in the window). Other shrewd buys include Spanish guitars, among the best in the world, handcrafted jewellery, embroidery and lace, and furniture (modern as well as antique).

Food shopping. Spain's thriving import market means that many international brands of canned and frozen foods and drinks are also available in Spain. All large towns have modern supermarkets that as well as food, stock a wide variety of goods as diverse as tableware, clothes, toiletries and hardware.

For those determined to integrate more fully into the Spanish way of life, or for those living far out in the countryside, there are smaller shops which sell the type of Spanish food and drink that they have always sold – before the tourists arrived demanding food 'like we get back home'. There are also the municipal markets (*ventas*) – controlled by the local governments, which offer the best prices and often the highest quality fresh produce. These *ventas* can provide a whole new world of gastronomic discovery. For example, hand-made (as opposed to industrially produced) sausages can still be found, offering a staggering variety of textures and tastes. The red *chorizo* sausage is the best-known Spanish sausage, consisting of ground pork and fat, paprika or peppers and garlic, pepper, oregano and nutmeg. *Longaniza* is the long, thin version of the *chorizo*, and the *chorizo de Pamplona* is a smoked variety. The *sobrasada*, *salchichón*, *morcilla* and *butifarra* sausages are but a few others available.

Most towns and all cities have a *venta*, usually open from 9am to 2pm daily where you can buy fresh produce (fish, meat, fruit and vegetables), and often other products such as dried fruits, spices, cut flowers and hardware may also be on sale. These markets are very popular and first thing in the morning you will see flocks of Spanish housewives out with their shopping baskets at the stalls. Prices at these indoor markets tend to be fixed.

Weekly outdoor markets are also very popular in Spain and most towns have at least one held in the main square, or some wide-open space. The large markets draw stallholders from all over selling anything from fresh fruit to cameras, shoes, fake perfumes, tools etc. Antique and flea markets as well as car-boot sales are held in many towns and cities, usually at the weekends.

Indoor and outdoor markets are found in every town and in many of the larger villages, and function as the centre-point for the exchange of local news and gossip. They offer a real and rare insight into Spanish small-town life. A helpful hint for the newly arrived is to investigate the villages of the nearby countryside, where prices can be lower still than in the markets which, although good value, sometimes raise their prices to suit the look of the foreigner's pockets.

Hypermarkets are now very popular in Spain and most large towns and cities have at least one, usually situated on the outskirts. The main hypermarkets in Spain are Alcampo and Carrefour (both French owned), as well as Eroski and Hipercor (part of the El Corte Inglés giant). Hypermarkets tend to be huge and sell everything. Prices are generally reasonable. Discount stores such as Lidl, Día and Plus have sprung up in towns and cities all over Spain and are popular for basic foodstuffs and hardware.

Some of the more remote areas of Spain are served by mobile shops (*ventas ambulantes*). Vans travel around selling most things required by the average household including fresh fish and meat. This service, amounting to what is practically a door-to-door supermarket, is especially helpful for those of restricted mobility; whether due to old age, lack of transport or having a baby to look after.

The Demon drink. The tax on alcohol is considerably less in Spain than in the UK and most of the prices in Spanish bottle shops are lower than duty-free prices back home. The languid, thirsty afternoons and warm, convivial evenings, coupled with the fine quality of Spain's wines, sherries, brandies and champagnes tend to bring with them the temptation to overindulge in alcohol. Excessive drinking is an affliction of many an expat, and, for those who have stepped over the line between social drinking and alcohol dependence, there are Alcoholics Anonymous meetings advertised in English-language publications in Spain.

Non-food shopping. Once famous for the high quality and low price of its leather, Spain is still known for the quality of its goods but bargain prices (especially in the larger, tourist frequented areas) are hard to find. The mass-market department stores and boutique-like souvenir shops dominate the larger cities and to find real bargains, which combine quality and value for money with authenticity and originality, you will need to travel out to the smaller towns and villages and into the backstreets. Consumer durables, such as refrigerators, washing machines, electronic and electrical equipment, and cameras, tend to be as expensive in Spain as back home while food, electricity, gas, public transport, tobacco and alcohol and, at present, cars, all tend to cost less.

The most important department store in Spain is El Corte Inglés, one of the country's most successful and profitable enterprises. There's an El Corte Inglés store in practically every city stocking as much and more than the *hypermercados*. El Corte Inglés offers customer services such as in-store cards, home delivery and free parking for cardholders. Prices, however, are on the high side. Other chain stores include the clothes shops such as Zara, Bershka, Pull & Bear and Massimo Dutti, DIY stores such as Leroy Merlin and Akí, and the ubiquitous furniture store, Ikea. Many of these stores can be found in shopping centres which increasingly feature as huge retail parks on the outskirts of towns and cities. English-language bookshops are scattered along the *costas* and in the big cities (try Julian's Library, Calle España 11, Fuengirola). In Madrid try the International Bookshop at Campomanes 13, or the Turner English Bookshop, Calle de Genova 3 in Barcelona.

Sales. Spain has two sales periods a year. Winter sales are held in January and February, Summer sales in July and August. The sales (*rebajas*) are particularly good for electrical and home appliances and clothes. Even small stores in towns and villages hold annual sales.

Shopping etiquette. The Spaniards generally do not believe in queuing, and although this is gradually changing many a heated dispute is had in shops over who arrived first and whose turn it is to be served next. A lot of shops and counters in *hypermercados* have a number system with illuminated numbers by the counter which change to let you know who's turn it is to be served. On arrival a customer collects a ticket with a number on it from a dispenser and waits for the number to come up on the counter. Walking into a shop where there are a lot of customers waiting to be served it is a good idea to ask, '¿quién es el último?' (who is the last in the queue).

Most purchases are paid for in cash in Spain, and most of the small shops in towns and villages will only accept cash payment. The use of debit and credit cards is not yet widespread outside of the big cities and resort areas. If you pay by debit or credit card you may be asked to show some form of identification. Payment by cheque is still rarely accepted. The price marked on goods in shops usually includes VAT (IVA), though on some items such as building materials IVA isn't included in the price.

Shop opening hours

Opening hours are strictly regulated in Spain and vary depending on the area, type of shop and the time of year. Most general stores are open

Monday to Friday from 10am to 1.30-2pm and then again from 4.30-5pm to 7.30-8pm and on Saturday mornings. In the larger towns and cities many shops also stay open on Saturday afternoons. In the south of Spain during the height of summer, some shops may not open up again in the afternoon until 6pm – staying open until 9pm or later. In some places, particularly in small towns and villages, there's often one day or afternoon a week when all shops are closed.

Most shopping centres and department stores are open continually (without closing) from 9.30am until 9.30pm or later Monday to Saturday. Some may also open on Sundays and public holidays, although this depends on the region and time of year.

Sundays. Nearly all shops stay closed on Sundays although bakeries are often open on Sunday mornings and may sell basics other than bread and cakes. If you are stuck for food on a Sunday the larger petrol stations often have a mini-market attached to the premises. And there are always bars open that will sell you tapas.

Shops are allowed by law, generally, to open on a maximum of twelve Sundays and public holidays a year, usually coinciding with the Christmas period and over the summer. In tourist areas, shops are generally allowed to open on Sunday mornings during the high season.

MEDIA

Newspapers

The circulation of the daily press in Spain is far lower than in most other European countries. Only eight newspapers in Spain sell more than 100,000 copies a day and it is estimated that only one Spaniard in every ten buys a daily newspaper. Freedom of the press was not established in Spain until 1978, but the removal of the censorship laws have not lessened a certain apathy in the Spaniard towards newspapers, and journalism in general. Spain has no real equivalent of the British tabloid newspapers.

The most popular daily newspaper in Spain is *El País* (Miguel Yuste 40, 28017 Madrid; www.elpais.es), which has a reputation for liberalism and is one of very few Spanish national newspapers to offer any serious political analysis and competent foreign news coverage. *El País* has an average daily circulation of about 450,000 (by comparison, in Britain *The Daily Telegraph* has a daily circulation figure of over a million). National dailies also have Sunday editions and sales of these are generally 50%-100% higher than those for the rest of the week.

ABC is the other leading daily newspaper of national circulation, and like *El País*, is published in Madrid (Serrano 61; www.abc.es), with regional editions in some of the Autonomous Communities. *ABC* is aligned very definitely right of centre in its politics as well as in its stringent moral dictums. Other leading national newspapers include, *La Vanguardia Española* (Pelayo 28, Barcelona; www.lavanguardia.es), *El Mundo* (Pradillo 42, E-28002 Madrid; www.elmundo.es), *El Periódico* (published in Barcelona and with a mostly Catalonian readership), and the sports papers *AS* and *Marca*.

Franco's death saw the re-creation of several daily newspapers printed in the vernacular of the Autonomous Communities: the Catalan newspaper, *Avui* has gradually gained a solid and established following while the Basque papers, *Eja* and *Egin* (a supporter of independence) are mostly printed in *euskara*. *El Alcázar* is a popular, blatantly ultra-right wing national newspaper whose circulation soared during the 1980s.

Magazines

None of the Spanish newspapers have an equivalent of the social diaries or gossip columns that are found in such abundance in British and American papers, and so Spanish magazine publishers have successfully exploited this gap in the market. There are now countless profitable glossy magazines devoted to the lives and loves of the rich and famous; a few of the most well-known include, *!Hola!* (which spawned *Hello!* magazine in the UK); *Pronto*; *Diez Minutos*; *Lecturas*; *Semana*; and *Garbo*. These magazines are known as the *Prensa de Corazón* (Press of the Heart) and are among the ten most popular magazines in Spain.

English Language Newspapers

Spain is well served for English-language publications. *SUR in English* is a free weekly paper distributed on Fridays through outlets such as supermarkets, bars, travel agencies, banks etc., and is published by *Prensa Malagueña,* Avda. de Marañon 48, E-29009, Málaga; ☎952 649 600; www.surinenglish.com. Another local English-language magazine is *Absolute Marbella* (Office 21, Edificio Tembo, c/ Rotary Internacional s/n; 29660 Puerto Bans, Málaga, Spain; ☎902 301 130; fax 952 908 743; www.absolutemarbella.com).

Other English-language publications in Spain include the weekly *Costa Blanca News* (Apartado 95, Benidorm, 03500, Alicante, E-03500; ☎ 96 585 5286; www.costablanca-news.com); *The Majorca Daily Bulletin* (c/ Dan Felio 17, 07012 Palma de Mallorca; ☎ 971 716 110; fax: 971 719 706; www.majorcadailybulletin.es); *The Island Gazette* (C/Iriarte 43 2°, Puerto de la Santa Cruz, Tenerife, Canary Islands) and *Tenerife News*

(Apartado 11, 38412 Los Realejos, Tenerife; ☎ 22 34 60 00; fax 22 34 49 67; www.tennews.com). *Barcelona Resident* (distributed free in the city) is a glossy magazine featuring articles are on all aspects of Barcelona life and includes adverts for services beneficial to expats.

Lookout magazine (Urb. Molino de Viento, C/Rio Darro-Portal 1, E-29650 Mijas-Costa, Málaga; ☎ 952 473 090; e-mail lookout@jet.es) is another very useful magazine for anyone thinking of living in Spain, with general interest articles, property trends, and useful legal advice; various property and other community services are featured. The same group also publishes *SunGolf* for golf enthusiasts; *SunProperty* and the annual *Property Guide for Southern Spain* (in English and German). Similar newspapers and magazines are to be found in those areas where there is a large expatriate population.

British newspapers and the *International Herald Tribune* are available in most of the larger Spanish cities and around areas popular with tourists. *The Guardian Weekly* (164 Deansgate, Manchester M60 2RR; ☎ 0161-832 7200; www.guardianweekly.com) is available on subscription. Rates for Europe are currently £41 for six months (£73 for a year). *The Weekly Telegraph* (☎ 01454-620070; weeklytel@cisubs.co.uk) is a similar news digest with a subscription costing £83.20 for a year.

Television

The Spanish, like the British and the Americans, are a nation of telly addicts. They watch more television than any other country in Europe, except Britain, and nearly every Spanish household contains at least one television set.

Televisión Española (TVE), the main Spanish television station, was set up as a state monopoly in 1956, and was subject to heavy censorship under Franco's regime. This censorship lasted well into the 1980s and had the effect of lowering the general quality of the programmes aired. TVE's two channels are called TVE-1 and TVE-2: the first directed to a more general public, while TVE-2 has a flexible programming which lends special attention to sports broadcasts and live broadcasts of important cultural events. TVE-2's coverage and audience have grown considerably over the last few years; however, TVE-1 has the larger audience with more than 20 million spectators (80% of total viewers). There are also three independent stations: Antena 3, Tele Cinco and Canal Plus. Various regional television channels also exist in Catalonia, the Basque Country, Galicia, Andalucía, Madrid and Valencia.

Spaniards prefer current affairs and serious discussion programmes to light entertainment (which makes up for the lack of a newspaper readership) and documentaries are particularly popular, as is TVE-1's main current affairs programme, *Informe Semanal.*

The introduction of commercial television, the formation of three new private channels and the arrival of satellite and digital TV has sparked some political controversy. The Grupo Prisa (which also owns *El País*) has launched a cable channel called *Canal Satélite Digital* (soon to be available by satellite) with pay-for-view football, something which the government is currently attempting to limit. A rival digital service has also been launched called *Via Digital* which offers 40 more channels. Various Spanish language channels (6 to 8 depending on the area) can be received free of charge.

Expats usually install a satellite system such as the Sky TV system in order to receive channels broadcast in their own native language. MMDS and Digital TV are other options but the latter is somewhat more expensive than its analogue counterpart. All satellite systems require the installation of a dish on the roof. In the case of those living as part of a comunidad de propietarios the community president must be advised of the intent to install a dish. If, after a period of three months a community dish isn't installed then permission cannot be denied to an individual to install a dish.

Radio

The first state network, Radio Nacional de España (RNE), launched by Franco in 1937, paralysed the development of the Spanish radio as news broadcasts were produced only by this government-controlled station and prohibited on all others. Only groups close to the Franco régime were given licences, and in 1960 all radio stations were legally obliged to broadcast simultaneously the news programmes produced by RNE. Once the censorship laws had been removed, however, the growth of new networks was so prolific that at one point Spain hosted some 450 radio stations. The largest public network is still RNE, which merged with *Radio Cadena Española* in 1988, although the audience level is actually lower than that of some of the private networks.

The most popular radio networks include *SER,* which has three different stations, *Los 40 principales,* directed mainly at young people, *Radio Minuto,* which alternates music and news, and *Cadena M80,* which is aimed primarily at an older audience. *COPE (Cadena de Ondas Populares Españolas)* is the second-largest system of private stations. *Antena 3* is a more recently established national network and groups together a number of FM stations that appeared after the concession of new licences in the 1980s. Most of the stations and networks are now on FM rather than Medium Wave (Spain has no long-wave stations). Spanish radio has a reputation for high-quality and entertaining programming and its audience is greater than that in any other European country.

The BBC World Service website (www.bbc.co.uk/worldservice/) has details of the best frequencies to pick up its broadcasts in Spain. You will also find details in the local English-language press as well as local radio stations broadcasting in English. For those who are worried that if they move to Spain they'll start missing Radio 4's *The Archers*, have no fear. From the end of January 2003 the Spanish radio station Onda Cero will be broadcasting the agricultural-based soap.

CRIME AND THE POLICE

Sadly, democracy in Spain has appeared to bring with it a rising crime rate. However, the Spanish figures for car crime and burglary are still significantly lower than in Britain.

One factor that has contributed to the increase of crime in Spain is a more sympathetic police force. It is said that reports of offences are dealt with 'more professionally'. Another cause of the increased crime rate is a growing drug problem. Drugs are relatively easy to come by in Spain and cannabis is widely used among the young, and largely tolerated by the Spanish police. Again, this problem is one that was born in the transition to democracy and the relaxation of social mores which followed. The Socialists in 1983 effectively decriminalised the use of cannabis for a time; a measure which was largely responsible for the easygoing attitude taken towards the use of soft drugs in the 1980s. The law was then revoked and now all non-prescribed drug use is illegal, but the effect has been irreversibly stamped on drug-users and police alike and the possession of a small amount of cannabis for personal use is unlikely to lead to a fine or prison sentence.

The core of the drugs epidemic, however, lies in the spread of hard drugs such as cocaine and heroin. Madrid's Barajas airport is a particularly popular entrance point for drugs from Latin America destined for the European marketplace. Across the Strait of Gibraltar in Morocco there are large farms producing the lucrative cash crops of cannabis and hashish, much of which gets smuggled into Europe via Spain. Spain also has increasing problems with crime syndicates from Morocco, Colombia, Italy and Eastern Europe.

Tourists can, unsurprisingly, be a target for criminals, with much petty theft located along the *costas* directed at the thousands of tourists who visit them each year. The varieties of crimes committed against tourists range from purse snatching and car break-ins to theft of belongings on beaches to armed burglary (a favourite with Spain's teenagers apparently). There is little you can do after such incidents and it is best to take preventative measures and to make sure that you have a good insurance policy. Those who choose to live away from the popular and tourist-saturated coastal areas are likely to enjoy a blissfully crime-free existence. Everybody tends to know everybody else's business in the more rural areas and so a thief will have a hard time remaining incognito.

The Police

Should you be in need of police assistance it is as well to recognise the roles and responsibility of the three main police forces in Spain. The *Policía Municipal* wear blue and white uniforms and are based in police stations called comisarías. They deal with crime in urban areas as well as holding the responsibility for issuing residence permits, identity cards, etc. These are definitely the people to approach in cases of minor disaster, if you are hopelessly lost or need to ask the time.

The *Guardia Civil* wear green uniforms and patrol the rural areas of Spain – also acting as border patrol and frontier guards – and have responsibility for roads and prisons. The *Guardia Civil* is a predominantly military force, which has failed to lose its reputation as a reactionary and somewhat hostile militia, called out to combat riots or strikes as well as more peaceful demonstrations. (It was a *Guardia Civil* colonel, Tejero, who held the Spanish Parliament hostage in the unsuccessful coup of 1981).

The third police force, the *Policía Nacional* (brown uniformed), was much hated for the violence and repression for which it was responsible during the Franco years. The *Policía Nacional* – and their machine-guns – can be found mounting zealous vigil over embassies, stations, post offices and barracks in most cities. Serious crime such as theft, rape or mugging should be reported to the nearest *Policía Nacional* station. The Basques and Catalans both have their own police forces; a result of the Spanish experiment with devolution in which both these Communities were granted home rule.

THE LANGUAGES OF SPAIN

The language that we call Spanish is actually Castilian and is the *lingua franca* spoken throughout the country. The Autonomous Communities, i.e. Catalonia, Galicia and the Basque Country, in addition have their own languages. In the province of Catalonia, the principality of Andorra, parts of the French Pyrenees and the Balearic Islands, Catalan (*catalá*), and its various dialects, are widely spoken. The province of Valencia also has its own language, which developed out of Catalan during the 16th century when huge numbers of Catalan-speaking labourers were moved from the north of the country.

Catalan. Catalan dates back to the ninth century and is currently spoken by six and a half million people. It is worth noting that there is no surer way to offend a Catalonian than to refer to his or her language as a *dialect*. Although Catalan bears a close resemblance to Provençal and therefore to French and Spanish, it is as distinct from each of these as, say, Italian and has as long a history. School children in Catalonia are now taught both Castilian and Catalan and you will find that many road signs and documents in this region appear in both Catalan and Castilian.

Basque. The Basque provinces also have their own language, *euskera* or *euskara*, which is spoken by about 700,000 people. Although some words have been absorbed into the language from French and Spanish, the basic vocabulary and structure are completely unrelated to any known tongue and predate the Roman conquest of Spain. Very few English words derive from Basque – one exception is 'bizarre'; from the Basque word for beard.

Galician. About four-fifths of the 3 million inhabitants of Spain's northwest province speak Galician (*Galego*), which includes elements of both Spanish and Portuguese (and has Celtic roots). Again this is a separate language, not just a dialect. Within Galicia three dialects of *Galego* are spoken.

Learning the language

Knowledge of literary Spanish (Castilian) is much more useful than a knowledge of Catalan, Basque or Galego since all Spaniards understand Castilian but very few outside their communities can communicate in the regional languages. If you choose to live in the great Catalan city of Barcelona or in Valencia, Castilian Spanish will usually be understood. In the more xenophobic parts of Catalonia and the Basque Country, Castilian is reviled, however foreigners are forgiven more easily than Spaniards for speaking Castilian. If you have children who will be going to local schools, be aware that it will be compulsory for them to learn the language of the region, possibly to the exclusion of Castilian.

It is strongly advised that anyone planning to move to Spain try to make some headway learning the language before leaving home. Castilian Spanish is one of the easiest languages to learn at a basic level, especially if the student has a prior knowledge of any of the Romance languages (e.g. French, Italian) and some understanding of the basics of phonology. Spanish is also an international language. After Chinese and English, it is the most prevalent language on earth, spoken by about 250 million people and is the primary tongue in 20 countries.

Language schools and organisations both in Spain and beyond its frontiers offer differing types of course. Some of the most popular forms of language-learning and the organisations which offer these courses are listed below.

Self-Study Courses

The advantage of self-study is that it allows students to work and absorb material at their own pace and in their own time. The BBC produces some excellent workbooks and cassettes at various levels. Further information is available from BBC Customer Services (☎0870-2415 490), via the website www.bbcshop.com or from BBC Education (www.bbc.co.uk/education/languages/spanish). The BBC now also offers an online beginners' course called 'Spanish Steps' as well as the self-study course *España Viva.*

Linguaphone (0800-136 973; www.linguaphone.co.uk) distributes more elaborate (and more expensive) self-study courses in the form of books, cassettes and compact discs which tend to be geared towards holidaymakers and business travellers rather than prospective residents. Consequently, the lessons focus on such subjects as sightseeing, how to order meals and drinks, shopping, making reservations, explaining symptoms to a doctor, etc.

Other books with cassettes currently on the market are *Teach Yourself Spanish* (Hodder & Stoughton), *Colloquial Spanish* (Routledge) and *Teach Yourself Spanish* (Hugo). These and other book-with-cassette courses are generally priced between £20 and £40 and are available from larger bookshops and some libraries.

The *Open University (OU)*, Central Enquiry Service, PO Box 724, Walton Hall, Milton Keynes MK7 6ZS; ☎ 01908-653 231; www.open.ac.uk offers courses leading to an undergraduate degree in Spanish. For example 'A Fresh Start in Spanish' is a level 1 course aimed at people who already have a grounding in the language. It runs from February to October and costs £325.

Language Courses in the UK

Evening language classes offered by local authorities and colleges of further education usually follow the academic year and are aimed at hobby learners or those wishing to obtain a GCSE or A level. Intensive Spanish courses offered privately are much more expensive.

A more enjoyable way of learning a language (and normally a more successful one) is to link up with a native speaker of Spanish living in your local area, possibly by putting an advertisement in a local paper or making contact through a local English language school.

Spanish Societies. It is a good idea to find out if any Anglo-Spanish clubs or societies exist in your area, as these will organise various social events and discussion groups. Check with your local further education institute, university, or local library. It is also worth obtaining details from the Hispanic and Luso Brazilian Council (Canning House, 2 Belgrave Square, London SW1X 8PJ; ☎020-7235 2303; www.canninghouse.com) about its cultural and educational programmes. It also has a library of 50,000 books on Spain, Portugal and Latin America, covering geography, history, current affairs, economics, sociology, natural history, literature, art, music and religion. The *Canning House Library* is open to the public from 2-6.30pm on Mondays and 9.30am-1pm and 2-5.30pm Tuesdays to Fridays. Borrowing facilities and a postal service are available to members only. The Hispanic and Luso Brazilian Council also distribute a free list of Spanish language conversation classes in and around London including addresses of organisations and private tutors offering day or evening language and conversation classes.

Additionally, the Spanish equivalent of the Alliance Française or the Goethe Institute of Germany, is the non-profit *Instituto Cervantes,* now the largest worldwide Spanish teaching organisation, with headquarters in Madrid (C/ Libreros 23, 28801 Alcalá de Henares, Madrid; ☎ 918 856 100; www.cervantes.es). The Cervantes Institute in London, sometimes referred to as the Spanish Institute (102 Eaton Square, London SW1W 9AN; ☎020-7235-0353), has an information and audio-visual department to which members have full access. Manchester also has an *Instituto Cervantes* at 322-330 Deansgate, Manchester M3 4FN; ☎0161-661 4200). The membership fee includes admission to events on their cultural programme such as flamenco performances, classical guitar concerts and exhibitions of paintings.

Total immersion courses in Spanish are offered by international language organisations such as *Berlitz UK* (Lincoln House, 296-302 High Holborn, London WC1 7JH; ☎ 020-7611 9640; fax 020-7611 9656; www.berlitz.com) and *inlingua* (Rodney Lodge, Rodney Road, Cheltenham, Glos. GL50 1HX; ☎ 01242-250 493; www.inlingua-cheltenham.co.uk). Both offer crash courses in Spanish which can be started in Britain and completed in Spain on request. The Berlitz School in Madrid is at Gran Via 80/4, while inlingua Madrid is at Calle Arenal 24 (☎ 915 413 246/7).

Language Courses in Spain

An annotated list of Spanish schools and universities offering Spanish language courses is available from the *Hispanic and Luso Brazilian Council* (Canning House, 2 Belgrave Square, London SW1X 8PJ; ☎020-7235 2303; www.canninghouse.com) for £4 and includes the current prices and details of the courses. Various regional associations of language schools can put you in touch with their member schools. For example the *Associacion de Escuelas de Español para Extranjeros de Andalucía* has links to 16 schools in the main towns of Andalucía (e.g. Cadiz, Córdoba and Granada) on its website at www.aeea.es.

Serious language schools usually offer the possibility of preparing for one of the internationally recognised exams. In Spain the qualification for aspiring language learners is the DELE (*Diploma de Español como Lengua Extranjera*) which is recognised by employers, universities, officialdom, etc. The DELE is split into three levels: *Certificado Inicial de Español, Diploma Básico de Español* and the *Diploma Superior de Español.* Most schools say that even the Basic Diploma requires at least eight or nine months of study in Spain. A prior knowledge of the language allows the student to enrol at a higher level and attain the award more quickly.

Language Schools in Spain. Out of the thousands of language schools offering Spanish courses for foreigners, a small selection is listed here. If you decide to pursue the language after you are established in Spain, look for relevant adverts in the press, for example in *Lookout* magazine, a useful source of information on living and working in Spain published in Málaga.

Aula Magna Castellana: Santo Tomas 1 3D, 40002 Segovia; ☎ 921 412 155; www.aulamagnacastellana.com. Specialised and intensive courses in Segovia from €1,200.

CLIC International House: C/Albardea 19, 41001 Seville; ☎ 954 502 131; www.clic.org. Recreational Spanish courses.

Eat, Sleep & Study Español: C. Doctor Fleming 4, Bjos 2a, 08960 Sant Just, Barcelona; ☎ 933 718 725. Specialises in one-to-one tuition, living, learning and socialising with the tutor.

ENFOREX Spanish Language School: Alberto Aguilera 26, 2°, 28015 Madrid; ☎ 915 943 776; www.enforex.es. Courses at 10 locations, year-round.

Malaca Instituto: Cerrado de Calderón, Calle Cortada 6, 29018 Málaga;

☎ 952 293 242; www.malacainst-ch.es. Variety of Spanish language and culture courses including practical Spanish for the older student, Spanish and Dance lessons (Sevillanas or Salsa), Commercial Spanish, intensive and one-to-one tuition.

Sociedad Hispano Mundial: Ribera del Genil 6, 1° planta (Edif. Real Center), 18005 Granada; ☎ 958 010 172; fax 958 101 173; www.shm.edu. Spanish language courses, plus Spanish civilisation and Hispanic studies courses.

Trinity Language School: PO Box 720, Calle Ave del Paraiso 6, 11500 El Puerto de Santa Maria, Cadiz; ☎ 956 871 926; www.trinitylanguageschool.com. A Mediterranean resort favoured by Spanish holidaymakers.

SIGNING AND ADDRESSING LETTERS IN SPAIN

In Spain, women do not take the surname of the husband when they marry. Instead, the maiden name of the mother is added to the surname of the couple's offspring. The second-to-last name in most Spanish names is the father's name (*apellido paterno*), and the last name is the mother's maiden name (*apellido materno*). Thus the child José, whose father is Arturo Sanchez López and whose mother before she was married was Sarah Perez Reverte, would be José Sanchez Perez. Additionally, a woman traditionally keeps her maiden name after marriage, but drops her mother's family name and replaces it with *de* plus her husband's family name. Thus José's mother is known as Sarah Perez de Sanchez. The Spanish equivalent of the hyphen you see in the occasional English surname (e.g. Olivia Harvey-Nicks) is the Spanish *y* ('and'), as in Gabriel Ramírez y López.

Addresses in Spain

Addresses in Spain are written in the form: C/Marco Polo 4, 2° dcha., 28015 Madrid. How this would translate is: Right-hand Apartment, 2nd Floor, Number 4, Marco Polo Street, Madrid. The postcode is added between the description of the building and the postal town. A post office box number is written as *Apartado de Correos*. Below is a short list of the abbreviations most often used in addresses. Note that in Catalonia, Galicia and the Basque country different spellings may be used which can cause some confusion, though addresses written in Castilian Spanish will always be understood.

ABREVIATIONS USED IN SPANISH ADDRESSES		
Almd	Alameda	Avenue/Boulevard
Av/Avda	Avenida	Avenue
C/	Calle	Street
Cllj	Callejón	Alley/Passage
Cno	Camino	Road/Way
Cril	Carril	Lane
Ctra/Ca	Carretera	Highway
Gta	Glorieta	Roundabout
P°/Po	Paseo	Avenue
Pje	Pasaje	Passage
Pl/Pza	Plaza	Place
Pllo	Pasillo	Passage
Pte	Puente	Bridge
Urb	Urbanización	Housing Estate
Ent	Entresuelo	Ground Floor
1°	1st Floor	
2°	2nd Floor	
3°	3rd Floor etc.	
cto.	Centro	Centre
dcha.	Derecha	Right-hand side
izq.	Izquierda	Left-hand side

PUBLIC HOLIDAYS AND FESTIVALS

The total number of national holidays per year, including the many regional ones, is fourteen. In addition, the various regions and localities have their own festivals and carnivals (often commemorating local saints, with dates liable to change from year to year) when very little apart from bars and hotels will be open for business. As in France, August is the month when all those who can take their annual holiday and at the end of the month up to 20 million Spaniards take to roads to get home as fast as possible – the majority heading from the coasts to the major cities. Many local amenities, especially in the larger cities, close for all or part of August and this should be noted when dealing with bureaucracy etc.

PUBLIC HOLIDAYS

1 January	*Año Nuevo*	New Year's Day
6 January	*Epifanía*	Epiphany
March/April	*Viernes Santo*	Good Friday
March/April	*Domingo de la Resureccion*	Easter Sunday
April	*Lunes de Pascua*	Easter Monday
1 May	*Fiesta del Trabjo*	Labour Day
15 August	*La Asunción*	Feast of the Assumption
12 October	*Día de la Hispanidad*	National Day
1 November	*Todos los Santos*	All Saints' Day
6 December	Día de la Constitución	Constitution Day
8 December	*Fiesta de la Hispanidad*	Feast of the Immaculate Conception
25 December	*Navidad*	Christmas Day

CONVERSION CHART

LENGTH (NB 12inches = 1 foot, 10 mm = 1 cm, 100 cm = 1 metre)

inches	1	2	3	4	5	6	9	12
cm	2.5	5	7.5	10	12.5	15.2	23	30

cm	1	2	3	5	10	20	25	50	75	100
inches	0.4	0.8	1.2	2	4	8	10	20	30	39

WEIGHT (NB 14lb = 1 stone, 2240 lb = 1 ton, 1,000 kg = 1 metric tonne)

lb	1	2	3	5	10	14	44	100	2246
kg	0.45	0.9	1.4	2.3	4.5	6.4	20	45	1016

kg	1	2	3	5	10	25	50	100	1000
lb	2.2	4.4	6.6	11	22	55	110	220	2204

DISTANCE

mile	1	5	10	20	30	40	50	75	100	150
km	1.6	8	16	32	48	64	80	120	161	241

km	1	5	10	20	30	40	50	100	150	200
mile	0.6	3.1	6.2	12	19	25	31	62	93	124

VOLUME

1 litre = 0.2 UK gallons — 1 UK gallon = 4.5 litres

1 litre = 0.26 US gallons — 1 US gallon = 3.8 litres

CLOTHES

UK	8	10	12	14	16	18	20
Europe	36	38	40	42	44	46	48
USA	6	8	10	12	14	18	

SHOES

UK	3	4	5	6	7	8	9	10	11
Europe	36	37	38	39	40	41/42	43	44	45
USA	2.5	3.3	4.5	5.5	6.5	7.5	8.5	9.5	10.5

Residence and Entry

CHAPTER SUMMARY

- **Regulations**. EU citizens (and those of Iceland and Norway) can enter Spain as a tourist without acquiring a visa for a period of up to six months.
  - To obtain a residence permit you will need to visit the *Oficina de Extranjeros* at the *Comisaría Provincial de Policía.*
  - Residence in Spain is not the same as citizenship. Those who wish to become a citizen will need to have lived there for ten years first.
  - If you own homes in Spain and in your native country you will be deemed to be resident in the country where your centre of interests lie.
  - Illegal residents run the risk of being thrown out of the country straight away and being forbidden to return for three years.
  - Non-EU nationals are not meant to go to Spain for the sole purpose of employment without prior permission.
- A *gestor* is a 'fixer' who can deal with all kinds of bureaucracy for you, and can prove to be a godsend when it comes to dealing with paperwork, permits and bureaucrats.

RESIDENCE PERMITS FOR CITIZENS OF THE EU

Spain is a member of the European Union and immigration procedures for Britons follow the pattern as for citizens of other EU countries. EU citizens (and those of Iceland and Norway) can enter Spain as a tourist (they do not need to apply for a visa) for a period of up to six months. If they wish to stay longer they will need to go to the Foreigners' Registration Office (*Oficina de Extranjeros*) in the larger cities or a local police station and apply for a residence permit (*permiso de residencia*). The process is fairly straightforward, although you cannot expect English or other foreign languages to be spoken by the police and taking along a Spanish-speaking friend or using the services of a *gestor* is probably a good idea if you are not conversant with Spanish.

Once in Spain, you are able to apply for permanent residence immediately. To obtain the residence permit you will need to present to the *Oficina de Extranjeros* at the *Comisaría Provincial de Policía* the following documents:

- completed application forms.
- a full valid passport.
- proof of residence (utility bills, rental contract, etc.).
- marriage documents (if applicable).
- four passport-sized photographs.
- a standard medical certificate from your doctor.
- bank statements showing your regular income.
- details of your health insurance (you will need a certificate from the health insurance company stating that full hospitalisation and treatment are covered, or evidence of registration with the Spanish Departments of Health/Social Security, the INSS).

Unfortunately, the list of required documents can vary from office to office and region to region but the process is relatively straightforward. You will be issued with a temporary residence visa valid for a period of one year, after which you will need to renew it. Renewal of temporary residence permits should simply be a formality (and most Britons and Irish citizens can receive a five-year or permanent one). If you move out of Spain or back to your country of origin, then once the residence permit has been handed in at the police station, your right to residency in Spain automatically ceases.

WORK AND RESIDENCE PERMITS FOR CITIZENS OF THE EU

As in other EU and EEA (European Economic Area) countries, nationals of EU member states may enter Spain as a tourist for a period of six months while looking for employment; they do not need work permits as such, but will need residence permits. Once a job has been found, the EU citizen will need to present the contract of employment and Social Security registration documents to the Foreigners' Registration Office (*Oficina de Extranjeros*) of the local police station. A *tarjeta comunitaria* (a residence and work permit) will be issued; valid for a year, after which it will be renewable for a period of five years. Usually, once work has been found, the employer will make the necessary arrangements for registration, otherwise the services of a *gestor* may be required. EU nationals entering Spain to set up a business or who are already in some form of self-employment will need to register with the local police upon arrival. Further details on self-employment can be found in the chapter *Making Money from your Property*.

VISAS AND PERMITS FOR NON-EU CITIZENS

Non-EU or EEA nationals applying to take up residence in Spain have much more red tape to cope with. However, the volume and variety of the bureaucracy will vary according to nationality (and if there are reciprocal health and tax agreements for example). All non-EU nationals should apply for a visa (and work permit if they are intending to take up employment) through the Spanish Consulate in their own country before leaving for Spain.

Non-EU nationals are not meant to go to Spain for the sole purpose of employment without prior permission, but it is worth noting that Canadian and American visitors with a valid passport do not require a visa to visit Spain for a period of up to 90 days; a time which may allow for the organisation of residence or work visas and permits if they happen to find work, and therefore cannot make these arrangements in advance.

Non-EU citizens will require a visa to *live* in Spain (although not necessarily to visit the country) and both a residence and a work permit if they decide to stay in Spain. Work permits can cost up to €300 and are normally issued for 1-5 years, and details of the different classes of permit are given below.

WORK PERMITS FOR NON-EU APPLICANTS

Non-EU citizens are supposed to complete the process legalising their work and residence status in Spain before starting work in Spain. Americans and others from outside the EU will also have to know which type of work permit to apply for: Class A, which covers seasonal or cyclical work; Class B, for 'a given occupation and activity in a given territorial area'; Class C, for those who have already been resident in Spain for some time and covering all categories of employment; Class D, for self-employment in a specific location for up to one year; and Class E, for all categories of self-employment. Class F only concerns you if you do not actually live in Spain but close enough to the Spanish frontier to commute to work in Spain.

Note that in recent years, the Spanish authorities have tightened up on entry and work regulations for non-EU or European Economic Area citizens; which in practice means that many temporary or short-term workers do not bother to apply; and more and more mainly young people who work in tourism or seasonal jobs and come from outside the EU are being expelled. Illegal residents run the risk of being thrown out of the country straightaway and being forbidden to return for three years. It is wise to make sure that all the procedures described below are followed, without taking any 'shortcuts' or trying to drift from tourist to resident status.

For non-EU applicants, the procedures for obtaining a work permit usually take several weeks. Applicants should specify what kind of work permit they are applying for (the different types are listed above). There are exemptions, for categories of workers from the USA or Canada, and elsewhere for foreign academic staff and media correspondents, for example, or representatives of religious organisations. A full list of these can be obtained from the nearest Spanish embassy or consulate. There are also categories for group work permits, trainees and au pairs.

Applications are not accepted by post in any circumstances, and instead should always be made in person or by a representative who has written consent from the applicant to act on his or her behalf. The following documents are required for each application:

- a certified copy of the applicant's passport details.
- a report on the employer's business and a job profile.
- four recent photos.
- a duplicate copy of the applicant's visa application.
- any relevant degrees and qualifications held.
- evidence (if applicable) that the applicant falls into one of the preferential categories noted above.
- evidence that the employer is registered with the Social Security Administration.
- the completed application forms.
- a medical certificate.
- a certificate of your criminal record (should you have one).
- written proof of the offer of employment.

If all the documents are in order, a copy of the application form, medical certificate and the photocopies of the passport, certified by the consulate, will be returned to the applicant as proof that he or she has applied for the visa. All three documents must then be sent to the prospective employer in Spain; who in turn should apply immediately for the work permit at the district department of the Ministry of Labour (*Ministerio de Trabajo*) or the relevant department. The granting of the visa is subject to the approval of the work permit by the Spanish authorities and this usually takes several weeks.

Successful applicants should collect their visas in person as soon as the consulate advises them to do so and must take with them their passports with at least one blank page to affix the visa, the consular fee, and the communication from the consulate stating that the visa is ready for collection. Once in Spain, a work permit can be picked up from the local police station or from the provincial departments of the Ministry of Labour and Bureaux for Foreign Persons; there will be no problem in obtaining this if the residence/work visa is presented.

The type and duration of the work permit will vary according to certain factors, i.e. the type of work undertaken, and the area in which it is done, but in no case will it exceed five years. Work permits will always be issued for the same duration as the residence permit. And their granting and renewal will depend on the following considerations: the level of unemployment in the specific activity for which the permit is applied for; and vacancies available in the profession in which the proposed activity is to be carried out.

A Spanish embassy or consulate can advise on the strict rules of taking up employment in Spain, (i.e. foreigners are normally prevented from doing work that could be done by the Spanish, or undercutting wages and conditions which apply locally) and advise on the documents you will need and the forms to be filled in. You may need to present evidence of qualifications or diplomas held; photocopies of your passport and visa application; a certificate relating to your criminal record (should you have one) and a medical certificate. If you can show evidence that your work is needed to 'organise and start up a foreign enterprise moving entirely or partly to Spain' or other documents that might favour your application so much the better. Unfortunately, the list of required documents can vary and will also depend (for non-EU citizens) on whether a work permit is being renewed at the same time. Excellent detailed information on the legal processes involved can be seen on the website of *The Broadsheet,* an English-language monthly magazine in Madrid (www.thebroadsheet.com).

Extending Work Permits and Other Procedures

Once you have your temporary residence permit or work visa you will at some point have to renew or extend it. The *Oficina* or *Departamento de Extranjeros* at the *Comisaría Provincial de Policía* deals with the renewal of residence or work permits. As with many administrative matters, this may be more conveniently tackled by a *gestor*.

A *gestor* is basically a 'fixer' who can deal with all kinds of bureaucracy for you, and can prove to be a godsend when it comes to dealing with paperwork, permits and bureaucrats. Their offices (*gestorias*) are listed in the yellow pages (*las páginas amarillas*). The simplification of procedures for EU citizens does not mean you will be able to do without the services of a *gestor* – even when it comes to something as relatively simple as renewing a residence permit. Often the only way for you to find out precisely what is required in many administrative matters is to queue at the counter of a *gestoria* along with your Spanish neighbours.

Get a good *gestor* – Stuart Anderson

To try and cope with all the bureaucracy on one's own in a foreign country is never worth it. With the purchase of the house, which was a private deal with the previous owners (i.e. no estate agents involved), we sought out an English-speaking abogada (using the helpful services of the local Collegio de Abogadas). Her work was thorough and she made all the necessary arrangements right through to the completion of signing in the presence of the notario and the processing of the escrituras (which duly arrived some three months later). For other purposes we have used a gestor, again extremely valuable and well worth a little extra expense. He led us through the steps required for obtaining residencia permits; arranging car insurance; private health insurance; property and contents insurance; and kindly reminding me before my 62nd birthday that I needed to arrange a medical test for myself in order to update my driving licence. A good gestor is worth his weight in gold and we found ours by recommendation.

TAX AND RESIDENCY

If you own homes in Spain and in your native country you will be deemed to be resident in the country where your centre of interests lie, i.e. the country where your personal and economic relations are stronger, or in the country where you live most of the time. If you sell your home in your native country and move to Spain permanently you will be deemed to be a Spanish resident. If you spend less than six months a year in Spain you will be classed a non-resident but will be required to carry out certain obligations:

- pay local rates.
- pay utility bills.
- pay income tax on any earnings through business activities in Spain.
- declare all capital assets in Spain and where necessary pay wealth tax on these.
- if you have a car you must pay road tax and have insurance.

Número de identificación de Extranjeros (NIE)

Obtainable from the *oficina de extranjeros* of the local police station the NIE is a tax identification number which is necessary for all property owners to possess whether they are officially resident or non-resident in Spain.

Residency and Citizenship Rights

Residence in Spain is not the same as citizenship. Those who wish to become a citizen of their new host country will need to have lived there for ten years first. Residents of Spain with overseas nationality have most of the rights and obligations of a Spanish national in employment, health and other fields; but no right to vote in elections and no liability to endure military service.

Spanish Residency – Registering with your Embassy

Once resident in Spain, as anywhere in the world, it is also advisable to register with your embassy or consulate: a list of these is provided below. This registration enables the authorities to keep emigrants up to date with any information they need as citizens resident overseas and, in the event of an emergency, helps them to trace individuals. Your embassy or consulate can also help with information regarding your status overseas and advise with any diplomatic or passport problems, and offer help in the case of an emergency, e.g. the death of a relative overseas. However, consulates do not really function as a source of general help and advice.

As a rule, British embassies and consulates interpret their role helping British citizens overseas more strictly than those of many other countries. As many who have needed their help in an emergency have found, diplomats tend to keep within the letter if not the spirit of their duties. Appeals for assistance in matters which fall outside these duties – explained in a leaflet available from embassies/consulates or the *Foreign and Commonwealth Office* (Consular Division, Old Admiralty Building, London SW1A 2PA; ☎ 020-7008 0232; www.fco.gov.uk) – often fall on deaf ears.

Spanish Embassies and Consulates in the UK

Spanish Embassy: 39 Chesham Place, London SW1X 8SB; ☎ 020-7235 5555; fax 020-7259 5392.

Spanish Consulate General: 20 Draycott Place, London SW3 2RZ; ☎ 020-7589 8989; fax 020-7581 7888.

Spanish Consulate General: Suite 1A, Brooke House, 70 Spring Gardens, Manchester M2 2BQ; ☎ 0161-236 1262; fax 0161-228 7467.

Spanish Consulate General: 63 North Castle Street, Edinburgh EH2 3LJ; ☎ 0131-220 1843; fax 0131-226 4568.

Consular Section: Spanish Embassy, 17A Merlyn Park, Ballsbridge, Dublin 4, Ireland; ☎ +353 1269 3444.

British Embassies and Consulates in Spain

British Embassy: C/ Fernando el Santo 16, 28010 Madrid; ☎ 917 008

200; fax 917 008 272; www.ukinspain.com.

British Consulate-General: Paseo de Recoletos 7/9, 28004 Madrid; ☎ 915 249 700; fax 915 249 730.

British Consulate: Plaza Calvo Sotelo 1/2, 03001 Alicante; ☎ 965 216 022/216/190; fax 965 140 528.

British Consulate-General: Edificio Torre de Barcelona, Avenida Diagonal 477-13, 08036 Barcelona; ☎ 933 666 200; fax 933 666 221.

British Honorary Vice-Consul Benidorm: to be contacted through Alicante.

British Consulate-General: Alameda de Urquijo 2-8, 48008 Bilbao; ☎ 944 157 600; fax 944 167 632.

Honorary Consular Agent: Plaza San Cristóbal 3, 18010 Granada; ☎ 669 895 053; fax 958 274 724.

British Vice-Consulate: Avenida de Isidoro Macabich 45-1°, 07800 Ibiza; ☎ 971 301 818/303 816; fax 971 301 972.

British Consulate: Edificio Eurocom, Bloque Sur, C/ Mauricio Moro Pareto, 2, 2°, 29006 Málaga; ☎ 952 352 300; fax 952 359 211 (Postal address: Apartado Correos 360, 29080 Málaga).

British Consulate: Plaza Mayor 3D, 07002 Palma de Mallorca; ☎ 971 712 445; fax 971 717 520.

British Vice-Consulate: Sa Casa Nova, Cami de Biniatap 30, Es Castell, 07720 Menorca; ☎ 971 363 373.

British Consulate: Edificio Cataluña, c/ Luis Morote 6-3°, 35007 Las Palmas de Gran Canaria; ☎ 928 262 508; fax 928 267 774.

British Vice-Consulate: Plaza Weyler 8-1°, 38003 Santa Cruz de Tenerife; ☎ 922 286 863; fax 922 289 903.

Honorary British Consulate: Paseo de Pereda 27, 39004 Santander; ☎ 942 220 000; fax 942 222 941.

Honorary British Consulate: Apartado de Correos/PO. Box 143, 41940 Tomares (Sevilla); fax 954 155 018.

Honorary British Consulate: ☎ 986 437 133; fax 986 112 678; email vigoconsulate@ukinspain.com.

Spanish Education, Labour and Social Affairs Office: 20 Peel Street, London W8 7PD; ☎020- 7727 2462; fax 020- 7229 4965; www.sgci.mec.es/uk/. For advice on work and social security in Spain; and publishes *Regulations for British Nationals Wishing to Work or Reside in Spain.*

Employment Service: Overseas Placing Unit, Rockingham House, 123 West Street, Sheffield S1 4ER; ☎0114-259 6000; www.employmentservice.gov.uk. Publishes information sheet on *Working in Spain.*

Other Embassies and Consulates

Spanish Embassy: 2375 Pennsylvania Avenue, NW, Washington DC 20037; ☎ 202-728-2330; fax 202-728-2302. There are Consulates in Boston, Chicago, Houston, Los Angeles, Miami, New Orleans, New York (☎ 212-355-4090), Puerto Rico and San Franciso.

Spanish Embassy: 74, Stanley Avenue, Ottawa, Ontario K1M 1P4, Canada; ☎ 613-747-2252/7293; fax 613-744-1224. Consulates in Edmonton, Halifax, Montréal, Québec, Toronto, Vancouver and Winnipeg.

United States Embassy: Serrano 75, 28006 Madrid; ☎ 915 872 200; fax 915 872 303; www.embusa.es.

Canadian Embassy: Edificio Goya, Calle Núñez de Balboa 35, 28001 Madrid; ☎ 914 233 250; fax 914 233 251; www.canada-es.org.

Further Assistance. In all your dealings regarding residence and entry requirements, whether to start a business, work, or retire, you should find the process nowadays is relatively straightforward, if at times somewhat time-consuming. Where difficulties do arise while you are in Spain you are recommended to contact solicitors *Cornish & Co.* at their Málaga office (Avda Ricardo Soriano 19, Planta Tercera, 29600 Málaga; ☎952 866 830; www.cornishco.com; e-mail cornish@mercuryin.es).

Part II

Location, Location...

WHERE TO FIND YOUR IDEAL HOME

Where to Find Your Ideal Home

CHAPTER SUMMARY

- **Location**. Many of the major new housing developments are now inland, or adjacent to golf clubs.
  - Foreigners tend to buy property on the Mediterranean *costas* and in the Balearics and Canaries. There are also large expat communities in the bigger cities, especially Barcelona, Granada and Madrid.
  - The Costa de la Luz (Coast of light) is becoming increasingly popular, as it is less developed than the Costa del Sol, with cooler seas and cheaper land.
  - Galicia rates with inland Andalucía as one of the least developed and poorer regions of Spain.
  - Madrid is the seat of the Spanish parliament and is famous for the Prado museum and the dizzy nightlife, which lasts from dusk till dawn.
- Many foreigners opt to buy either new build or off-plan properties.
- It is sensible to spend time during different parts of the year in the area where you would like to buy property.
- The Law of the Coasts (*Ley de Costas*) prohibits building within 100 metres of the high-water mark.
- **Golf**. Spain has over 200 golf courses. The Costa del Sol is often called the 'Costa del Golf'.
- **Services.** The main points to look out for with rural properties are the provision of utilities gas, electricity, sewerage disposal, telephone links and water.
- **Buy to let**. If a property is more than an hour's drive from the nearest airport potential tenants are likely to think twice about renting from you.

OVERVIEW

For many years Spain has been the property buyer's paradise. Traditionally, cheap property, the availability of timeshares, as well as offshore banking and a welcoming atmosphere for expats, have all contributed to its attraction for second-home buyers and potential residents. Currently, however, although many bargains are still available, the Spanish property market, especially in the tourist-saturated areas along the coast, is upgrading itself; and Spain is not the buyer's market it once was (except in some of the less well-known regions where expatriates are still thin on the ground).

Trends. The *costas* are becoming less fashionable than they once were and with the bad publicity which mass tourism has attracted, many of the major housing developments are now inland, or on sites adjacent to golf clubs or similar facilities to attract the more up-market purchaser. There are purpose-built complexes nowadays for retired people as well; and estate agents have become almost like travel agents, offering everything from inspection visits, car hire, and even paying all the bills. Many property developers are now copying the tourist trade and offering an all-inclusive service with the same leisure facilities and amenities that a holidaymaker might expect.

Many foreigners opt to buy either new build or off-plan properties and you are likely to find that this is the area that most estate agents concentrate on; prices for this type of property are generally higher than for the small traditional cottages that may be found in the unfashionable inland areas – expect anything for under £50,000 along the *costas* to be an apartment rather than a villa. Brits still overwhelmingly opt to buy property along the Costa del Sol and the Costa Blanca because of the ease of access by air, the vast array of available properties, some of the best beaches in Spain and good leisure facilities, particularly for golfers. The Costa Brava attracts those who are looking for beautiful surroundings rather than constant sunny weather – it can get pretty cold during the winter months. If winter sun is your criteria then you should consider buying in the Canary Islands, although the summers can be Saharan. The Costa Calida and areas around Murcia are less developed, and have attracted mainly Spanish buyers, however this is changing as prices on the other *costas* have risen.

Comparative Costs. Prospective buyers can keep up with trends by reading the property and travel sections of some of the broadsheet and Sunday newspapers. Obviously, property costs vary greatly according to location. Some of the cheaper areas include the depressed market of the Costa Blanca, while the periphery of the Spanish hinterland (e.g. Castilla La Mancha) is at last beginning to open up to the international property buyer (and more tourists) through the extensive refurbishment of road communications and the revival of interest in these little-discovered and scenically unspoilt areas.

Fashion also dictates property prices. Marbella, once the dream destination of the more affluent expatriate, is now out of favour with the same; so some real property bargains are currently available. For instance, at the time of going to print, a one-bedroomed maisonnette with a large patio, next to the Conception Lake in the Marbella mountains would cost about £55,000 ($80,000). The price range in Marbella is from £30,000 for a one-bedroom flat to £50,000-£55,000 for a larger two-bedroom flat with patio or garden to £100,000 ($145,000) for a three-bedroom town house. In nearby Sotogrande, a luxurious three-bedroom house with private pool costs considerably less than its British equivalent, with one advertised for £150,000 ($215,000). In contrast, Mallorca, which was once relatively unspoilt (especially the north of the island) and Ibiza are enjoying a period of renewed popularity, reflected in the often younger visitors to the islands, and the escalating property costs. All the Balearics seem to have become home to the very rich; who manage to live in secluded isolation from their less affluent British neighbours and can easily pay one and a half million pounds for a holiday home.

WHAT YOUR MONEY WILL BUY

The following are given for guidance. The habitable surface area is given at the end of each entry, where available.

€30,000 – small 2-bed cottage in need of renovation in Salobreña village, on the coast South of Granada.

€40,000 – small property of 160 sq.m in need of renovation on two floors on 3,500 sq.m plot; utilities connected, 40km from La Coruña, Galicia.

€47,000 – semi-detached *cortijo* in need of restoration with outbuildings and utilities connected; 400 sq.m of garden; Almanzora Valley, Andalucía.

€92,000 – 1-bed townhouse on *urbanizacíon;* short walk from beach and community pool, Torremolinos.

€92,000 – 2-bed rustic house with almond, olive and fig trees; good access; 3,700 sq.m plot, Almería.

€97,000 – 2-bedroom apartment with balcony in Puerto Santiago, Tenerife.

€102,000 – 900 sq.m plot for self-build, with water and electric connection; 10km from Denia town.

€105,000 – character property of stone and wood with potential to renovate and expand; gardens and garage; 4km from Salamanca near Zarapicos golf course.

€108,000 – new-build apartment of 62 sq.m with balcony on *urbanizacíon* in La Calera, Gomera, Canary Islands.

€110,000 – 2-bed apartment with terrace and shared pool on *urbanizacíon*, Addaya, Menora.

€126,000 – 1-bed apartment 150m from beach with sea views, Costa Blanca South.

€134,000 – 2-bed cottage in need of updating in fishing village near Salobreña with roof terrace and sea views.

€137,000 – 2-bed apartment with sea and sierra views; garaging; Mijas Costa. €146,000 – 2-bed, 2-bathroom terraced house with roof garden on *urbanizacíon* by golf course, Costa Blanca South.

€152,000 – 3-bed *finca* on plot of 1,000 sq.m, San Vicente.

€160,000 – 4-bed house with small pool; 4,000 sq.m plot, El Rio, Costa Azahar.

€166,000 – 2-bed flat in new complex in Poble Nou, Barcelona.

€166,000 – 1-bed renovated flat in Palma old town, Mallorca.

€179,000 – 2-bed detached house on plot of 500 sq.m situated by San Jorge golf course, Costa Azahar.

€210,000 – new-build 2-bed semi-detached villa on *urbanizacíon*, Calpe.

€210,000 – new-build house on plot of 450 sq.m 5km from Alicante and 15 minutes from beach.

€390,000 – luxury apartment with sea views on Bendinat Estate, Mallorca .

€390,000 – 10-bed chalet with terraces and garden. Potential to be converted into four apartments; 10km from Palma, Mallorca.

€450,000 – 3-bedroom 260 sq.m *masia* on plot of 2,500 sq.m near French border.

€700,000 – 4-bed *finca* with living area of 325 sq.m on 12,000 sq.m plot with garages, pool, guest house and views into National Park; near Algeciras.

€1,021,000 – 6-bed villa with sea views and pool, Marbella.

€1.26 million – 5-bed 400 sq.m country house set on 25,000 sq.m plot with gardens, pool and independent detached villa, Alayor, Menorca.

Here and elsewhere, living costs have risen; and in Mallorca your everyday expenses will be noticeably more (around 20%) than they are even in London; although prices for food, electricity, water charges, and so on are more or less the same as those in Britain away from the islands, and outside the more expensive Madrid and Barcelona areas.

Golf

Spain has over 200 golf courses: 16 in the Balearics, 10 in the Canaries, 24 in the central areas of Spain around Madrid, 23 on the Costa Blanca (the majority around Torrevieja and north of Benidorm), 35 on the Costa Brava, 14 on the Costa le la Luz, 7 on the Costa Tropical (East and West of Almería), 18 in the northwest of the country, 21 in northern Spain, 7 in western Spain and 34 along the Costa del Sol. Bearing these figures in mind, and the climate of the regions, the Costa del Sol is the place for the golfer. The 'Costa del Golf' is well known as a winter golf resort which grew out of a boom period in the late eighties. Between 1985 and 1991 no fewer than 17 new golf courses appeared, bringing the total along the 50-mile stretch of coast up to thirty.

When Valderrama was chosen to host the Ryder Cup in 1997, the Costa del Sol received universal recognition as the finest winter golf resort in Europe, which has in turn led to many new golf courses being constructed. Golf course owners are re-investing in their courses to further improve the quality, and every course has its own particular challenge on the well-kept fairways and greens. In 2003 there were 60 golf courses already built or planned in Andalucía.

For those looking to find the choicest locations for a life of leisurely golf, several websites have details of Spain's golf courses. As yet there isn't a guidebook on the market outlining the pros and cons of the courses but www.siestaland.com has a good rundown of what's on offer, and there are a number of other sites such as www.golfeurope.com and www.golfinspain.com which give the golfer a description of the courses available. There are also a number of complexes built around golf courses and these are a godsend for the enthusiastic golfer – though prices are steep because of the demand for such properties.

Information Facilities

A good starting point when looking for information on Spain in your home country is the Spanish National Tourist Office. The SNTO (www.tourspain.es) can provide national maps, railway guides and brochures for all the main Spanish towns and regions. In Spain itself you will find an SNTO in every large town and from these you can obtain specific local guidebooks and information on hotels, car hire, the principal sights, and so on. In addition, there are tourist information bureaux (*Turismo*) run by individual municipalities. Generally speaking, the tourist offices and bureaux only carry information on their own particular region. The *Mapa de Comunicaciónes España*, which can be supplied by the SNTO, lists details of each of the local tourist information offices, with information on customs posts, driving in Spain and speed limits, motorway assistance, railway information, useful telephone numbers, and *paradores* – government-run inns and hotels.

The central reservation number for Spanish *paradores* is 915 166 666; fax 915 166 657 (Paradores de Turismo, Requena 3, 28013 Madrid; www.parador.es). In Britain, *Keytel International* (402 Edgware Road, London W2 1ED; ☎ 020-7616 0300; fax 020-616 0317; e-mail paradors@keytel.co.uk) will send you a booking form and general information including insurance and car hire details, and a Directory of Paradores in Spain. To arrange accommodation in advance *Room Service* (42 Riding House Street, London, W1W 7EU; ☎ 08704-430 530; fax 08704-430 529; www.room-service.co.uk) also has a brochure for Spain, featuring some charming and affordable hotels and pensions from £25 a night for a double room throughout the country. Flights, car hire and tailor-made itineraries can also be arranged.

When looking for possible estate agents in the area that you are hoping to buy in a useful resource is the website www.themovechannel.com. The website acts as a portal for estate agents and property companies dealing in the various regions of Spain.

THE REGIONS OF SPAIN

In Spain, foreigners have tended to buy property on the Mediterranean *costas* and in the Balearics and Canaries, however, there are also large expat communities in the bigger cities, especially Barcelona, Granada and, of course, Madrid. The average price of a second home in Spain is £129,000/ €194,790; the most sought after properties being newly built complexes. The Canary Islands, the Balearic Islands and the area stretching from Denia on the northern stretches of the Costa Blanca down towards Murcia are particular favourite locations for second homes. Prices obviously vary depending on the size of a property and the location. For example the average cost of a property in Alicante is £74,340; on the Canaries £68,144; while on the Costa del Sol average properties sell for £167,265.

Spain as we know it today has grown out of a number of separate states and kingdoms (for example Asturias, founded in the tenth century), making it a complex country with a mix of peoples and cultures. The regions and provinces described below represent the current political make-up of Spain. Although most people seeking to buy property in Spain are likely to find themselves in the better-known regions of the country, there are vast areas of Spain, such as Extremadura, which are practically ignored by both tourists and house-hunters alike. *Spain Off the Beaten Track* by Barbara Mandell and Roger Penn (Moorland Publishing Co.) is an excellent guide to some of these more out-of-the-way destinations.

THE MEDITERRANEAN REGIONS

ANDALUCÍA

Main cities and provinces: Almería, Cádiz, Córdoba, Granada, Huelva, Jaén, Málaga and Sevilla (Seville).

Andalucía is the second largest autonomous region of Spain and has its own parliament, allowing it a large amount of self-government. The region covers 17% of Spain's total area and has on average 300 days of sunshine a year. It is the most populated region of Spain with around seven million inhabitants and takes its name from al-Andaluz – the stronghold of Muslim Arabs and Berbers who crossed from North Africa in the eighth century, virtually took over the Iberian Peninsula in less than four years and were finally driven from their last stronghold in Granada by the Christians in the mid-fifteenth century. Andalucía's Moorish past can be seen in the great monuments that survive from that period, most notably the cities of Córdoba, Seville and Granada. The Alhambra Palace in Granada is regarded as one of the world's greatest buildings.

Andalucía is also the home of the gypsy guitar and flamenco. However, in contrast to its culturally rich past Andalucía today displays extremes of poverty and wealth. Part of its coastline, the Costa del Sol, is one of the most popular tourist destinations on earth and home to an estimated 200,000 foreigners – the majority of whom are Brits – while the region itself has one of the highest unemployment rates in Europe (over 20% in some areas), where peasants eke out an existence on smallholdings and through seasonal work.

The Costa del Sol

More than 60% of British people looking to buy property in Spain choose properties on the Costa del Sol and most of the development so far has taken place west of Málaga, with perpendicular concrete running virtually all the way to Marbella. The western reaches of the Costa del Sol – between Málaga and Cádiz – has one of the most developed coastlines in Europe. The notorious tourist centres of Fuengirola, Torremolinos and Calahonda are along this stretch, as well as the more upmarket towns such as Marbella, Estepona and Puerto Banús. Property for sale along this stretch is either new or fairly new resale buildings. The highest prices will be asked for property lying between the N340 and the sea and in the environs of Marbella. Inland there are still some bargains to be had but the more beautiful the setting (e.g. towns such as Ronda and Mijas) the higher the price of property.

East of Málaga concrete is also proliferating – principally around the resorts of Nerja, Almuñécar and Salobreña. The main coastal road, the N340, is known locally as the *Carretera del Muerte* ('highway of death'). Virtually a motorway, the road runs through urban areas and fatalities are common – caused by pedestrians jaywalking and those unfamiliar with the Spanish Highway Code (often intoxicated British package holidaymakers) trying to run across it.

East of Málaga development has been a little less rampant and there aren't the long swathes of beach as along the west of the *costa*. Prices are cheaper here and the area has managed to hold on to its roots. Fincas in need of renovation can be found for around £50,000 and a beachside villa complete with pool will be cheaper here than to the west of Málaga.

West of the Costa del Sol

West of the Costa del Sol – between Estepona and Tarifa – is a less built-up area of coastline, and about halfway between these two towns lies Gibraltar, still British and a banking and money moving centre, but a thorn in the side of any prospective Anglo-Spanish political alliance. Luxury housing developments are beginning to sprout in the vicinity, notably Sotogrande and La Duquesa; and many people choose to live not too far from English-speaking Gibraltar where they can shop at Marks and Spencer and Mothercare and visit the local Safeway supermarket. This region is also the easiest to get to by way of Málaga airport. In August 2002 the final stretch of motorway linking Estepona to Sotogrande was completed and this has meant that travelling to the western Costa del Sol is reachable from Málaga within 50 minutes. This ease of access will inevitably have a knock-on affect

Bay of Biscay
Corunna
Lugo
Galicia
Asturias
Cantabria
Pontevedra
León
Orense
Burgos
Palencia
Atlantic
Ocean
Castile and
León
Zamora
Valladolid
Segovia
Salamanca
Avila
Madrid
Cáceres
Toledo
Castile la
Estremadura
Ciudad Real
Badajoz
Córdoba
Jaén
Huelva
Andalusia
Sevilla
Granada
Gulf of Cadiz
Málaga
Cádiz
N
0
100
200 Kms
0
50
100 Miles

Regions & Provinces of Spain
The Basque Country
Biscay
Guipuzcoa
Alava
Navarre
Rioja
Huesca
Lérida
Gerona
Aragon
Catalonia
Soria
Zaragoza
Barcelona
Tarragona
Guadalajara
Teruel
Cuenca
Castellón
Balearic Islands
Menorca
Mallorca
Mancha
Valencia
Ibiza
Albacete
Formentera
Alicante
Murcia
Mediterranean Sea
Almeria
La Palma
Lanzarote
Gomera
Tenerife
Hierro
Fuerte-Ventura
Gran Canaria
The Canary Islands

upon house prices in the region.

There are two Spanish outposts of Melilla and Ceuta on the North African (Moroccan) coast, which are officially parts of Andalucía and beg the question of Spain's hypocrisy in demanding the return of the Rock while still claiming sovereignty over two towns in Morocco. Further west along the coast from Gibraltar is another landmark of British history – the Cape of Trafalgar – and beyond that the Gulf of Cádiz, an area of relatively unspoilt coastline that eventually meets the Portuguese border. The famed Coto Doñana wetland wildlife park can be found in this area.

Andalucía also contains some of Spain's largest mountain ranges: the Sierra Morena, and the highest range – the Sierra Nevada – dominates the Moorish town of Granada. There are ski resorts in both ranges. The province of Jaén behind Granada is famed for its olives, while Almería is partly desert – parched vistas, cacti, tumbleweeds and all. Several Westerns have been filmed in this region. There is a small collection of foreign-owned villas in and around the hill town of Mojácar near Almería city though most are inhabited during the mild winter months only, as summers tend to be too hot and dry. For those interested in exploring the region from the UK, Ramblers Holidays offers a range of walking tours through the countryside as well as the larger towns. Contact them on 01707-331 133 or visit their website at www.ramblersholidays.co.uk. If you have a passion for golf then Andalucía will certainly be the right place for you: there are over 60 courses in the region – thirty of them in the 50 miles or so between Málaga and Gibraltar.

Andalucían Property

Property prices in Andalucía at the lower end of the scale fell by around 15% in 2002, but are expected to rise in the long term. Prices peaked in the 1970s but are picking up again. UK residents account for 650,000 of the permanent population of the Costa del Sol and it is the fastest growth area of population in Europe according to a report by the property firm Hamptons International (www.hamptons.co.uk). A top end villa with pool located a few miles from the sea will fetch around half a million pounds. A villa on a smaller scale on the coast will sell for around £250,000 depending on location. Smaller houses in good condition away from the sea can go for £150,000, while it is still possible to buy one bedroom flats in golf complexes for about £75,000. In general you will find that prices are lower on the eastern side of the Costa del Sol (east of Marbella), and inland (although a property in the white villages will not be cheap).

Andalucián Cuisine

Andalucía has a vast array of food to offer due to its proximity to the sea, the climate and its Moorish heritage. Fruit and vegetables grow in abundance – oranges, lemons, olives, grapes, tomatoes, melons, pears and cherries. Because of the number of foreigners living in Andalucía there is also a great many restaurants and pubs serving staple dishes that you would find back in the UK, in Germany, Holland, and Scandinavia. Traditional Andalucían dishes include *gazpacho* (chilled soup – often tomato-based but also almond-based), *calamares* (squid), *Pescaito frito* (fried fish), cured ham, bean stews and dishes such as *migas* that were common when the region was at its poorest. Andalucía is home to the refreshing garlic-almond soup, tasty olives and world-famous sherries.

SOME ANDALUCÍAN SPECIALITIES	
Alfajores	nut and honey dessert
Habas con Jamón	fava beans with ham
Heuvos a la Flamenca	baked eggs with sausages and vegetables
Menudo	chick-pea and vegetable stew
Pestiños	fried pastries with honey
Polvorones	sugar biscuits
Rabo de Toro	oxtail soup
Riñones al Jerez	kidneys in sherry sauce
Tocino de Cielo	caramel flan

The Costa del Sol

Marbella

This small but cosmopolitan city has long been associated with decadent discos and nightclubs, chic boutiques and palaces built for rich Arabs and the jet-set. The pretty town is conveniently located half an hour's drive from Málaga airport and the old town, dating from the Middle Ages, has been carefully restored. Nearby is Puerto Banús harbour with its floating gin palaces, and behind the town is the spectacular Juanar mountain reserve. Marbella boasts 27km of coastline with 24 beaches within its city limits, as well as mountains topped by the unmistakable La Concha peak. Some of the world's finest golf courses are situated nearby.

In 2002 a rash of new properties came onto the market, pushing prices down by 15%. The journey from Málaga airport to Marbella takes 35 minutes and just under an hour to get to Gibraltar by car. When searching for property be aware that some have been developed on rustic and greenfield sites – planning permission may have been given illegally and banks will refuse mortgages on such properties. Cash buyers should also be cautious and get everything thoroughly checked by their lawyers. Prices of property in and around Marbella are some of the most expensive in Spain and villas, especially at the top end of the market, are highly sought after.

Mijas

Mijas is located on a mountainside 8km inland of Fuengirola and apart from being billed as a typical Andalucían white village with Moorish origins, it also has a fair amount of holiday and second home developments – both *urbanizaciónes* and villas. The walled town is picturesque with winding lanes and little squares filled with restaurants and shops and a miniature bullring. Mijas is the place of choice for many permanent expat residents. The many hilltops surrounding the town and along the descent to the coast are natural attractions for a dream villa with magnificent views.

Nearby attractions include the new horseracing venue, the Mijas Hipódromo, the first of its kind on the Costa del Sol, and the Tivoli amusement park. While enjoying the tranquillity of the mountain setting, the coast is only minutes away at Fuengirola and Benalmádena. Marbella is about 15 minutes drive to the west while Málaga airport – to the east – is closer still. Property in Mijas is not the bargain it once was.

Estepona

Estepona is a modest jewel of the Costa del Sol, the whitewashed old buildings of its historic town centre sandwiched between a wide, glistening beachfront and a dramatic mountain backdrop. It is a town large enough for major shopping and entertainment but small enough to cover in a comfortable walk and to offer an intimate ambiance. Located just beyond the areas of mass tourism, Estepona retains an authentic flavour of small-town Andalucía. Located on the western side of the Costa del Sol, Estepona is between Marbella and Gibraltar. Malaga airport is around 45 minutes away along the N340 while Gibraltar airport can be reached in about 30 minutes. Travel to the western Costa del Sol has been improved with the extension of the dual carriageway from Estepona through to Sotogrande.

The old town centre has winding narrow lanes with white townhouses and plazas. Estepona port has numerous bars and restaurants and plans are afoot for the expansion of its marina into a major port with berthing for cruise liners. Other draws are the renovated beach promenades and seafront, the Estepona Equestrian Centre and riding school, the Estepona and nearby Duquesa golf courses, plus a dozen or so others dotted around Marbella and

Sotogrande. Nearby attractions include the gigantic wildlife park, Selwo, and the white villages such as Casares and Gaucin. The British enclave of Gibraltar and flash Marbella lie less than half an hour to either side. Estepona is a long-time favourite of many foreign residents and property is still quite cheap, especially flats in older apartment blocks in town.

Manilva

Eleven kilometres southwest of Estepona this traditional small town is located on a hilltop overlooking the coast backed by the Sierra Bermeja. Fishing and agriculture have been the main occupations of its inhabitants throughout its history but tourism has steadily developed, and the town is now surrounded by residential developments, La Duquesa Golf Club, and a marina.

Despite its prime location on the coast, Manilva lacks the anonymous concrete towers that typify much of the real estate on the Costa de Sol. The majority of residents live in the commercial centre, which covers just two kilometres, 128 metres above sea level. The surrounding area is mainly agricultural. Manilva is 98km from Málaga.

Sotogrande

As well as having some of the most expensive and exclusive properties on the Costa del Sol Sotogrande also has some of the best sporting amenities. Since the 1960s when the western end of the Costa del Sol still consisted of little more than windswept dunes and small Andalucían villages, Sotogrande has stood as an exclusive getaway for the wealthy. The original resort, designed to attract the well-heeled, spreads among the broad beachfronts near Gibraltar and has since grown into a full-fledged community with numerous residential developments.

Sotogrande is situated at the far west of the Costa del Sol, close to La Linea, the Spanish town across the border from Gibraltar. Estepona lies some twenty minutes away to the east, Marbella only another 20 minutes drive further up the coast. Málaga airport can be reached by car in an hour and a half, though the new dual carriageway between Estepona and Sotogrande will cut this time significantly. Gibraltar airport is only minutes away but has fewer flights to choose from than Málaga.

Sotogrande remains an exclusive location offering some of the highest quality property, along with the highest prices, on the Costa del Sol. In addition to the villas of Sotogrande proper there are more recent apartments available in the port. The range of the development is so extensive that it is almost a small town. Sotogrande has the finest golf courses on the Costa del Sol with the Valderrama,

> Almenara, La Cañada, San Roque Club and Real Club de Sotogrande courses close by. Sotogrande also has a large marina, polo and horse riding facilities, commercial services and an excellent international school. Property in Sotogrande is uniformly expensive.

La Duquesa

A prestigious and well-managed development, the port of La Duquesa offers full marina services for boating enthusiasts as well as the promenades encircling the port offering a variety of restaurants, bars and cafés. Two nights a week the port hosts a unique Crafts Market, popular with local residents as well as visitors. La Duquesa Golf and Country Club boasts an 18-hole course. In addition to golf, the club offers many facilities including tennis, squash, and a fully equipped gym. Close by are the Alcaidesa Links course overlooking Gibraltar; Valderrama, host of the Ryder Cup and World Championship; Sotogrande, a parkland course; and La Cañada. San Roque, host to the qualifying schools, is also only a few minutes away. There are another 40 or so courses within an hour's drive or under construction. Winter and spring skiing is available only two hours away in Granada.

Casares and Ronda

Casares, fifteen minutes drive from La Duquesa, is the quintessential Andalucían hilltop village. Its incredible setting, perched on the edge of a cliff topped by a medieval castle, has made Casares the most photographed village in Spain. Ronda (45 minutes away) is an historical city with its famed and spectacular bridge straddling both sides of the huge gorge bisecting the town. Ronda has beautiful churches and monuments which serve to highlight the incredible scenery surrounding the city. And again – often an additional bonus in this area – the drive to Ronda is an event in itself as it passes through ancient hilltop villages along rugged mountain ridges. Prices vary depending on the state of the property and the view.

Puerto Banús

Puerto Banus, just west of Marbella before you reach the town of San Pedro de Alcántara, has an impressive mountain backdrop and ocean views. Since its inception some forty years ago, the leisure port has steadily grown and now features a casino, commercial shopping centre, an El Corte Inglés department store, boutiques, a marine observatory and a multi cinema. The beach adjacent to Puerto Banús holds a European blue flag.

San Pedro de Alcántara

San Pedro de Alcántara, just 10km west of Marbella and 20km east of

Estepona is also just a few minutes drive away from the Sierra de Ronda mountain range. In the second week in October San Pedro also has the last summer fair (*feria*) in Andalucía. There is an ancient basilica and necropolis in woods next to the Bora Bora Beach Club on the town's sea front. Nueva Alcántara is the beach side area by San Pedro, home to a great deal of new development with thriving shops, restaurants and hotels.

Benalmádena

Benalmádena is located to the west of Málaga and Torremolinos, although due to the expansion of both Benalmádena and Torremolinos it is difficult to say where one resorts ends and the other begins. Benalmádena's tourist explosion occurred later than Torremolinos' and so has managed to avoid some of the uglier 1970s developments that make up the latter.

The new Puerto Marina has an 'international' feel to it and the area is crammed with a variety of nightclubs and bars playing the latest music and staying open until sunrise (or later). The town boasts a sea-life centre and the Tivoli theme park and Benalmádena Costa has aimed for a more family-based clientele than the 'young, fun-in-the-sun' image associated with Torremolinos. The municipality of Benalmádena is divided into three areas: Benalmádena Pueblo, Benalmádena Costa and Arroyo de la Miel. Benalmádena Pueblo, the original village, remains largely a typical Andalucían village 280 metres above sea level in the foothills of the mountains sweeping down to the sea. Benalmádena has a fair amount of affordable property away from the marina.

Salobreña & the Costa Tropical

An hour's drive east from Málaga airport, Salobreña is due south and 45 minutes drive away from the mountains of the Sierra Nevada and the villages of La Alpujarra. Located 2km inland from the coast, Salobreña is surrounded by a tropical plain. In winter you can, if so inclined, ski in the Sierra Nevada in the morning and sunbathe on the coast in the afternoon. The ski fields are approximately an hour away by car. Salobreña has a maze of narrow streets leading up to an old Moorish castle. At the bottom of the town is the commercial centre where you will find shops, supermarkets, banks and the town hall. The long black sandy beach below the town stretches all the way to the port of Motril. Beside the beach is a golf course. For a property needing some renovation work expect to pay around £100,000; a three bedroom villa with a swimming pool and view will cost around £300,000.

Eastern Costa del Sol and Inland Andalucía

Nerja

Nerja, some 55km east of Málaga on the N340 coastal highway, marks the eastern end of the Costa del Sol. Once a quiet fishing village the town now has a population of over 12,000 but development has seen more villas than concrete tower blocks being erected. Nerja boasts 16km of beaches and is flanked by the dramatic Sierra Almijara. All major water sports are available here, including water skiing, scuba diving and sailing.

The town's old quarter has narrow, winding streets and whitewashed houses with wrought iron terraces. The spectacular Balcón de Europa has a magnificent promenade along the edge of a towering cliff, giving panoramic views of the Mediterranean and the small coves and beaches below. A few km from Nerja are enormous natural caverns containing paintings over 20,000 years old and other pre-historic remains. One of them has been transformed into a concert hall, where many performances are staged during the summer. The N340 coast road is only dual carriageway as far as Torre del Mar which is about 20km distant. This section of the coast road can be slow especially at peak periods. Prices in and around Neja vary from a modest 110,000 euros for a 2-bedroom apartment to a quarter of a million euros for a villa with views.

RioGordo

RioGordo, half an hour's drive inland from Málaga airport, has some of the most beautiful countryside of rolling hills and farmland, and views over the Sierras down to the sea. It is an area dedicated to olive and almond farming. The towns and cities of Antequera, Nerja, Málaga and Granada are all close by. This inland region of Spain offers far better value for money than equivalent properties on the coast.

Antequera

The largest town in the province in terms of area, most of the municipality of Antequera is made up of fertile plains devoted to olive and cereal production 540 metres above sea level, surrounded by the El Torcal and El Arco Calizo Central Sierras. The attractive town stretches across the side of a hill at the foot of the Sierra del Torcal. It lies 50km inland from Málaga.

The Costa de Almería

> The Costa de Almería lies in the southeast corner of Andalucía. It is a dry land with 190km of coastline with clean, long beaches. Not yet as overcrowded as

most other Spanish tourist resorts, the Costa de Almería has bays, inlets and cliffs and is an ideal place for those who want to get away from it all and want to live in a more traditional Spanish environment. The climate in Almería is subtropical, with an average winter temperature of 16° Celsius. It has the most sunshine hours of the whole of Spain. The area is great for water sports and there are a number of golf courses – such as the 18-hole golf course Marina Golf at Almería's main resort, Mojácar Playa. The area also has famous archaeological sites as Los Millares and El Algar. The subterranean caves at Sorbas are of great interest and include the most important Gypsum Karst in Europe. There is also the Mini Hollywood theme park in the desert near Tabernas where a few fistfulls of Spaghetti Westerns were filmed. There is an international airport 8km from Almería city (which also has a train station), and other airports at San Javier in Murcia and Alicante serve the area. The resorts and main towns of Almería are served by the main Mediterranean coast road that runs from the border with France all the way to Cádiz. Depending on the time of year travel times can be fast or crowded and slow. Coastal property in this region is still among the cheapest you will find.

Mojácar

The upper Moorish fortress town of Mojácar Pueblo stands on a towering crag overlooking the modern beach resort of Mojácar Playa – a strip of beach 7km long. In the 1960s Mojácar had become a ghost town after most of its inhabitants went north to find work in the factories of the Barcelona region. To attract new residents, the town's mayor gave land away to anyone who promised to build within a year. Mojácar started to grow and in the following decades tourist developments started to spring up. Directly south of Mojácar is the Cabo de Gata nature reserve. Around the area of Mojácar and Vera there are seven golf courses. Road access is excellent in this area, and the airport at Almería is approximately 45 minutes away by car. Prices are still pretty cheap around Mojácar with a 2-bedroom apartment fetching in the region of 50,000 euros.

The Costa de la Luz

The Costa de la Luz (Coast of light) is becoming increasingly popular as it is less developed than the Costa del Sol, with cooler seas and cheaper land. This coastline is at the western end of the Andalucían coastline, facing out to the Atlantic. The temperatures are slightly milder in the winter than on the Costa del Sol and the beaches are more spread-out, and often backed by sand dunes and pine trees. This part of the coast has not yet seen the high-rise hotel development of other areas. At present, property prices on the Costa de la Luz are rising fast as more and more people are discovering the potential of the region. The estate agents are cashing in on this interest and upping their price lists.

Tarifa

The southernmost point in Europe is situated at the point where two seas meet – the Mediterranean Sea and the Atlantic Ocean. Its name comes from 'Tarif Ibn Malluk', a Berber chief, and the town began with the construction of a castle in the 10th century. Tarifa is only 14km away from Africa and has nearly 38 kilometres of beaches in the municipal area, which are a considerable draw for surfers from around the world. Further inland, there is the Los Alcornocales Natural Park. Other activities, markedly different to the golfing and leisure industries on the Costa del Sol, include the rearing of fighting bulls and horses, windsurfing and underwater fishing.

Conil de la Frontera

Conil de la Frontera is a small town with a traditional Spanish atmosphere. Although becoming an increasingly popular tourist resort it is still a typical Andalucían town with narrow cobbled streets, tapas bars and an open-air market at weekends and pavement cafes around the main plazas. There are a number of beaches around Conil from sandy beaches to coves backed by cliffs.

Chiclana de la Frontera

Chiclana de la Frontera is situated at the south of Cádiz Bay. To the east is the river, Cano de Sancti Petri, separating Chiclana from San Fernando and Cádiz. At the mouth of this river on the Atlantic coast lies the beautiful island of Sancti Petri, and very fine sandy beaches. The ideal coastline and hotels and sports complexes makes Chiclana a high quality destination. Six kilometres from Chiclana, is the beautiful eight kilometres long Barrosa Beach. Within its 8km, La Barrosa offers an urbanised promenade with shops and bars and restaurants as well as virgin beach, which has won a European Blue Flag Award for clean beaches.

Sancti Petri

Sancti Petri is situated between Chiclana de la Frontera and Conil, near La Barrosa Beach. Sancti-Petri is a large, 4,000 hectares, *urbanización* with 4km of coast. It has apartments, chalets, and lots of land available to build overlooking the Atlantic Ocean in addition to numerous bars, shops, restaurants and a golf course. The area also boasts horse riding and eight tennis courts. The golf course here was designed by Severiano Ballesteros, and features four water obstacles. In Sancti Petri harbour nearby, there is mooring capacity for 724 boats, a yacht club, a chandlery and a sailing and windsurfing school. Jerez de la Frontera airport is 50km away by car to the north.

Sanlúcar de Barrameda

Situated on the mouth of the Guadalquivir River next to the Parque Nacional Doñana, Sanlúcar de Barrameda has a typical fisherman's quarter 'Bajo de Guia' and bodegas where the Manzanilla wine is produced. The town has good sports facilities, a yacht club and a bullring. Horse racing is held on the fine beaches here in the month of August.

Arcos de la Frontera

The starting point of the White Villages Route, this village is one of the most atmospheric in Spain, surrounded as it is by olive and orange trees, and fertile farmland. The surrounding countryside is engaged in the rearing of bulls and horses. Since 1962 the old quarter has been declared area of historical artistic interest for its natural beauty.

Vejer de la Frontera

Vejer de la Frontera is a pretty town perched on top of a 200m hill, about 15km from Cádiz. The white houses are crowded together on this hill and from the *Castillo* on the very top you have a beautiful panoramic view of the whole area. Vejer is a perfect example of Moorish/Andalucían architecture. It is a favoured area for the practise of gliding, and being only 9km from the coast, it is also known for its beaches and underwater fishing and surfing.

Ronda

Most people tend to search for property within a 12-mile radius of Ronda for reasons of access. Equidistant from Málaga and Seville, Ronda attracts a number of artists. Surrounding whitewashed villages remain Spanish/Andalucían to the core and you may find that little English is spoken. In the more rural areas there will be no telephone and electricity lines and the populace rely on wells for their water supply. Because of the nearby nature reserves in the Sierra de las Nievas and Sierra de Grazalema there are strict building regulations and though you may be lucky enough to find a ruin and get planning permission to restore it, you will not be allowed to extend the property.

Prices of properties in and around the 'white villages' such as Ronda can be bargains – it is possible to pick up houses in villages for around £40,000 and less but expect a fair amount of renovation work to be done on such properties. Prices for villas with pools can go as high as £1 million. Fincas sell for around £100,000+ though it is possible to find a finca in need of repair for about £65,000. The further away from Ronda, the more rural the setting, the cheaper the property.

MURCIA AND VALENCIA

Provinces and main cities: Murcia, Alicante, Castellón and Valencia.
The provinces of Murcia and Valencia between them make up nearly 7% of the area of Spain and are home to just over 12% of the population. Murcia is separate from, though adjacent to, the region of Valencia but there could hardly be a greater contrast between Murcia – the driest place in Spain – and Alicante, Valencia and Castellón which make up Valencia (*País Valenciano*), one of the most fertile. Valencia has strong historical associations with the Catalonian/Aragonese partnership, which conquered it in the twelfth century, and shares a linguistic heritage with Catalonia, although arguments still rage as to whether Valencian is in fact a language in its own right or a dialect of Catalan.

Murcia does not have as strong a regional identity as its Valencian neighbour and in the thirteenth century was a part of the united territory ruled over by the dynasties of Castille and Aragon. The Aragonese kingdom at that time also encompassed Catalonia. The historical link between Catalonia and Murcia led many inhabitants of the region to pour into Catalonia after the Spanish Civil War in search of work. It was at this time, too, that Murcians seem to have acquired an unfortunate and unmerited reputation for being uncouth and violent, which has become part of national lore to the extent that to many Spaniards 'Murcian' is a term of abuse. The main port of Murcia, Cartegena (named after the Carthaginians who founded it) is a large naval base whose nightlife is described by one guidebook as 'lively, if somewhat dangerous.'

To the east of Murcia is the province of Alicante, on whose Costa Blanca ('White Coast') are the beaches and resorts frequented by package tourists and residents alike: Denia, Jávea, Calpe, Altea, Benidorm and Villajoyosa to name but a few. Access to the Costa Blanca is easy from Alicante airport.

It is not until you reach the city of Alicante, away from the hotels and villas, that you feel you are truly in a foreign country. Inland from Alicante the landscape is more exotic, with palm groves originally planted by the Moors centred on Elx ('Elche'). The fame of this town rests almost exclusively on an ancient bust discovered at the turn of the century and known as *La dama de Elche*, although you will have to go to the

Archaeological Museum in Madrid to see it.

Valencia

North of Alicante lies Valencia. Somewhat confusingly, this is also the name of the province, and of the autonomous region comprising the three provinces of Valencia, Alicante and Castellón. The modern-day city of Valencia has sprawling suburbs of high-rise blocks and its fair share of beggars and gypsies; however, the city is forever linked with the romantic figure of El Cid. Valencia, a city of cultural and commercial prestige is the third most important – and third largest – city in Spain. It has a population of 800,000 inhabitants; 1,500,000 including the population of the surrounding suburbs and towns. Valencia is easily accessible with links to Spanish and other European cities through its port, motorway, airport and railway network. The appealing climate includes mild winters and warm summers.

El Cid, otherwise known as Ruy Diaz de Bivar, was a soldier of fortune in the dark days of the Moorish occupation and he became through his chivalric exploits the hero of one of Spain's earliest epic poems the *Cantar de mío Cid* as well as the subject of folk legends and ballads. The reality was probably more prosaic; he fell out with his monarch, fought for the Moors, then became reconciled with his ruler by changing sides once again and was rewarded with the governorship of Valencia. The story of El Cid is a pointer to the Spanish politics of the future in many ways.

Mediterranean cuisine

Mediterranean cuisine is associated with the staples of bread, olives and wine but also makes full use of rice, garlic, vegetables, meat, fish and dairy products and masses of fruit. Catalonian cuisine is perhaps one of the most exciting of the Mediterranean region with a wide range of fish dishes and inland dishes such as *escudella* (a meaty broth with pasta) *carn d'olla* and roasts.

Valencian cuisine mixes typically Mediterranean dishes – fish, green vegetables and fruit – with soups and game stews. Rice, served dry, moist or in a variety of *paellas* is the most famous Valencian dish, while the Moorish influence can be seen in the preponderance of sweetmeats, *turrón* and ice cream.

SOME SPECIALITIES OF THE REGION	
Anguilas All-i-Pebre	eels in garlic sauce
Arroz a Banda	rice cooked in fish broth
Arroz Murciano	rice in fish soup with red peppers
Arroz Negro	black rice with squid
Fesols y Naps	rice, bean and turnip stew
Fideuá	pasta prepared in the style of *paella*
Paella a la Marinera	rice with seafood
Paella a la Valenciana	rice with rabbit, snails and broad beans
Paella Mixta	rice with seafood, chicken, *chorizo* and vegetables
Turrón	almond sweet

The Costa del Azahar

The coastline north of Valencia, the Costa del Azahar ('Coast of Orange Blossom'), is lined with small summer resorts, perhaps the best known of which is the ancient fortified town of Peñiscola. The capital of the Costa del Azahar is Castellón de la Plana. Surrounded by the extensive, spectacular La Safar mountain ranges and excellent white sandy beaches, the Costa Del Azahar offers views of stunning and contrasting landscapes. Properties along this lesser-known coastline are bought mainly by Spaniards, but may well appeal to foreigners as prices remain reasonably low and access is relatively quick and direct from Valencia airport.

Oropesa

One of the more developed tourist resorts on the Costa del Azahar, Oropesa's beaches spread from Torre La Sal at Ribera de Cabanes as far as Benicasim. There are property developments all around these beaches and on the nearby hilltops and a recently built marina.

Torreblanca

Torreblanca is a traditionally agricultural community which in recent years has experienced a notable boom in tourism particularly around the area of Torrenostra beach, which has apartments right beside it.

Torre La Sal beach, a little further south from Torrenostra, belongs to the township of Cabanes, which stretches from the mountains to the sea. The waters of this section of the coastline are reputed to be very clean and this area was chosen as the location for a Marina Biology Research Centre concerned with the breeding of such species as king prawns, sole and bass.

Peñiscola

Peñiscola is perched on the Rock of Peñiscola, rising majestically out to sea, and fortified by large solid sections of wall dating back to the time of the Knights Templar.

The town is very attractive and is a favourite tourist destination for both Spanish and foreign tourists alike. The old town of Peñiscola has been preserved practically in its entirety. Tourist development hasn't destroyed the monuments within the town nor those buildings that line the beach on the road between Peñiscola and Benicarló.

Benicarló

South of Tortosa, Benicarló has a fishing port as well as excellent beaches, which stretch as far as Peñiscola. A coast road links both towns. The resort area between Benicarló and Peñiscola is so built up that it is difficult to know where one town ends and the other begins.

MURCIA AND THE COSTA CALIDA

> The Costa Calida – between Almería and La Manga – still has reasonably priced property with a lot of new developments springing up. New marinas are planned at Alguilas and at Mazarrón. Also planned are seven sea-front golf courses and more hotel development. It is hoped that the developers of the Costa Calida will have learned from the 'too much too soon' construction of some of the other costas and so will manage to retain some of the coast's present charm. La Manga is a very popular destination for tourists and owners of second homes.

Journeying south along the N-332 motorway towards Mazarrón, the spectacular sea views of La Manga give way to smaller coves and sandy palm lined beaches set against a dramatic backdrop of rugged mountains. Here, pretty fishing harbours and quaint hillside villages sit in harmony with modern golf courses and yachting marinas. A new airport near Corvera is planned but the area is still rural with local amenities limited and even mains electricity fairly restricted. You may need to look into generators and solar panelling. Alicante to Bristol is a 2½ hour flight. The heat during mid-summer may be a little intense for some.

Mazarrón

Mazarrón is a small Spanish town. Spaniards have been buying holiday homes here for generations and the lack of big hotels means that this is not a resort but rather a typical Spanish town frequented by the Spanish.

Situated in the province of Murcia, Mazarrón is actually two towns in one: there is the main town with its town hall, indoor market, banks, medical facilities, shops etc., and less that five minutes drive away there is its little seafront sister, Puerto de Mazarrón. Here you find a harbour and marina along with superb sandy beaches and secluded coves. There is 35km of shoreline here, with a backdrop of the high mountain ranges of the Sierra Espuña. Murcia, the provincial capital, and Cartagena, an ancient coastal city, are within a thirty minute drive from here. The region is famous for farming and agriculture. For skiers, Granada and the Sierra Nevada are two and a half hours drive away and the Sierra Espuña National Park is a twenty minute drive from Mazarrón.

Costa Blanca South

This southern region of the Costa Blanca is generally cheaper to buy property in than the northern reaches. Inland fincas can be bought for around £50,000; while small studio apartments on the cost can be had very cheaply – £20,000 or so.

Torrevieja

Torrevieja is both overdeveloped and one of the fastest growing resorts on the Costa Blanca but that fact doesn't mean that one has to write off the whole area. With a superb climate, great beaches, first class sport, recreation and health facilities and the low cost of living, as well as being just 35km south of the airports at San Javier and Alicante, there are a few reasons to look for property here. Apart from its beaches, Torrevieja offers stunning cliff walks, many natural beauty spots and a well-served marina.

> Torrevieja is at present one of the growth areas for property with many new *urbanizaciónes*, villas and flats being built by development companies. Because of the glut of new properties, prices around Torrevieja are cheap though many are used as holiday homes only, and during the tourist season the town and the beaches are packed to capacity.

South of Torrevieja there are excellent golf courses (the area is fast becoming a Mecca for golf enthusiasts of all handicaps), a dozen varied beaches, two good marinas and plenty of restaurants and bars. The city of Murcia is a short drive away, and offers fine shopping, culture and architecture in equal measure. This area is sometimes known as the Orihuela Costa after the *platyas de Orihuela* – the beaches along this coast.

Santa Pola

The port town of Santa Pola boasts several miles of superb beaches and is home to the Mediterranean's largest deep sea and coastal fishing fleet. The town is also famous for its salt flats – miles of protected wetlands, which combined with the continuing commercial salt production, are important sources of both revenue and natural beauty for this popular town. Santa Pola is the main embarkation point to Isla de Tabarca – a little island in the bay once used as a prison and now home to a small fishing community.

Guardamar del Segura

Guardamar lies at the mouth of the Río Segura to the north of Torrevieja. There are several miles of popular beaches nearby, set against a backdrop of palm groves planted on the dunes. Guardamar is well known for its cuisine – langoustines being the local speciality.

Cabo Roig

One of the most exclusive developments along the Costa Blanca situated 8km from Torrevieja, Cabo Roig is characterised by broad palm lined avenues and landscaped gardens and is just a few minutes drive from the superb Villamartin golf complex. There are excellent restaurants at the Cabo Roig marina and a maritime walk follows the coastline of the peninsula.

La Manga

To the north of the Costa Calida, La Manga ('the sleeve') sits on a narrow strip of land that stretches 22km out into the Mediterranean Sea creating the largest saltwater lagoon in Europe – el Mar Menor – 170 square kilometres in area. With a maximum depth of only eight metres, the water in the 'lesser sea' remains at a constant 18°C throughout the year. As a result there are all types of water sports available here with no less than 13 scuba schools and 19 sailing clubs. You will be equally spoilt on land with a vast choice of leisure activities, including a centre for professional football, ten tennis clubs and three international golf courses. There are a number of other mature golf courses nearby with many more planned or already underway.

La Manga is very popular with Spaniards and foreigners alike, and it gets very busy. Access to La Manga is improving. Driving along the new A37 you can make Alicante airport in under an hour. The airport at San Javier is about 20 minutes away and handles daily flights to the UK. Property in La Manga is sought after and expensive.

South of La Manga towards Mazarrón the spectacular sea views make way for smaller coves and sandy palm-lined beaches set against the backdrop of the sierras. The coastline here is characterised by pretty fishing harbours and quaint hillside villages sit in harmony with modern golf courses and yachting marinas.

Alicante and the Costa Blanca North

Alicante was called 'Lucentum' – City of Light – by the Romans. Close by is the maritime town of El Campello, with a modern marina and a fine blue-flag beach. Alicante has good medical care facilities and an infrastructure that supports the large number of retirees who have decided to move into the area. South of Alicante property is relatively cheap, and there is plenty of it, though over the last three years prices have increased by 20% a year. The area running from Denia to Murcia is a favourite place to buy in Spain at present, along with the Canary and Balearic Islands.

As the main city of the Costa Blanca, Alicante has much to offer with the architecture, arts, crafts and cuisine a wonderful fusion of styles, together with miles of coastline. While tourism has replaced port activity as the main source of revenue in the region, Alicante still has a bustling and vibrant harbour. The San Juan de Alicante beach is to the east of the city and is over 7km long. Gran Alacant, at the southernmost reach of Alicante's influence, is located just south of the regional capital and close to the airport. It is also convenient for Benidorm, Terra Mítica and the North Costa Blanca, making it a very popular resort town. The town has benefited from continuing massive investment, creating high quality residential and business developments.

North of Alicante the coastline can be quite spectacular and except for the blot of Benidorm (once a little fishing village now bombed out of all recognition by high rise development) the northern reaches of the Costa Blanca have had restricted development which has led to a rather exclusive and expensive area of property acquisition. The 'golden triangle' of Denia, Jávea and Calpe are sought after and property prices are high compared to those south of Alicante. For example, an exclusive three bedroom villa with views can be expected to fetch £460,000; an attractive villa with pool a few minutes walk from the beach will sell for around £300,000 or more. Smaller properties on developments will be cheaper and a good sized villa can be bought for £130,000.

Busot

The village of Busot is located amid spectacular scenery some 20km from Alicante – the international airport can be reached by car in less than 30 minutes. Close by – between Busot and Muchamiel – is the Bonalba golf club complex with its restaurants, bars and shops. Several other courses are just south of Alicante. Nearby are the beaches and coves of El Campello and San Juan. El Campello is a bustling little resort with numerous hotels, bars, cafés and restaurants serving its 5km of coastline. Midway between Alicante and Benidorm, El Campello is close to the airport and there is quick access to Costa Blanca North.

Denia

Denia is an old town sitting at the foot of the Montgó Mountain, which shelters the town from the hot winds of the *meseta*, offering a microclimate with an annual average temperature of 19°C. Denia has a marina and is ideal for those hoping to sail a lot and there are seven beaches, ideal for water sports. A short distance inland is the La Sella golf club. The Montgó Nature Park offers walks, trails and horse riding and is a haven for the region's flora and fauna.

Jávea (Xábia)

Jávea is a favoured venue for naturalists, scuba divers and water sports enthusiasts due to its many submerged caves, rock formations and marine life. Jávea consists of three parts with the pretty and laid-back old town lying inland, and the port and harbour and marina 3km away. Nearby is the main beach resort of El Arenal – the beginning of 25km of coastline.

Calpe

Calpe is overlooked by Peñón de Ifach – a stunning rocky peak resembling the rock of Gibraltar which rises 332 metres above the town. Once used as a watchtower to forewarn of Barbary Coast corsairs, it is now a national park with a trail leading to its summit. Below the Peñón de Ifach are two large bays where a harbour and the town itself are situated. Playa Levante to the north of the rock has had a great deal of development and is popular.

Altea

Altea has retained its charm and the town's whitewashed old quarter features winding cobbled streets which lead you to the main square by a magnificent church with its cupola roof inlaid with deep blue and white tiling. From here the views over the town to the sea are stunning. The beaches are pebble, rock and sand around Altea and there are secluded coves. Development here has been restrained and is mainly located on the seafront. Property in Altea is expensive. Ten kilometres south of Altea is Benidorm.

Benidorm

Benidorm, for those seeking noise, has it all – great beaches, water sports, restaurants, cafés and bars and heaps of nightlife. Millions visit Benidorm every year, and many have decided to buy property there. Inland is Terra Mítica – a theme park on the scale of Euro Disney – designed (allegedly) to reflect Mediterranean history and attracting many thousands of visitors every year. Because of the vast amount of real estate that has transformed Benidorm from the tiny fishing village it once was property prices here are low.

THE BALEARIC ISLANDS (LAS ISLAS BALEARES)

Main town: Palma (Mallorca).

The Balearic Islands lying off the Valencian and Catalonian coasts have been under Spanish sovereignty since the Romans incorporated them into their province of Hispania (which comprised the whole of the Iberian Peninsula). Together, the four main islands of Mallorca, Menorca, Ibiza and Formentera comprise less than 1% of the area of Spain with a total population of around 750,000.

The largest island of the group is Mallorca, which attracts an estimated three million tourists a year and is home to an estimated 15,000 British residents. Tourist development is mainly concentrated in small areas of the coast, notably around Palma and in the northeast around Pollensa. A three bedroom beachside apartment at Pollensa sells for around £215,000.

The other islands are mainly summer resorts and fairly quiet (and sometimes chilly) out of season. The liveliest and most up-market is certainly Ibiza, which gained its reputation for tolerance towards foreign visitors in the sixties when it became popular with hippies and several rock stars bought properties there. More recently, aficionados of house music and rave culture have made it a popular destination among the young. Menorca (where the entrepreneur Richard Branson has a summer home) is more sedate and family-orientated. Michael Douglas and Catherine Zeta Jones have a house there. Menorca is an island of 48km by 23km and has at one point been home to Greeks, Romans, Moors and Phoenicians. Menorca is relatively unspoilt and peaceful and safe, however, property is expensive, as strict controls have limited the amount of development allowed. In the last three years prices have increased by 75%-100%. There is also the *tramuntana* to contend with – a buffeting continuous cold and dry mistral that hits the eastern side of the island. Property in the Balearic Islands is a good investment as the islands are a very popular tourist destination. Prices continue to rise and there is a healthy rental market

SOME SPECIALITIES OF THE BALEARIC ISLANDS

Arroz Brut	rice, pork and vegetable casserole
Butifarrón	cured sausage with pine nuts and herbs
Caldereta de Langosta	lobster stew
Escaldums	chicken and meatball stew
Frit	sauté of liver, peppers and potatoes
Greixonera	bread pudding
Queso de Mahón	semi-soft cow milk cheese
Sobrasada	soft seasoned sausage
Sopas Mallorquinas	thick vegetable soup
Tumbet	sautéed potatoes, peppers, eggplant and zucchini

Other Balearic specialities include fluffy pastries known as *ensaimadas*; the islands also gave the world mayonnaise (*salsa mahonesa*).

Mallorca

Demand has pushed prices up and Mallorca has some of the highest property prices compared to mainland Spain, the other Balearic Islands or the Canaries and detached cottages and fincas within 15-20 minutes of Palma are always in short supply. If you decide to live in a fairly heavily touristed area, particularly the east coast of the island, be aware that the end of season exodus of holidaymakers, and the subsequent closing of businesses and empty villas can get slightly depressing.

Even on a relatively small island such as Mallorca, climate variations occur and the areas west and north of Palma enjoy the most favourable winters. The availability of leisure facilities as well as the opportunities for mixing socially will also vary and buying in one of the more beautiful but remote corners of the island will necessitate a certain amount of travelling about. The round trip taking the kids to and from school twice a day will be compounded by extra school and sports activities and the kids wanting to visit friends on the other side of the island etc. Some International Schools provide a collection and drop-off service but only in a limited radius and often subject to there being sufficient need. Some families decide to relocate after a year or two from an idyllic coastal setting to somewhere more compatible with family life.

The more highly populated southwest corner of Mallorca, with its better weather, popular coastline and exclusive residential areas, attracts the greatest numbers of foreign buyers. Inland villages are attracting more and more buyers due in part to lower prices and the lack of tourist activity. Golf courses can be found throughout the island, particularly in the southwest, and marinas and boat yards are a big draw in the southwest corner. The southwest corner also has the majority of international schools, is close to the International Airport, and has some excellent restaurants. Mallorcan natives, especially villagers, have something of a reputation for being rather inward looking and wary of incomers.

There are large expat communities on each of the three major islands of the Balearics but prices have become inflated in recent years. Access from the UK is easy as there are numerous charter flights all year round. There are also ferry connections to Ibiza from Denia and Barcelona, and from Valencia to Ibiza and Palma, as well as to Menorca from the mainland. In winter there are fewer flights to Ibiza and Menorca than to Mallorca. The smallest island, Formentera, is the quietest and the least developed of the islands.

CATALONIA (CATALUÑYA)

Main cities and provinces: Barcelona, Girona, Lleida (Lérida), Tarragona.
Catalonia, whose first ruler was the hirsutely-named Guifré el Pelós ('Wilfred the Hairy'), is one of the regions of Spain which has its own distinct historical – and some would say national – identity, with its own Catalan culture and language. Although covering less than 7% of the total area of Spain, Catalonia is home to over six million inhabitants; about 16% of the total population of Spain. This has long been one of the most exciting and cosmopolitan parts of Spain, and Barcelona a fascinating centre of politics, fashion, commerce and culture.

In the twelfth century, Catalonia was an autonomous part of the kingdom of Aragon, an alliance that enhanced its political influence and brought far ranging cultural influences to Aragon from Provence and Roussillon in France by way of Catalonia. The Catalan language is closely related to the Langue d'Oc, still spoken in some parts of southern France that once formed part of a united kingdom with Catalonia. Catalonia was one of the Mediterranean powers in the Middle Ages and today there is still a Catalan-speaking outpost on the Italian island of Sardinia.

The decline of Catalonian wealth and power in the fourteenth century weakened Aragon to the extent that Castile became the dominant regional power. For the next five centuries the Catalonians attempted to consolidate their autonomy while successive Spanish dynasties tried to stake a claim to it. Towards the end of the nineteenth century, the broad-based nationalist movement of Catalanism began to gather momentum and attracted the attention of Madrid, which offered a limited autonomy to the region. This was subsequently repressed by the dictator, Primo de Rivera, and any further thoughts of autonomy were interrupted by the Civil War, during which Barcelona became the final refuge of republicanism and anarchism and held out against Franco's armies until the bitter end in 1939.

Franco's retribution against the Catalan language and culture took the form of book-burning and the changing of street and place names. However, in the decades following the end of the Civil War, Catalan nationalism mellowed and Catalanism became characterised more by bravura than violence and extremism. Perhaps one of the reasons for this change is that during most of this century the Catalonian region has been settled by many migrant workers from poorer parts of Spain, attracted by the industry and wealth of the area. The result is that about half of the people of Catalonia are descended from immigrants, which has led to a bilingualism similar to that of Wales, with Spanish universally spoken, but Catalan favoured in schools and universities. This immigration has also contributed to the dilution of some of the strong nationalist feelings in the region.

The province of Barcelona includes part of the Pyrenees. It is also home to one of the national symbols of Catalonia, the monastery of Montserrat built around the legend of the Black Virgin, an icon reputedly hidden on the site by St. Peter and rediscovered in the ninth century amidst the sort of miraculous happenings usually associated with such shrines. During the Franco era the monastery clandestinely published the Montserrat Bible in Catalan and became a centre of nationalist gatherings.

Barcelona

Much to the chagrin of the capital Madrid, Barcelona is held by many to be the most lively and interesting city in Spain. Not only is it a huge industrial centre and port (with a population of three million), and the spiritual home of individuals of such startling originality as the architect Gaudí and Pablo Picasso, it is also the most liberal (or decadent, depending on your viewpoint) city in Spain. The notorious red light district, the *barrio chino*, is now used as the term for similar districts elsewhere in the country. The sheer energy and sophistication of the place is a great attraction, especially for European nightclub goers, and the city is near enough to the Costa Brava (where many foreign residents are based) to make it a regular port of call for those who want a change of pace.

Work on the famous Gaudí cathedral, La Sagrada Familia, started in 1882 and left unfinished for a time after the architect was killed by a tram in 1926, has continued (controversially) and the cathedral is likely to be completed in the next twenty years or so. For years it remained open to the skies and many Barcelonans would have preferred to see it left that way, as a monument to its creator. The facilities left behind by the Olympic Games in 1992 are another attraction, as is the Picasso Museum on the Carrer de

Montcada.

Barcelona airport, Prat, is 14km from the city centre; and there are ferries from Barcelona to the Balearic Islands. Those seeking work may find it in the many English language schools in Barcelona and in the growing number of high-tech industries that have grown up to match those across the Mediterranean in southern France.

Period two-bedroom apartments in the Ciutat Vella fetch around £97,000-£160,000, while large three bedroom apartments in Eixample can fetch between £150,000 and £525,000. In top notch central areas expect to pay around £3,950 per square metre of apartment. The price drops the further away from the centre of the city a property is. Cheaper and more outlying areas such as Gracia, west of Eixample, have real estate selling at around £660 per square metre. One company dealing in property in Barcelona and which has a web presence is Cinnamond & Co. (www.cinnamondco.com; ☎637 521 453).

The Catalonian Coastline

The coastline running from Girona up to the French border is known as the Costa Brava (the 'rugged coast') and is home to many northern Europeans, the majority of whom have retirement or second homes. The well-known holiday resort of Lloret de Mar is situated just south of the mediaeval walled city of Girona, and Girona airport serves all the Costa Brava holiday resorts. Further north is Figueres, the birthplace of Salvador Dali and home to the museum celebrating his life and work.

The town of Tarragona, to the south of the Costa Brava, is a large industrial port with chemical and oil refineries and can be divided into two parts: an old walled city and an ugly modern one. Historically, Tarragona has had trading links across the Mediterranean; the Romans built a splendid city here and many fine examples of their architecture remain in the old part of the town and its environs, notably the forum, Scipio's Tower (*Torre de Scipio*) and a triumphal arch (*Arco de Bara*).

The Lleida province of Catalonia is situated inland and is a mixture of fertile plains and parts of the Pyrenees. Lleida (or 'Lérida' in Spanish) town has a magnificent former cathedral which has been used as a military barracks since the eighteenth century.

The northern *costas* were the first to be invaded in the 1950s by tourism and property development. There is a large Spanish presence among the property owners in this region so it has remained pretty culturally intact, unlike the Costa del Sol. Because of Catalonia's proximity to the French border overland travel between UK and Spain is pretty fast. A motorway running along the east coast connects southern France to the South of Spain. The completion of a high-speed train line in 2004 will mean that travel times between Barcelona and Madrid and northern Europe will improve considerably.

SOME SPECIALITIES OF CATALONIA	
Amanida	salad of cured meat, cheese and fish
Bacallá a la Llauna	salted cod with beans
Bacallá amb Mel	salted cod with honey
Butifarra	white cooked sausage
Canalons	rolled pasta with meat, fish or vegetable filling
Crema Catalana	custard glazed with caramelised sugar
Empedrat	cod and bean salad
Escalivada	grilled peppers, tomato, eggplant and onion
Esqueixada	cod with peppers, tomato and onion
Faves a la Catalana	fava beans with mint
Formatge Llenguat	strong cow milk cheese
Fricandó amb Moixarnons	veal stew with wild mushrooms
Fuet	salami
Llagosta amb Pollastre	lobster with chicken
Mel i Mató	honey and cheese
Múrgules Farcides	stuffed morels
Oca amb Peres	gosling with pears
Sarsuela	mixed seafood stew

The Costa Brava

For many the Costa Brava is the only place in which they would consider buying property. The beauty of this coastline, with its cliffs and coves led to the beginnings of mass tourism in Spain, which in turn has led to the over-development of the area. Between Blanes and Sant Feliu de Guixols some of the worst aspects of mass tourism can be seen, but the further north toward the French border you travel the less sprawling the development. Property is still being developed along the coast and is in increasing demand. There is also a great demand inland, especially for the large country houses (*masia*) with land. Prices for such properties, even if they are in need of restoration, go for about £350,000 due to the demand for a sparse supply.

At the northern end of the Costa Brava are the small and unspoilt resorts of Calella de Palafrugell, Figueres and Cadaques. The main airports serving this coastline are at Barcelona and Girona. Demand for property here is driven by Spanish buyers and property inland will be cheaper than that on the coast, especially if you are prepared to renovate. Apartments and townhouses near Cadaques are selling for about £100,000, while a two bedroom house on an urbanización near Pals sells for around £126,000. Renovation projects are not particularly cheap near the coast: an average price for a village property in need of work will cost around £68,000, while a sprawling masia in need of renovation can sell for as much as £600,000.

St. Feliu de Guixols

St. Feliu de Guixols is one of the most attractive resort towns on the Costa Brava with its small streets, yacht harbour and medieval architecture to explore. The town is built alongside a horseshoe-shaped sandy bay and is set against the backdrop of Sant Elm – a mountain topped by a ruined Benedictine monastery offering wonderful views. St Feliu is a busy, clean, welcoming resort with beaches, cafés, bars and restaurants.

Tossa de Mar

Tossa de Mar, 13km north of Lloret, dates from Palaeolithic times and retains evidence of the occupation of the Romans and the Moors. The *Vila Vella* (old town) is divided from the rest of the town by a well-preserved 12th century wall. Tossa has a narrow natural harbour formed by the surrounding cliffs, and four beaches. It is renowned for its charm, superb seafood restaurants and excellent nightlife.

Blanes

About an hour's drive north of Barcelona and situated at the southern end of the Costa Brava, Blanes is a colourful resort town. The long sandy beach is one of the longest on this stretch of coast and the town is popular with Spaniards due to its proximity to Barcelona. The international airports at Girona and Barcelona are half an hour and just over an hour away respectively. Local road and rail links are excellent. There is a marina, a port, an aquarium and two botanical gardens. For golf aficionados there is the Club de Golf l'Angel; other courses in the area include Santa Cristina d'Aro, Caldes de Malavella and Playa d'Aro. There are two water parks and skiing can be had in Andorra – two hours away by car.

L'Escala

L'Escala was once the most important fishing port in the region. The promontory on which the town is built juts out into the sea to form a sheltered bay ideal for mooring a traditional Mediterranean fishing fleet. Running to the west and east of the town are several kilometres of beach as well as rocky coves. L'Escala is a relatively small resort offering a gentle pace of life to its residents along with good access to the northern Costa Brava – the Golf de Roses, the town of Figueres – home of the Salvador Dalí museum, and Cadaques, the pretty fishing village where Dalí lived for many years.

L'Estartit

L'Estartit is a popular and lively tourist resort both during the day and at night. L'Estartit has a large marina that serves those keen on watersports. The Islas Medes, less than a kilometre offshore, form a marine wildlife reserve boasting excellent snorkelling and diving. L'Estartit's has a wide sandy beach 6km to the east.

Torroella de Montgrí

Torroella de Montgrí, situated 5km inland from L'Estartit, is a town with a strong historical tradition, noted for the 13th century castle overlooking the town from the top of the 300 metre Montgrí hills, and its 14th century gothic church. Famed as the town of the *sardana*, the traditional Catalan dance, Torroella also hosts an International Music Festival through July and August every year.

Pals

Eight kilometres north of Palafrugell is the medieval village of Pals with its many excellent seafood restaurants and a peaceful hilltop setting. Much of Pals' recent popularity can be attributed to the stunning views, three local golf courses and the huge variety of water sports available nearby at Platja de Pals – a popular and small beach surrounded by dense pine forest which leads inland almost as far as Pals.

Platja d'Aro

Platja d'Aro is a lively beach resort set at the mouth of a river valley. There are many good shops and several excellent seafood restaurants in this busy resort, all of which offer great value. Platja d'Aro has a 3km long stretch of well-serviced sandy beach and the town is also ideally located for day tripping – Barcelona can be reached in less than two hours. Inland from Platja d'Aro begin the foothills of the Gavarres range – ideal for hiking, walking and horse-riding.

The Costa Dorada

The Costa Dorada (the Golden Coast), running south of Barcelona to the Delta de l'Ebre, is less wild than the Costa Brava and the closer you are to Barcelona the higher the cost of property. There are fewer coastal centres of population along this coast, with most development around Vilanova i la Geltrú and Torredembarra, and the terrain becomes less attractive and flat as you head south toward Tarragona. Sitges, a fashionable resort since the late 19th century, is the star of this stretch of coast but because of its status property here is more expensive than elsewhere and apartments in town especially can be very hard to find. For this reason many people looking to buy in the area decide to check out Vilanova, only 5km south of Sitges.

> Further away from Barcelona, and inland, property is considerably cheaper than on the coast. However, summer up in the hills can be exhaustingly hot and there may be problems with water supplies, communications and, in the winter, access. At the time of writing the medieval walled town of Montblanc – an hour's drive from Barcelona – was being touted by estate agents as a good place to buy.

The Costa Dorada is less of a draw to holidaymakers than the Costa Brava or Costa del Sol and for this reason property is somewhat cheaper than those coastlines. Against this is the fact that many of the resorts along the Costa Dorada become ghost towns during the winter, and both the busy main coastal road (the N-340), and the Barcelona-Valencia railway line run parallel to the beaches.

Calafell, Cubelles, Altafulla, Cambrils and Tarragona are all places worth looking for property due to their proximity to the beaches. Salou is one of the oldest and most famous resorts on the Costa Dorada and remains popular with northern European tourists as well as with the Spanish. There are several marinas along this coast and four golf courses. There are waterparks and Port Adventura, the largest theme park in Spain, is situated 7km west of Tarragona.

Although the Costa Dorada does not have the density of foreign residents of other places in Spain, the number of foreign visitors to the area means that there is access to English-language newspapers and magazines as well as the supermarkets stocking certain foods from 'back home' and pubs and restaurants catering for those after non-Spanish cuisine. There are hospitals in Tarragona and due to the proximity of Barcelona there should be no problems getting to the medical services there in an emergency.

Most visitors to the Costa Dorada fly in to Barcelona Airport, which is about an hour's drive from Salou. The small airport at Reus – north-west of Tarragona – handles an increasing number of charter flights. If you will be working anywhere along the Costa Dorada, the Barcelona-Valencia railway line serves the main towns and resorts as it runs all the way along the coast.

Miami Platja

Miami Platja is a resort situated on the coast 6km from Cambrils, 15km from Salou and 110km from Barcelona. Its gift is the 12km of beaches, a mixture of rock and sand, some of which have merited the Blue Flag of the EU for their quality and services. Miami Platja is close to the golf club of Bonmont Terres Noves.

Cambrils

Cambrils has more than 9km of beaches and more than 4km of illuminated seafront promenade. Home to the fishing fleet, Cambrils port is also home to the yachting marina; the place to come for sailing and all other sports related to the sea. The historic centre of Cambrils still has a distinct medieval air within its fortified walls and watchtowers. The most popular Cambrils dishes include the different types of *romesco* sauce, fish *suquets*, rice and noodle *rosejats*, grilled or fried mixed fish platters, seafood, *paellas* and *sarsuelas*.

Salou

Salou is the liveliest resort on the Costa Dorada. Summer visitors are attracted by the sandy beaches which run virtually all along the seafront and also Universal Studios Port Adventura theme park just outside the resort. Many of Salou's beaches are long and wide, others nestle in small, secluded coves, along the foot of the rocky Cape Salou.

Tarragona

Tarragona, is the southernmost provincial capital of Catalonia. Two airports, Reus just 7km away, and Barcelona's International airport just 90km away, provide easy access. Its seaport is one of the most bustling on the Mediterranean. Motorways link Tarragona with Alicante and the French border and the rest of Europe and with Madrid and the Basque Country.

Tarragona is a city open to the sea, with an important seaport as well as a large fishing port. Its 15km of coastline boasts long beaches with fine sand, coves sheltered by rocky outcrops and dotted by green Mediterranean pine groves. Water sports including sailing, windsurfing, rowing, water skiing, scuba-diving are all served by the facilities and equipment at the city's Nautical Club and Maritime Club. Tarragona has become an important commercial centre, with good shopping in its pedestrian-only shopping districts.

Calafell

With five kilometres of fine sand, the coast around Calafell is flat and the water warm, rich in iodine, clean and very shallow. Calafell offers a number of facilities that enable everyone to practice the sport that they most enjoy and the resort also has a modern multi-sport pavilion and an attractive sport harbour.

Sitges

Few resorts can boast the prime location of Sitges – fifteen minutes from Barcelona airport, twenty minutes from Barcelona city centre, seventeen beaches stretching along four km of coastline, and a full cultural life and busy festive calendar. The intense cultural life and the organisation of mass events like film, theatre, music, jazz and tango festivals make Sitges today a cultural capital of prestige. Sitges has three pleasure ports: Aiguadolc, Garraf and Port Ginesta, a golf course, horse riding, tennis, swimming, bicycle promenade, bowling, the Natural Park Garraf (10,000 hectares of green), etc. The nightlife in Sitges is unbeatable. Discos, bars, pubs and cafés make Sitges one of the most fun and vibrant places on the Mediterranean. Because of its popularity, property prices are high in Sitges.

THE PYRENEAN REGIONS

ARAGÓN

Provinces and main cities: Huesca, Teruel and Zaragoza (Saragossa).
The northern part of Aragón incorporates a section of the Pyrenees while the southern region slopes down toward the Ebro valley and rises again in Teruel. The Aragonese provinces comprise 9.5% of Spain but, like Extremadura, are heavily underpopulated with a total of only around 1.2 million inhabitants.

The historical kingdom of Aragón was created by Sancho the Great of Navarre, who reigned from 1000 to 1035. Later, in the fifteenth century, Aragón and Castile became one kingdom under the joint rule of Ferdinand and Isabella. Places of interest include the magnificent castle of Loarre about 25 miles/40km from Huesca which was built by Sancho the Great as part of his forward defences against the Moors. Pyrenean Aragón, particularly around the Ordesa National Park, is fast becoming popular with hikers. There are also several ski resorts of which the most chic is Benasque. The town of Jaca, the capital city of former times, is also on the pilgrim route to Santiago de Compostela, and Zaragoza is a lively city with some interesting Moorish architecture, notably the Ajaferiá Palace. It is also the fifth largest city in Spain.

The province of Teruel extends south and is one of the most unexplored areas, with few inhabitants and poor roads. Property in Aragón is scarse.

SOME SPECIALITIES OF ARAGÓN	
Ajo Arriero	dried cod and red pepper stew
Chuletillas de cordero	lamb chops
Cuajada	rennet pudding
Melocotón al Vino tinto	peaches in red wine
Pollo Chilindrón	chicken and red pepper stew
Queso Tronchón	semi-soft sheep milk cheese
Ternasco	roast lamb

NAVARRA (NAVARRE)

Main town: Pamplona.

Navarre is one of the smaller regions comprising 2.06% of Spain's area and home to 1.35% of the population. A stretch of the Pyrenees runs along the northeastern part of the province and includes the historic pass of Roncesvalles (on the route taken by mediaeval pilgrims to Santiago). The south of Navarre is on the northeastern edge of the *meseta* and is a region of vineyards and agriculture. The main city of the region is Pamplona, whose bull-running festival – Fiesta of San Fermín – takes place in July and attracts capacity crowds from all over Spain and beyond.

The origins of the kingdom of Navarre can be found in a ninth century battle between the Basques and the Franks. The Franks, in the process of retreating after an unsuccessful campaign against the Moors, were ambushed and routed by Basque separatists in the valley of Roncesvalles. Thereafter the Basques declared the area around Pamplona independent. The event is immortalised in the *Chanson de Roland* which, however erroneously, claims the attackers were really Moors not Basques. During the eleventh century, the kingdom of Navarre included Basque territory on both sides of the Pyrenees, linking the area's history with that of France as well as Spain. Navarre remained an independent kingdom playing its own part in European power politics until 1512, when King Ferdinand of Aragón and Castile annexed it in order to give his armies a safe corridor to attack the French on the other side of the Pyrenees. Once this had been accomplished he allowed the Navarrese their autonomy, which they have retained almost uninterruptedly ever since. It is largely due to this continued independence that Navarre never became incorporated into the Basque country, in spite of its foundation by, and close links with, the Basques.

Northern cuisine

The north is a wet verdant region renowned for its meat and fish dishes. The Basque Country has local specialities such as *marmitako* (potatoes with bonito) and *txangurro* (clams and spider crab) and the city of San Sebastián has a tremendous concentration of five-fork restaurants serving some of the finest food in Europe. Asturias has a similar cuisine, with its own local dishes such as the *fabada* (haricot bean and pork stew), regional cheeses and cider. Cantabria meanwhile offers beef, anchovies and dairy products and Galicia has the *pote* (a soup made with ham, haricot beans and turnips), *caldeiradas* (bouillabaisse, followed by the fish), *pulpo* (octopus), a wide variety of fresh shellfish, from scallops and mussels, dairy products and pastries as well as the famed Albariño and Ribeiro wines.

The fertile valleys across Aragón, La Rioja and Navarre produce fruit and vegetables – asparagus, peppers, borage, cardoon, peaches and pears, potatoes, cabbage hearts, pochas and trout. Specialities include meat marinades (*chilindrones*) and *confits*. Desserts include cheeses, milk puddings and fruit (fresh, chocolate-coated or preserved in syrup).

SOME SPECIALITIES OF NAVARRE	
Bacalao al Ajo Arriero	cod with pimento and tomato
Canutillos	custard-filled pastry rolls
Cochofrito	lamb stew with garlic and lemon
Pichón a la Cazadora	pigeon in wine sauce
Queso del Roncal	cured sheep milk cheese
Trucha a la Navarra	trout with cured ham

THE BAY OF BISCAY AND THE ATLANTIC COAST (THE GREEN COAST)

PAÍS VASCO (THE BASQUE COUNTRY)

Provinces: Alava, Guipuzcoa, Vizcaya (Biscay).
Main cities: Bilbao (Vizcaya); San Sebastián/Donostia (Guipuzcoa); Vitoria/Gasteiz (Alava).
The Basque Country (*Euskadi*) is one of the more heavily populated regions of Spain, representing about 1.5% of the surface area and 6% of the population. Most Basques see themselves as an ethnic or national minority within Spain and, in common with Catalans, seek greater autonomy, or independence. The region also has the most determined separatist movement, and a terrorist organisation, *Euskadi ta Azkatasuna* (ETA), which came into being as a direct result of the repression of the Basques – their culture, language (*euskera*) and national aspirations – by the Franco regime. Its campaign continues today and ETA is in some respects the Spanish equivalent of the IRA.

It is widely said that the Basques are descended from the original aboriginal inhabitants of Europe who lived in the region before the farmers and settlers arrived from the Middle East 10,000 years ago. There may be some connection with the now-extinct Picts in Scotland. Early skeletal remains featuring a distinctive elongated head, which is characteristic of Basque people, have been unearthed in the region although many subsequent invasions have left their mark on the Basque country. Historians have ascertained that the Romans managed to subdue the province to the extent of building roads and settlements.

After the Romans left, the so-called barbarians (the Franks and the Visigoths), who settled in much of the rest of Spain, never managed more than a partial conquest of the area. The region was also one of the last corners of Europe to adopt Christianity and to build towns, and the Basques habitually ambushed pilgrims on the route to Santiago. Nominally ruled by the dynastics of Castile and Navarre, the Basques managed to keep a large measure of autonomy through the grass roots governorship of their own nobles and chieftains. Through their long association with the Castilian crown they also prospered, providing administrators for the Hapsburgs and producing such notable historical figures as Ignatius Loyola, St Francis Xavier and the explorer Lope de Aguirre.

The strident nationalism associated with the region was unknown before the nineteenth century and arose in response to the spread of centralist government, and ultimately as a reaction to the French Revolution. During the so-called Carlist Wars, the Basques were split between the urbanised supporters of Madrid, and the rural peasantry who sided with Don Carlos (who made an unsuccessful attempt to usurp his brother's throne). As punishment, Basque areas had their autonomy rescinded, which upset the loyalists who had sided with Madrid and caused a festering discontent. In the early twentieth century Basque industry, based around rich natural resources such as iron ore and timber, made the area around Biscay a hub of wealth, industry and banking. The Basque Nationalist Party – the PNV – was founded in 1910 with support broadly based in the liberal middle stratum of society. The Civil War of 1936 re-opened the old gulf between the peasantry and the middle-classes: the coastal provinces of Guipúzcoa and Vizcaya sided with the Republicans, who rewarded them with autonomy, while the inland province Alava sided with the government.

In 1937, the Basque Country was the scene of the most appalling brutality when the small but historic town of Guernica was bombed and over a thousand of its inhabitants massacred as they fled. It took four hours to reduce the town centre to rubble. The bombardment was carried out by the German air force, sent in in support of Franco's forces. Miraculously perhaps, the ancient *Guernikako Arbola* (Tree of Guernica) under which the Basque Parliament used to meet survived the attack.

Franco's attempt to bludgeon the Basques into submission has become immortalised in the Picasso painting depicting nightmarish scenes juxtaposed with modern technology representing the horror of war and the artist's reaction to it. The huge canvas was only brought to Spain after the dictator's death – as Picasso requested – and now hangs in the Centro de Arte Reina Sofia in Madrid.

In recent years, the industrialised north of Spain has suffered economic setbacks, with iron and steel works around Bilbao being put out of business by the recession. With high unemployment, and its reputation for terrorism, the Basque country may not seem an attractive prospect for property hunters, however, there *are* possibilities, and away from the main industrial areas around Bilbao there are rural areas of a greenness reminiscent of Ireland, and Basque farmhouses resembling Swiss chalets may appeal to some. The Basque Country is famous for its cuisine.

Basque Property. The biggest drawback to living in this part of Spain would probably lie in mastering the Basque language, which bears no resemblance to other European languages and would prove more difficult to learn than Spanish. The port of San Sebastián is a well-known, attractive resort popular with the Spanish. The Basque Country is popular with Spanish and foreign holiday makers alike who are looking for milder weather and greener landscapes during the summer season.

Because of the cooler sea temperatures and the amount of annual rainfall most northern Europeans choose not to buy in the area and you will be something of an oddity if you choose to live here. However, there are properties to be had, especially if you are looking to buy in order to renovate, and traditional Basque farmhouses (caseríos) can be found. There are few holiday homes for sale and as yet the holiday rental market is nowhere near that of the coastal resorts of the south (except in the resort of San Sebastián, which has very high property prices).

Because of the cooler climate, winter in the Basque Country is rather quiet with few tourists visiting the region. Unless you speak Spanish you are likely to find life rather isolating here as there is virtually no access to English-language media and foreigners are few and far between. There are regular ferry services between Plymouth and Santander and between Plymouth and Bilbao during the summer.

SOME SPECIALITIES OF THE BASQUE COUNTRY	
Angulas a la Bilbaína	baby eels in garlic sauce
Bacalao a la Vizcaína	salted cod in red pepper sauce
Bacalao al Pil-Pil	salted cod in garlic sauce
Kokotxas a la Donostiarra	hake cheeks in green sauce
Leche frita	fried custard
Marmitako	bonito and tomato soup
Merluza Koskera	hake in green sauce
Pochas	broad bean stew
Queso de Idiazábal	smoked sheep milk cheese
Txangurro	stuffed spider crab

CANTABRIA & ASTURIAS

Main towns: Santander, Oviedo.

The spectacularly mountainous regions of Cantabria and neighbouring Asturias were considered too remote and inhospitable by the eighth century Moorish invaders, and so they left the area unconquered. The result was that Christians and the remnants of the Visigoths fleeing the Moors found it a useful place of refuge. Protected from the south by the natural barrier of the Cantabrian Cordillera – one of Spain's highest mountain ranges – the Christian northerners were then able, by a combination of violent sorties and general creeping encroachment, to push back the frontier of Moorish Spain. In 718AD, there was a notable Asturian victory at Covadonga under Pelayo, who founded a small Asturian kingdom and from these modest beginnings the kingdom of Asturias spread out westwards and southwards until it reached León on the *meseta*. Eventually expansion reached the point where it allowed the Christian north to make a determined push against the Moors and complete the reconquest of most of Spain in the eleventh century.

In the nineteenth century, Asturias became a centre for mining and steel production and was fiercely Republican during the Civil War and produced one of its greatest heroes, the communist, Dolores Ibarruri *La Pasionaria* (the Passion-flower), an Asturian miner's wife who incited the housewives of Asturia to defend their homes with boiling oil. A legendary orator, she returned to Spain from exile on Franco's death. During the war Franco sent Spanish legionnaires and North African troops with a reputation for barbarity to subdue the region; an irony which was not lost on the Asturians who prided themselves on their historical resistance to the Moors.

A range of mountains – the Picos de Europa – forms a natural barrier between Asturias and Cantabria to the east. The small region of Cantabria, of similar area and population size to La Rioja, is centred on the port of Santander. Once patronised by royalty, Santander is an elegant resort, popular with Spaniards from the capital. There are many smaller resorts east of Santander, including Laredo, which is to the French what Benidorm is to the British (and where the summer population increases the off-season population by a factor of ten).

Property Possibilities. Finding property in Cantabria and Asturias will involve spending time in the area, preferably with someone who speaks Spanish fluently. Although property is available in these regions, those that buy it are mainly Spaniards and therefore estate agents will not be as used to dealing with foreigners as frequently as their colleagues on the *costas*.

Both the coastline and the interior of these regions are capable of stunning the visitor and there are some of the least spoilt parts of Spain's coastline here. However, the coastline is not known as la Costa Verde (the Green Coast) for nothing and the rainfall and cool temperatures here may put off some prospective house hunters. These regions are heavily agricultural and are far from developed – especially inland where lines of communication are hampered by the mountainous terrain and national parks. Property is a lot cheaper than that found on the Mediterranean coastline and hinterland and there are many properties for restoration available to those with the ambition and money to take on such a project in this traditional area of Spain. The main places to look are Santander, Gijón, Cudillero, Laredo, Comillas, Castro Urdiales, Llanes, Noja and San Vicente de la Barquera. The majority of summer clientele to these towns and resorts are Spanish and French. Santander hosts an international music and cultural festival throughout August every year.

SOME SPECIALITIES OF CANTABRIA AND ASTURIAS	
Almejas a la Marinera	clams in wine sauce
Anchoa en Cazuela	braised anchovies and onions
Cocido Montañés	mountain chickpea soup
Marmite	fish stew
Truchas a la Montañesa	trout in onion and wine sauce
Quesada Pasiega	cheese tart
Queso Picón	blue cheese
Arroz con leche	rice pudding
Entrecote con Queso Cabrales	steak with blue cheese sauce
Fabada Asturiana	bean stew
Fabes con Almejas	clam and bean stew
Merluza a la Sidra	hake in cider sauce
Pulpo con Patatines	stewed octopus and potatoes
Queso Cabrales	Asturian blue cheese
Sardinas asadas	grilled sardines

GALICIA

Provinces and main towns: A Coruña, Lugo, Orense, Pontevedra.
It is hardly surprising that Galicia rates with inland Andalucía as one of the least developed and poorer regions of Spain and its inland provinces of Lugo and Orense have a reputation of being among the most parochial in the country.

Galicia sits on the northwest corner of the Iberian Peninsula, geographically isolated and with relatively poor communications with the other regions. Its sizeable, mainly rural population of nearly three million has steadily diminished through emigration, while those who remain work mainly in agriculture and fishing. The region has a Celtic past, of which traces survive including the bagpipes (*gaita*) and the Galician language, *galégo* (which also gave rise to Portuguese). *Galégo* is a distinct language spoken by about 80% of the inhabitants of Galicia, in a variety of dialects. This region is often compared to Ireland because of a shared Celtic heritage, a similar climate and a west coast shaped into deep inlets by the Atlantic. Other similarities include a past in which famines led to mass emigration. Cornered by the Atlantic to the north and west, and Portugal to the south, the emigrants were forced southwards into Léon, Castile and Portugal or to Latin America to seek their fortunes.

Before history made Galicia such an isolated backwater, it had been the focal point of Christian nationalism in Spain by virtue of a miracle which took place on its soil: a shepherd was supposedly led by a guiding star to discover the remains of St. James the Apostle who, legend has it, preached there. From that moment on the Christians gained a holy patron *Santiago mata-moros* (St. James the moor-killer) in whose name they waged battles against the invaders. Near the site of the miracle a city, Santiago de Compostela (St. James of the Field of the Star) grew up. The saintly relics were housed first in a church and then in a great cathedral, and the latter became a famous place of pilgrimage throughout Europe in medieval times (even Chaucer's Wife of Bath had been there) and this cathedral remains to this day – along with the city surrounding it – one of Spain's premier tourist attractions. Two of Galicia's most famous sons are Fidel Castro – the product of Galician emigrants, and General Francisco Franco – a native-born Galician.

Although in 1936 Galicia voted for home rule in a regional referendum, the Civil War interrupted its implementation. There is virtually no heavy industry in the area and, without the radicalism that organised labour and industrialisation can produce, the politics of the region have remained largely conservative.

Property Possibilities. In contrast to the countryside, the coastal cities of La Coruña, Pontevedra, Vigo and Santiago de Compostela are relatively prosperous; and tend to be Castilian-speaking. Galicia has charm with its mixture of the traditional and the modern. Increasingly, new highways make it easy to discover the beautiful Atlantic coast, which has some of the best beaches in Spain. Madrid is three hours away from La Coruña by road. In spite of Galicia's charm and the low price of property (a three bedroom house with all mod cons in the country costs around £52,000), there are relatively few foreigners living in the region. Lines of communication with the rest of Spain are poor and it's a long drive from France, though there is a motorway running between Galicia and Porto in the north of Portugal. The main airport in Galicia is Labacolla, 13km east of Santiago de Compostela, which handles flights daily to London and several other European cities.

SOME SPECIALITIES OF GALICIA	
Caldo Gallego	beans, greens and potato soup
Empanadas	savoury meat or fish pies
Filloas	pancakes
Lacón con Grelos	boiled ham hocks, potatoes and vegetables
Merluza a la Gallega	hake with potatoes and paprika
Pimientos de Padrón	fried green peppers
Pulpo a Feira	octopus with oil and paprika

Queso de San Simón	smoked cow milk cheese
Vieiras con jamón	baked scallops with cured ham

INLAND SPAIN

CASTILLA-LEÓN (OLD CASTILE)

Provinces and main cities: Avila, Burgos, León, Palencia, Salamanca, Segovia, Soria, Valladolid, Zamora.

The nine provinces of the region of Castilla-León make it the largest region of Spain, covering almost a fifth of the surface area, though it has less than half the population of the next largest region, Andalucía. Modern Spain grew out of the old kingdom of Castile (which was an independent country ruled by its founder Count Fernán Gonzalez in the tenth century), and a kingdom ruled by King Ferdinand in the eleventh century. The new kingdom quickly swallowed up León, becoming the combined kingdom of Castile and León on and off until the thirteenth century. In the fourteenth century the three kingdoms of Portugal and Aragon-Castile were united by the marriage of King Ferdinand of Aragon and Isabella of Castile. Castilla-León is frequently referred to as Old Castile, while the region of Castile/La Mancha to the south is referred to as New Castile. Aragon-Castile became known as Spain in the wider world.

The great river Douro flows right across the *meseta* of Castille-León and on through Portugal to Oporto at its mouth. The *meseta* is characterized by its huge prairies – given over largely to cereals – and by its sparse population.

Some of the most beautiful cities in Spain are to be found here: Salamanca, León, and the walled city of Avila. The most scenic province is probably Soria, which has many of the fine castles (*castillos*) that give rise to the region's name. The city of Burgos was the former capital of Old Castile, though its significance nowadays derives from its position as an important garrison town.

Meseta cuisine

The food served in the central plateau (the *meseta*) of Spain differs again from other regions of this big country. In Castilla-León cooking is based on vegetables, haricot beans (*la bañeza* and *el barco*), chickpeas (*fuentesaúco*) and lentils (*la armuña*). Pork (raised on acorns and chestnuts) is flavoursome, and game is used in *botillo* (mountain sausage from León), savoury *morcilla* from Burgos, and the red Segovian sausage known as *cantimpalo*. Other local dishes are based around roasted baby lamb, kid and sucking pig, trout and cod, and there are plenty of local cheeses made from goat's, ewe's, and cow's milk. Sweets and pastries, such as *yemas* and *hojaldres* (puff pastry) are the remnants of Moorish cuisine.

Ham and pork are also staples of Extremaduran cuisine: *calderetas* (stews) and *cochifritos* (lamb seasoned, garnished and casseroled in an earthenware dish), cold *escabeches* (marinades), wild mushrooms, cardoons and leeks and cheeses.

Castile-La Mancha has its saffron, *la alcarria* honey and *manchego* (ewe's milk cheese). There is *salpicón (salmagundi)* and *duelos y quebrantos* (a cattle-drover's and shepherds' dish of a fry-up of eggs, bacon and brains). Country cuisine includes *morteruelos* (chopped pig's liver braised with seasoning and breadcrumbs) and roast lamb and kid. Sweets include varieties of the Moorish-inspired marzipan of Toledo. Madrid's traditional dishes include *cocido madrileño* (broth followed by the soup-meat, chick-peas, potatoes and greens), cod and *callos* (tripe). Sticky *torrijas* (sweet fritters), desserts and sweetmeats complete a pretty tableau. Valdepeñas and Ribera del Duego make exceptional red wines.

SOME SPECIALITIES OF CASTILLA-LEÓN	
Chuletitas de cordero	lamb chops
Cochinillo asado	roast piglet
Cocido	chickpea stew
Cordero asado	roast lamb
Judías con Chorizo	bean stew with *chorizo*
Queso de Burgos	sheep milk cheese
Sopa Castellana	garlic soup

LA RIOJA

Main city: Logroño

Mention Rioja to most Brits and they'll think you are talking about a type of wine. La Rioja is the smallest of the Spanish regions, occupying just 1% of its surface area; and home to a mere 0.67% of the population (a little over 50,000). Historically part of the mediaeval Castilian kingdom, La Rioja has nevertheless so far chosen to remain independent. This single-province region takes its name from the Rió Oja, a minor tributary of the great Ebro river which provides the water for the famous vineyards of the region. The main city of Logroño is on the pilgrim route to Santiago; and is the next main stop after Pamplona in Navarre.

Guidebooks tend to gloss over La Rioja. There isn't a great deal to the province unless you are interested in wine and looking to buy a vineyard. Most of the vineyards are owned by large commercial concerns though there are a few family-owned *bodegas* still.

MADRID

Located on a high plateau with impossible extremes of climate, the town of Madrid had little else going for it other than its strategically central and easily defended position until the capital of Spain was moved here in the seventeenth century. Madrid is 2,200 feet/670 metres above sea level and all distances in Spain are measured from *Puerta del Sol* in the city centre. Madrid is the seat of the Spanish parliament and famed for the Prado museum and its dizzy nightlife, which lasts from dusk till dawn.

Madrid and the surrounding area form the autonomous community of Madrid, which is the most densely populated region of Spain with about 600 inhabitants to the square kilometre. Madrid city has a population of around three million – referred to as *Madrileños.*

Unfortunately, in common with other giant metropolises, Madrid has its fair share of eyesore high-rise suburbs and, to its chagrin, it is considered by some as the runner-up to trendy Barcelona as a place to live and work. However, living in the capital has many advantages for those not wedded to the sun, sea and sand lifestyle offered by the Mediterranean coasts: limited heavy industry and strict pollution controls, and a programme of tree-planting that has transformed the cityscape. There are scores of English-language schools, and a number of UK and American companies operating in the city, as well as the opportunities provided by any capital city, with a wide range of commercial and business activities. Some of Spain's most stunning sights are within easy visiting distance of the capital, notably the cities of Segovia, Avila and Toledo.

> The price of property here is the highest in Spain and mainly consists of apartments and flats. A two-bedroom apartment can fetch anything from 150,000-450,000 euros or more. Depending on what you are looking for Madrid can be a dream or a nightmare. Madrid is a large busy, noisy city that gets very cold in the winter and while it is one of the cheapest capital cities within the European Union, it is one of the most expensive places to live in Spain.

Madrid is the hub of all lines of communication in Spain and is served by Barajas Airport, which lies 16km east of the city and can be reached by metro from the city centre. There are a large number of foreigners living and working in Madrid (about 100,000) and because of this there are the facilities available to cater for their needs. There are social clubs, Anglican churches, English-speaking doctors and dentists and international schools. There are also two English-language free sheets (*The Broadsheet* and *Guidepost*), which are published monthly.

SOME SPECIALITIES OF MADRID	
Callos a la Madrileña	tripe and *chorizo* stew
Caracoles a la Madrileña	snails and *chorizo* in paprika sauce
Churros	fritters
Cocido Madrileño	chickpea soup
Cordero asado	roast lamb
Leche Merengada	cinnamon-scented iced milk
Soldaditos de Pavía	batter-fried cod
Sopa de Ajo	garlic soup
Tortijas	battered toast
Buñuelos de viento	doughnuts

EXTREMADURA & CASTILLA-LA MANCHA (NEW CASTILE)

Main towns and provinces: Badajoz, Cáceres, Albacete, Cuenca, Ciudad Real, Guadalajara, Toledo.

Extremadura and Castilla-La Mancha are two of the regions of the *meseta* (the central tableland) which together comprise about a quarter of Spain's surface area but contain just over a sixth of its population. Extremadura is dominated by ranges of mountains and reservoirs. There are plans to enhance the agricultural prospects of this little known and bleak region, which is often passed through by travellers between Madrid and Portugal but otherwise virtually ignored by outsiders. Cáceres, the main town, was originally built with spoils from the activities of the local nobles in the New World. There is a famous six-arched Roman bridge at Alcántara near the Portugese border and further extensive Roman remains at Mérida.

The plain of La Mancha is probably best known for its windmills, and Cervantes' mournful Don Quixote who tilted at them and brought the word `quixotic' into the English language. Nowadays the plain is highly cultivated and agriculture an important part of the local economy, as in much of Spain.

Castilla-La Mancha contains what is probably one of the most beautiful towns in Spain – Cuenca, perched precariously on the side of a cliff. It

A HOME IN

Spain

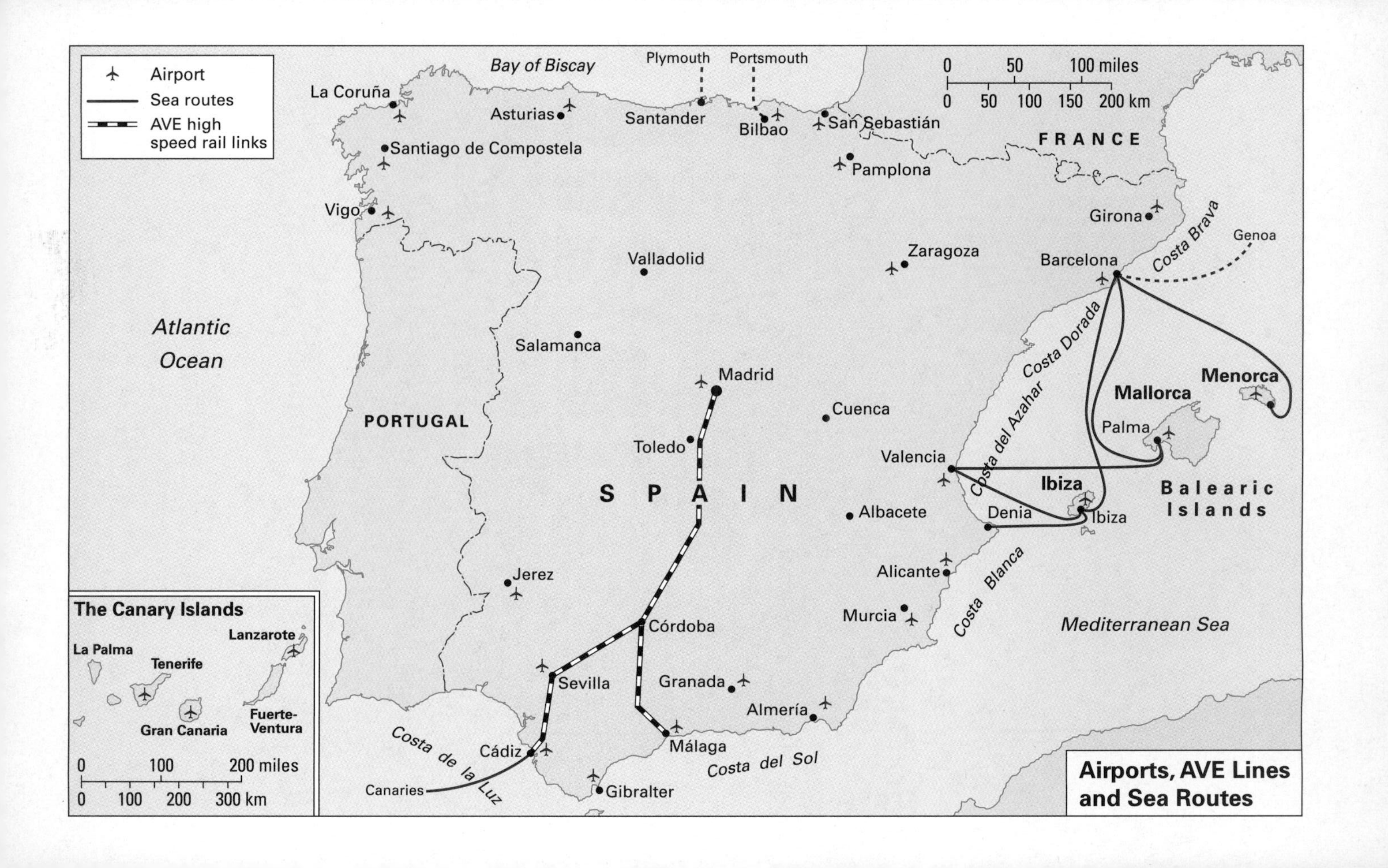

Airports, AVE Lines and Sea Routes

Village houses, Aragon

Old Castille, Leon Province, Castrillo de los Polvazares

Seaside houses, Sitges, Costa Dorada, south of Barcelona

Ramblas, Barcelona

Cadaqués seafront, Catalonia

Town houses, Mijas, Costa del Sol, Andalucia

Harbour apartments, Costa del Sol

Camposol, Costa Calida, near Cartagena 3/4 bed linked detached villas at €175,000

Camposol, 2 bed terraced villa around €100,000

New town house in Ciudad Quesada, near Alicante on the Costa Blanca

Villa terrace, Majorca

Historic village of Deyá, north coast of Majorca

also has one of the most famous – the medieval capital of Spain, Toledo, which sits on a craggy rock in a loop of the Tajo River. Toledo was once synonymous with crafted steel, especially sword blades, but its fame also rests on other achievements including scholarship, architecture, building, and the paintings of El Greco. This city also has connections with El Cid, who captured it in the eleventh century. Although redolent with history, Toledo's importance declined in the sixteenth century when the capital was moved to nearby Madrid.

Few foreigners live in the region and estate agents are not used to dealing with foreigners looking to buy. As with many other regions of inland Spain the prospective house buyer will need to spent time in the region ideally accompanied by a Spanish-speaker.

SOME SPECIALITIES OF EXTREMADURA AND CASTILLA-LA MANCHA	
Caldereta de Cordero	lamb stew
Faisán al Modo de Alcántara	pheasant with truffles and foie gras
Frite	potted lamb with paprika and garlic
Gazpacho Extremeño	white gazpacho
Queso de los Ibores	aged goat milk cheese
Queso Torta del Casar	semi-soft sheep milk cheese
Ajo Arriero	dried cod and potatoes
Flores Manchegas	fried pastries with honey
Mojete	dried cod and tomato salad
Morteruelo	meat and bread paté
Perdiz Estofada	stewed partridge
Pisto Manchega	vegetable stew
Queso Machego	sheep milk cheese

THE CANARY ISLANDS (LAS ISLAS CANARIAS)

Principal islands and resorts: Gran Canaria – Las Palmas; Lanzarote – Arrecife; La Palma – Santa Cruz; Tenerife – Santa Cruz.

The Canary Islands became Spanish territory as long ago as the fifteenth century. The best known of the Canary Islands are also the largest: Gran Canaria, Lanzarote and Tenerife. There are seven islands altogether, located about 70 miles off the Moroccan Western Sahara coast. The smaller islands are Fuerteventura, Hierro, Gomera and La Palma. With the exception of Lanzarote, which is comparatively flat, all these islands are characterised by high central mountains, and the consequent change of climate and spectacular scenery, a legacy of their volcanic origins. The climate is surprisingly mild considering their location, with the North-East Trade Winds bringing moisture-laden air – the 'horizontal rain' that supports much of the islands' vegetation. Ferries and jetfoils run by Transmediterranea and *Fred Olsen* link each of the islands and communications with the rest of Europe are good.

The central island, Gran Canaria, is described as a 'miniature continent', with a range of climates from dry and desert-like around the periphery; lush and sub-tropical; to a more temperate climate as you climb the central mountains. The mountains are volcanic, like the islands themselves, which emerged from the Atlantic some 40 million years ago. There are legends woven around the islands, enmeshed in their history, like Homer's Garden of the Hesperides, or Atlantis (which we can report did not sink into the sea around here). Both the ancient Greeks and Phoenicians knew of the Canary Islands and there were originally aboriginal inhabitants, probably related to the Berbers of nearby North Africa, whose fate when the Spanish arrived is not recorded in the guidebooks. Gran Canaria has a *Columbus Museum* in the atmospheric Governor's Residence in its bustling main town (and port), Las Palmas, which records the visit of the explorer who discovered America. Colonists from the Canary Islands also went on to settle in North and South America.

The atmosphere of Gran Canaria today is surprisingly cosmopolitan, with an important fishing industry, import-export companies taking advantage of the islands' favourable tax regime and tourists from continental Europe as well as Britain thronging its beaches, notably in the tourist developments around the Playa del Inglés and Maspalomas in the south.

Gran Canaria is not a backwater. Ikea and Benetton have stores there as does El Corte Inglés, the ubiquitous Spanish chainstore. The capital, Las Palmas, has all the facilities of any large Spanish city and its own beach – a centre for sunbathing and socialising – while the coastline further to the southwest has Puerto de Mogan, which retains its old-fashioned charm and is a favoured stopping-off point for yachts. The north is less developed and has strong local traditions. Getting away from it all would mean living inland, near the town of Teror with its famous annual fiesta. The facilities make Gran Canaria an excellent place to live and work, especially away from some of the overcrowded resorts. The *Patronato de Turismo Gran Canaria* can be contacted at: León y Castillo 17, 35003 Las Palmas de Gran Canaria; ☎ 928 219 600; fax 928 219 601; www.turismograncanaria.com.

> The Canaries have greater autonomy from central government than other regions of Spain and the two provinces they form are regulated from Las Palmas-Gran Canaria and Santa Cruz-Tenerife. The three main islands have long been popular with tourists from all over the world and in recent years they have also become increasingly popular with timeshare and villa owners, many of whom have holidayed in the islands before settling there. The year-round warm climate is a great attraction that outweighs the inconvenience of travelling to the islands.

Apart from the scenery and the wildlife there is much of interest culturally and historically, and if you are interested is sailing and ships this is a good place to be. Other points of interest are the mysterious aboriginal inhabitants, and the (almost) unique whistled language that used to be 'spoken' by shepherds on the island of Gomera.

In past times, the Canaries were a useful last-stop for ships bound across the Atlantic. Today, the Japanese tuna fishing fleet and many cargo vessels still stop off here and every November the ARC transatlantic yacht race takes off from Las Palmas.

The most popular places for foreign residents are also the tourist centres: in the Orotava Valley of Tenerife, and the south of Gran Canaria where there are several tourist developments including the Playa del Inglés and San Agustin. Apart from the three main islands there are also smaller foreign communities in Fuerteventura, Lanzarote and La Palma.

Hierro and Gomera are less visited and further from the convenience of facilities and services that many expats expect. Gomera is only a few miles away from Tenerife but completely different in its culture and the cost of property. Ferries travel to Gomera from Los Cristianos on Tenerife 5 times a day costing around £24 return. A population of 40,000 – mainly involved in farming and fishing – is now down to around 17,000 as the young have left, over-fishing has closed the tuna factories and cheaper produce has been discovered elsewhere. What this means for house hunters, is that there are plenty of properties on offer. The catch is that many properties have not being formally registered yet, or even put on the map.

Property Possibilities

Property prices are rising in the Canary Islands by up to 20% a year. The British tend to plump for property on Tenerife (and many retirees relocate to the main towns like Playa San Juan or the resorts along the Costa Adeje), Lanzarote and Fuerteventura. Property on the northern coast of Tenerife is still cheaper than that in the south as it rains more. Two-bedroom flats along the south coast will set you back around £115,000 while a detached villa with pool can be found for about £250,000. Prices in Lanzarote and Fuerteventura are slightly cheaper (by 10%-15%) than on Tenerife. Because of an embargo on new developments on all the Canary Islands prices on new builds (those being completed now are due to planning permission being granted before the embargo) are likely to rise considerably due to less property coming onto the market. Germans seem to abound in Gran Canaria, and to a lesser extent are buying up properties in the smaller off the track islands of Gomera, La Palma and Hierro. The local tax in the Canary Islands on new homes is 5% compared to the 7.5% on the mainland. Tax on building plots remains 5% compared to the 16% on the mainland which is an incentive for those who are prepared to tackle the bureaucracy involved in self-build.

SOME SPECIALITIES OF THE CANARY ISLANDS	
Mojo	potatoes and fish in sauce
Patatas Arrugadas	'wrinkled' potatoes
Potaje de Berros/Zaramago	watercress/mustard green soup
Puchero Canario	chick-pea soup
Quesadilla	cheesecake
Sancocho Canario	salted fish, sweet potatoes, spicy sauce

CHOOSING THE RIGHT LOCATION

It is sensible to spend time during different parts of the year in the area where you think you would like to buy. Compare the traffic density, the climate and the number of holidaymakers over the seasons. Hire a car and take a look around the area, check out the surrounding towns and villages. Take photographs and a video camera so that once back home you can live the moment again rather than relying on an increasingly fading memory of places visited. Check out the estate agents' windows in the area to get a feel for the price you'll have to pay for the type of property you are looking for. Make a shortlist of places that you consider suitable and then revisit them – preferably with a good friend whose advise you respect.

Choosing a Location – Lindy Walsh

We didn't want to be on the coast in an English ghetto. We needed minimal support from other English speakers while we learned Spanish. We loved the scenery; we liked the attitude of the Spanish locals towards us. There were a few (very few) English and Dutch living nearby whom we could call on. The property is ten minutes drive from the town, which has a police station, a petrol station and mechanic, a 24-hour health centre, a bank and shops. It covers our basic needs.

If you are intending to move to Spain permanently then it is a good idea to spend some time in rented accommodation in the area that you are interested in buying. This will give you time to get to really know the area with all it's pitfalls (every place in the world has its pitfalls – there are no utopias on earth) and allow you time to make contacts who may be able to turn up something that you had not previously considered, or a bargain.

If you are retiring then you may be looking for different criteria than if you are intending to work in Spain, or if you hope to partly finance life in Spain by engaging in the tourist trade by renting out your apartment. Are you a true urbanite who needs the bustle and crush of at least a decent sized town or are you looking for tranquillity and solitude? A lonely farmhouse at the end of a rough track may be the stuff that dreams are made of, but how far away are you from medical facilities, public transport and company? Will the rough track become practically impassable after a week of winter rain? Will the sun turn the surroundings into a virtual desert during the summer? Don't assume that plumbing, telephone and electricity will be laid on as standard as they would be back home. Have you enough capital to live without engaging in the wider world outside? When you get older and frailer will you be able to cope out there?

Buying a property abroad involves thinking about a lot of additional factors. Below are some of those you should take into consideration. A growing number of house hunters are choosing to buy properties inland, which offer better value for money and escape the crowded, concrete *costas.* The Federation of Overseas Property Developers, Agents and Consultants' website (www.fopdac.com) has details of over 40 member firms specialising in old and new properties. The average house price in 2002 (according to Abbey National) in Alicante was £74,340, in the Canary Islands £68,145 and along the Costa del Sol £167,265.

More advice for buyers – Lindy Walsh

I would advise a potential first time buyer to spend the extra money and take the extra time to visit the chosen area for at least a week in the height of summer and the depth of winter. Find out if the water supply goes down to two or three hours a day in temperatures in the high 30s when even at night it's too hot to sleep without artificial cooling. Find out if your area floods – it may only flood every few years but then leave you totally marooned for a couple of days. How cold does it get at night in February? Who are your neighbours, and are they permanent residents? It isn't only foreigners who have second homes. Are you assuming you'll be able to get mains water and electricity (I waited nine years for electricity) and if they are already connected how reliable is the supply? I know someone who bought a house with a barn, which he intended to use as a workshop. He found out too late that he could only get half a kilowatt of power – not enough for a fridge or a TV as well as lighting; and forget the welding equipment!

Shopping

How much of a shopaholic are you and the members of your family? Could you survive without the close proximity of numerous shops and variety? Spain, like the rest of Europe, has increasingly embraced the hypermarket and supermarket culture and outside many towns and tourist areas there are vast shopping centres (Hipercor, Carrefour, Lidls, Mercadona and Alcampo are the biggest players) selling everything from fridge freezers and clothes to the humble croissant. Elsewhere you will find smaller local supermarkets where you will be able to buy the necessities for the kitchen. However, fresh fruit and vegetables may well not be as fresh as those found in local markets (*mercados*) or in the hypermarkets.

Remember that much of the best quality fruit and vegetables grown in Spain are exported. The *mercados* are especially good for meat and fish where the stallholders will prepare produce for you while you wait. Becoming a devotee of the *mercados* is also a great way to improve your Spanish as well as becoming accepted into the community by the locals. What you will find, however, especially away from the main areas of foreign occupation, is the lack of those basics that you have been accustomed to back home. Tea, marmite, biscuits, Walkers crisps, marmalade and breakfast cereals; all these things will be hard to find, though are obtainable in Gibraltar. If you miss the old home cooking ask friends and family to bring supplies when they come to visit you.

Note: If you are used to living in a place where people form orderly queues to buy a ticket at a cinema or while waiting to pay at a newsagents then you will need to readjust your sensibilities. The concept of mañana doesn't extend to hanging about in a queue waiting to give away one's money. Don't be bullied into giving way and speak up if someone tries to step in front of you if your Spanish is fluent enough.

There isn't yet a culture of high street chains such as exists in the UK and you will find many of the shops are small, family-run enterprises. The most famous department store in Spain, a forerunner to the hypermarkets, is El Corte Inglés which sells clothing as well as electrical goods, kitchenware etc. Sales take place in the winter (January-February) and in the summer (July-August).

TYPES OF STORE IN SPAIN	
Alimentación	grocery store
Carnicería	butchers
Charcutería	delicatessen
Droguería	hardware store
Farmacía	Chemists
Ferretaría	ironmongers
Fruitería	fruitsellers
Lavandería automática	laundrette
Panadería	bakers
Pastelería	cake shop
Peluquería	hairdressers/barbers
Pescadería	fishmongers
Quiosco	newsstand
Tabac/estanco	tobacconists (also sells stamps, phonecards, etc.)
Tienda de ropa	clothes shop
Zapatería	shoe shop
Ganga	bargain
Ofertas	discounts
PVP (precio de venta al público	RRP
Rebaja	sale

Location Counts

How well do you really know the area where you think you want to live? Spend a month or so in the area getting to know it. Depending on where you are looking to buy property, winter, or the low season, is the time to visit property. At that time of year it is cheaper to rent a short-term let in which to base yourself while house hunting. You will also be seeing the area at its least crowded time when many of the restaurants will be closed and the bars quiet and practically empty (or deserted!). However, the winter is the high season in the Canary Islands and it is better to visit here in the summer when you will get a feel of the high temperatures. If you are not in a rush to buy, go back to the area and spend another month during the high season to see the changes that occur. Do you feel comfortable with the temperatures? The amount of tourist traffic? The activity or lack of it at these times of the year? Are there difficulties with obtaining cheap flights at certain times of the year? If you are thinking about living high up in the *sierras* are there problems with access due to flooding or snowdrifts during certain times of the year?

If you are determined to buy as quickly as possible there are short escorted visits laid on by developers and agents who will be able to whisk you around a number of properties, show you a good time and try and convince you that you can't find better than what they have shown you. If you do find something to your taste on one of these inspection flights, take your time and return again on your own to have a general look around at the location, the finer details of the property and surrounding area and local infrastructure.

Spending part of a holiday looking at property can be a fun and dreamy exercise, but you should allow yourself an extended period of time to view properties, and try to set up meetings with agents and vendors in Spain beforehand. Hopefully you will have already focused in on and know a fair amount about the area where you are looking to buy.

Living beside the sea is a dream for many people. And why not? During the hot summer months the sea breezes make the temperatures more bearable and the appeal of water sports for many is a big draw, sailing out into the Mediterranean, surfing, swimming, beachlife etc. After the cold of northern Europe with its grey choppy seas the desire to live beside an azure sea, calm as a millpond, is easily understandable. The downside of the dream, of course, is the reality. In Spain, more so along the Mediterranean than the Atlantic coast, during the summer months the tourist hordes invade and take over those once quiet beaches, pack the roads and verges with hire cars and motorbikes and coaches and party loudly into the early hours. It is true that money can be made from the hordes if one is renting property or working in the catering and leisure business, and this could be another draw to buying property on the coast. But properties within spitting distance of a beach and the sea are now fiercely fought over and as a consequence are very expensive. There may also be problems with building regulations if you plan to buy a property, or build one on land within a kilometre of the high water mark due to the 'Law of the Coasts'.

The Law of the Coasts. Fifteen years ago the Law of the Coasts (*Ley de Costas*) was introduced to stop the hotels and villas that were being built blocking the view of the sea. It is now prohibited to build anywhere on the coast within 100 metres of the high-water mark. This obviously hit a lot of property developers who owned such land and some shoreline developments were pulled down, though some still remain. If you wish to own or build a home on a seafront plot there are strict guidelines that will need to be adhered to. In Spain all beaches are publicly owned. There are no private clubs leasing beaches and restricting access to members only. Additionally, the military has rights over the first fifty metres inland from the coast, and in theory the army could commandeer a beach property, though this is very unlikely to occur. One way to tackle the building restriction is to buy an existing property, demolish it and then build your own. Beachfront plots are obviously very hard to come by. Such places do exist, but Mallorca is said to be impossible while the Costa Blanca, west coast of Fuerteventura, around Alicante, and at present the Atlantic coast, may be better bets.

Much of Spain, inland and away from the *costas* is still pretty sedate and what is strangely termed 'real Spain' still survives. Plots of land can be had much cheaper here than on the coast and though the infrastructure may be less developed there will be a more established sense of community and, depending on how you integrate yourself into a community, you may find it more rewarding being the foreigner on the hill than merely one of many thereabouts. Because foreigners *are* resented for the changes that have been wrought on the Spanish way of life along the *costas* in order to satisfy their needs.

The main points to look out for with rural properties are the provision of utilities such as gas, electricity, sewerage disposal, telephone links and water. If the desired property lacks some or all of these things then you should question why you want such a property and what you are going to do with it. How are you going to get round the inadequacies of the property? Can you afford to put in a septic tank? Install solar panelling? Use only a radio or mobile phone? Live without access to the Internet? If water provision is going to prove a problem, bang goes your idea for a swimming pool and the installation of several en suite bathrooms. If you have had an urban upbringing and are used to the noise, bustle and easy access of things in general in a town or city will you really be able to take to the slow pace of life in a village, or out 'in the middle of nowhere'? If you are certain that you can then go ahead and live the dream, if not then it will be more sensible to rent somewhere in the country to see it you 'take' to the way of life there.

Advice for first-time buyers – Lindy Walsh

Buying 'inland' is totally different from buying on the coast. Buying rural is as different again from buying inside a town or village boundary. Don't take anything for granted. I know awful cases of people buying land with water running through it, but not being allowed to use one drop; of buying land with trees and finding out too late that they hadn't bought the trees (or their harvest); of buying a 'house' (it looked like a house) and finding that it was registered as a chicken shed and not able to be registered as habitable because it didn't conform to the newest building standards. Check and check again and don't part with any money until you have a copy of a registered escritura that has been looked over by a local (but perhaps not too local as he may be the vendor's brother) gestor or abogado. Better a local gestor who doesn't speak English, and pay the extra to a translator, than an English speaker who doesn't know the area.

The plus of a place in the country is that you are likely to get more for your money and, depending on planning restrictions, location, etc., those additional outbuildings could be converted into holiday lets and the land turned to some use. How big a project are you looking to take on? Do you just want a bolthole for a few weeks every year, or a complete change of lifestyle? Just how self-sufficient are you and your family? You will need to seriously consider all these questions. Living on one of the islands can be different again. Everything from foodstuffs to furniture to flights are likely to be more expensive than living on the mainland.

When viewing properties, try to make several visits at differing times of the day to find out how dark, or sunstruck the rooms become. A quick flick of a light switch by the estate agent on entering a property can deceive the potential buyer into thinking that a property is brighter than it really is. Additionally find out the direction in which a property faces. A property advertised as 'cool in the summer' may be positioned so that it faces north and therefore receives no direct sunlight. This may be fine if you are only going to be living there during the hot summer months but the house will need to be heated during the cool winters. A south-facing house may be shockingly hot during the summer but pleasantly warmed in the winter.

What's the Weather Like in Your Part of Spain?

The only place where you will be guaranteed sunshine and warm sea temperatures throughout the year is in the Canary Islands. Elsewhere, even on the Costa del Sol, winter temperatures, though pleasant, are mild rather than baking. Further north, along the Costa Brava winter can get distinctly chilly and if you are buying up in the Sierras remember that you can go skiing here in winter! You will need to pack warm clothes and make sure that the property has adequate insulation and heating. Another point related to climate is the risk or otherwise of flooding and forest fires, which in some parts (mainly in the north) of Spain are yearly occurrences.

The Desirability of a Property

There are a number of factors influencing the desirability of a property and these need to be considered, whether you are thinking about buying to rent, buying to reside, or buying as an investment. A property needs a selling point, be it a sea view, its proximity to golf courses or the beach, being at the hub of the nightlife, or in a national park. A unique property (something strange or out of the ordinary) is also an attraction for many people, as is the area in which it is located. A beautiful, huge detached villa in a run-down *barrio* will command a lower price than a smaller one in a chic neighbourhood or in an up and coming area of town.

At present, with the Spanish property boom going from strength to strength, any modern property is likely to be a good investment if you plan to sell on in the future. However, if you are planning to buy in order to command an income from renting your property out to holidaymakers, you will need to choose a location that is desirable, where people will want to stay, perhaps come back and stay year after year. You will not be the only person with property for rent in a particular area. There will be competition and some will be able to spend more on marketing their property than you, others will have less to spend. You can get the edge on the competition by carefully weighing up the cost of a property against its location.

Ease of Access

If you are looking to buy to rent, you need to be aware that if a property is more than an hour's drive from the nearest airport potential tenants are likely to think twice about staying with you. This factor will also be an important factor in the purchase price of a property, both when you buy it and when it comes to selling on. Ease of access to communication networks, be they rail or road links are of considerable importance when weighing up the cost against the location of a place. Add to this local and regional transport in the area; the ability for you or a tenant who hasn't a car to get to areas of interest, the beaches and the commercial centres.

Leisure Facilities

Depending on what your leisure interests are – golf, sailing, skiing, equestrianism, water sports or bridge, how close to the property are the nearest facilities? Brochures tout some Andalucían properties with the promise of a sail in the Mediterranean in the morning followed by the possibility of skiing in the afternoon. Theoretically this may be possible, but you may end up spending more time driving between the Mediterranean marina and the snowfields of the Sierra Nevada than actually sailing or skiing. Distances can be deceptive, especially when the tourist season is in full swing and the coastal roads are packed. If you are addicted to golf and it will be of primary importance while you are in Spain, why not consider buying property in one of the golf resorts, or as close as possible to one of the courses along the Costa del Sol.

Medical Facilities; The Local Municipal Council

What is the medical facilities provision in the area where you are hoping to buy? Are there English-speaking staff? Good places to find out this sort of information (if you are hoping to buy on or near the *costas*) are the English-language magazines and newspapers, as well as other expat property owners. Your local lawyer may also be able to give you an idea of what is offered and local bars are often founts of information for the newcomer. Depending on how well run the town hall (*ayuntamiento*) is, you may find that local facilities, services and schools are very well run and efficient, that any planning and building regulations that need to be looked after and sorted out are cleared up quickly and efficiently, or on the other hand that things are badly run and disproportionately expensive to remedy.

Spain is the third largest country in Europe after Germany and France and different regions have very different characteristics when it comes to local politics. It is unhelpful to generalise about Spain – to find out how regions are run you will need to spend time where you are looking to buy, get to know the area, the local ambience. Everyone will have criteria personal to themselves – the laid-back atmosphere of an Andalucían village, for example, may be total anathema to the social butterfly looking for the hustle of a Barcelona or Madrid.

Do You Want to Live Among Your Compatriots?

Because of the sheer volume of foreigners who have bought property in Spain over the years, you will be unlikely to find a property too far away from another owned by someone from Germany, Holland or Britain or Scandinavia unless you have decided to buy in the *meseta*. Even houses in the villages up in the hills and hinterland behind the *costas* are increasingly being bought up by foreigners. These villages remain very Spanish and because the foreigners have moved there for precisely that reason, they try to integrate into the Spanish community as best they can. Don't be under any illusions that you will find a 'traditional' and culturally intact village up in the hills where you will be the only foreigner – those days are long gone, or if not quite, are fast disappearing. Globalisation has made big strides into post-Franco Spain as it has throughout the rest of the world.

> If you are buying an off-plan property, find out if there are likely to be further buildings planned – a possible Phase 2 or 3 where your bijou set of apartments is going to be reduced to being merely one of a number of such apartments, part of a small town complete with café, club house and social centre. There are *urbanizaciónes* where all the owners of the villas or apartments are foreign and where the only native Spanish face you see will be that of the gardener. Much like the compounds for foreigners found in Saudi Arabia these places are often insular worlds where there is no need, and no desire, to mix with the local community.

The Manageability and Security of a Property

Do you really need a large property with an inordinate number of bedrooms that requires a great deal of ongoing maintenance to the house and garden? If you are planning to retire to the property in Spain how far away is the house from the local shopping and medical centre, from neighbours and places to indulge your interests and/or hobbies. A beautiful view is wonderful for a time, but it will eventually merge into the general scenery and become everyday and you will ultimately take it for granted. If you are buying an isolated property how are you going to fill your days? If you are only planning on visiting the property for a few weeks or months a year then you should consider whether you really need a garden or whether you should get it paved over and add pot plants. Likewise a swimming pool will need continual maintenance and if a property is to be left unattended for lengthy periods of time this can become an inconvenience. Most properties will already have security grilles (*rajas*) fitted on ground floor windows and doors but depending on how much use is going to be made of a property you will need to look into how secure it is. Grand isolated properties may be expensive to insure, especially if they are only occupied for a certain number of weeks or months a year.

Seasonal Population Fluctuations

The summer crowds, the quiet winters. If you decide that you want to buy a property in town is it near a main thoroughfare that gets a lot of tourist traffic, or just a lot of traffic all year round? Remember that Spaniards tends to begin their evening socialising much later than we are accustomed to back home and revellers often party into the early hours. Restaurants open their doors late and remain open late. If you are looking to buy in a busy downtown area are you prepared to put up with noise below your flat through the night?

Is your property part of a development where neighbouring properties are let out continually to holidaymakers intent on a raucous two-week knees-up throughout the high season (when you may well want to enjoy some peace and quiet away from the stresses of your life back home) and then left entirely empty over the winter? During the tourist season finding a parking space near to your property may prove difficult and the demand for increased services (sewerage, water, electricity, beer or tapas!) may lead to temporary shortages and restrictions that you may find tolerable for one season, but which may begin to annoy you if endured year after year. For those seeking peace it may be better to look for property inland in order to avoid the tourist hordes.

Water Shortages

Areas that get little annual rainfall will naturally succumb to periods of drought when water restrictions come into force. Bang goes your dream of a house with a pool, of beautiful lawns irrigated by the soft pulse of sprinklers. Are there alternative water supplies at hand, e.g. a well or a storage tank? Such considerations are particularly important if you are looking to buy in Andalucía, as well as up the Mediterranean Coast along the Costa Calida and into the Costa Blanca. Although there has been a massive investment in water resources in Spain, transferring water from the northern and central areas of Spain to the south via a system of irrigation canals and reservoirs, water is an expensive commodity. The drought of 1995 meant that 10 million people were affected by water rationing. Talk to the locals and other foreigners who have lived in the area for some time.

Personal Plans

Another, perhaps obvious, point to consider is what are you going to do with your house in Spain. Are you going to use it as a holiday home, or are you going to live there full-time? Are you moving your life to the Iberian Peninsula? Are you retiring there? Are you going to have to find some way of earning a living in Spain? If you are self-employed are you confident that your business will be able to carry on once you are in Spain? What are you going to do? What will your spouse do? Where will your kids go to school? Is there a decent choice of schools in the area where you are hoping to go and live? Or are you looking to send them to an English-language International school or to a Spanish school? Is there one of these at a sensible distance from the property? Are there enough kids around of the same age group to create some sort of social life for your own? Do you have any contacts/entrées into the social scene there? How's your grasp of the Spanish language?

> Retirees often head for Mallorca, where a two-hour plane ride will see you anywhere in Europe you'd wish to be. The second most popular destination for retirees is Andalucía with its varied landscape – the mountains and skiing in the Sierra Nevada, the beaches and the sherry in Jerez. Costa Blanca is the third most popular area in which retirees settle – and is one of the cheapest costas in which to buy. The Costa Brava is more traditionally Spanish than other costas, as is the isolated but beautiful (and chilly) Galician coast.

FINDING THE RIGHT PROPERTY

Property Fairs and Seminars

Look in the property pages of any broadsheet newspaper and you will find advertisements taken out by companies such as *Homes Overseas*, *Intereality* and *Ocean Estates International*. These companies organise large events where a number of estate agents and property developers specialising in overseas property assemble under one roof to show off their wares. There are also seminars given on the Spanish property market, on the financial aspects and the law connected with buying in Spain. It should be stressed that the exhibitors at these events deal primarily with the most popular areas in Spain: the Costa del Sol, the Costa Brava, the Balearics, Canary Islands etc, and with developments and *urbanizaciónes*. If you are looking for something out of the ordinary then a property exhibition may not be the best place to find such a property, but it will be worth going along to one to pick up information on various aspects of property buying in Spain as well as making some useful contacts.

However, you should be wary of falling for the charms of the salesmen and saleswomen at these shows: they are looking for closure, hoping to persuade you to take a trip out to Spain to view their property and buy what they have to offer. Use the opportunity to get hold of as much information, brochures, ideas of the kind of prices and properties available. Go prepared – pin down the criteria you have for buying a place and scout around. Listen in to some of the conversations taking place between agents/developers and potential clients before getting into conversation.

Useful Addresses

Homes Overseas: Blendon Communications Ltd, 207 Providence Square, Mill Street, London SE1 2EW; ☎ 020-7939 9888; fax 020-7939 9889; www.blendoncommunications.co.uk.

Homebuyer Events Ltd.: Mantle House, Broomhill Road, London SW18 4JQ; ☎ 020-8877 3636; fax 020-8877 1557; www.homebuyer.co.uk.

Interealty: Avda. Ricardo Soriano, 25. Edif. Sierra Blanca. 29660 Marbella; ☎ 952 900 550; fax 952 765 278; www.interealtynet.com.

International Property Show: 7 The Soke, Alresford, Hampshire, S024 9DB; ☎ 01962-736 712; fax 01962-736 596; www.internationalpropertyshow.com.

Spain on Show: 15 The Triangle, Bournemouth,Dorset BH2 5RY; freephone 0500-780878; www.spainonshow.com.

World Class Homes: 22 High Street, Wheathampstead, Herts AL4 8AA; freephone 0800-731 4713; ☎ 01582-832 001; fax 01582-831 071; www.worldclasshomes.co.uk.

World of Property (Outbound Publishing): 1 Commercial Road, Eastbourne, East Sussex BN21 3XQ; ☎ 01323-726 040; fax 01323-649 249; www.outbound-newspapers.com.

The Internet

The World Wide Web is being used increasingly by estate agents and property developers as a marketing tool – as a cheap way to get their name out there into the homes and offices of prospective clients. There are portals such as Hamptons (www.hamptons.co.uk), www.primelocation.com (which includes property from 250 estate agents), www.propertyfinder.com (property from 900 agencies), and newskys.co.uk., which deal exclusively with property abroad. Depending on the budget that a company has to develop its website, a site may include 3-D walkthroughs of selected property or photographs and specifications as we are used to seeing in estate agents' display windows. Other sites may have been created by individuals – owners of property in Spain who are looking to sell privately. Using a search engine such as www.google.com or a web directory such as www.yahoo.com will lead you into a selection of websites dealing solely with Spanish property for sale.

Because of the vast amount of information (as well as misinformation and downright junk) that is posted on the Internet you will need to narrow down any search to specifics. Rather than just typing in 'property, Spain' or 'villas for sale, Costa del Sol' name the specific area or town you are looking to buy in. If you have the name of a developer that you are thinking of doing business with then use the web as a research tool. Find out as much as you can about the developers. You can make initial contact with vendors of property that interests you using email (you can get a free email address at such places as www.hotmail.com, or yahoo.co.uk) but be very wary of any company or individual who asks for payment of any kind over the web. Although e-commerce has come a long way and although those who have the money to invest in Internet security have made it virtually impossible for a 'hacker' to get hold of clients' credit card details that are given over the web, smaller operators may not have. If you decide to continue with negotiations after initial contact over the Internet better to set up a face to face meeting as soon as possible.

Part III

THE PURCHASING PROCEDURE

FINANCE

FINDING PROPERTIES FOR SALE

WHAT TYPE OF PROPERTY TO BUY

RENTING A HOME IN SPAIN

FEES, CONTRACTS & CONVEYANCING

BUYING FOREIGN CURRENCY FOR YOUR PROPERTY

If you're buying a property abroad for the first time, you've probably got enough to think about without worrying about exchange rates. You've found your dream home and secured the price of your property, and now all you have to do is look forward to your new life abroad. Right? Well, partly. Somewhere along the line you will have to change your pounds into euros, and that's where the dream can become a nightmare if you don't plan ahead. Whether you're buying a property outright or buying from plan in instalments, protecting yourself against exchange rate fluctuations can save you hundreds, if not thousands of pounds on the price of your new home.

Foreign Exchange markets are by nature extremely volatile and can be subject to dramatic movements over a very short space of time. In some ways it's all too easy to leave your currency exchange to the last minute and hope that the exchange rates fall in your favour. But if you don't take steps to protect your capital, you could find yourself paying a lot more than you bargained for.

As a matter of course, many people will approach their banks to sort out their currency, without realising that there are more cost-effective alternatives in the marketplace. There are a number of independent commercial foreign exchange brokers who can offer better rates and a more personal, tailored service. Their dealers will explain the various options open to you and keep you informed of any significant changes in the market. They will also guide you through every step of the transaction so that you are ultimately in control and able to make the most of your money.

If you're not still not convinced of how planning ahead can help you, take a look at the following example:

You've found your dream home and agreed the price of €200,000. When you signed your contract and paid your deposit in August 2002, the pound stood at 1.60. Just six months later when your next instalment was due, changes in the political and economic climate have caused the pound to weaken. You now only get 1.49 for your pound.

Agreed Price of Your New Home	Date	Rate	Cost in Pounds
€200,000	August 2002	1.60	**£125,000**
	February 2003	1.49	**£134,228**

In just 6 months the price of your home has **increased** by over **£9,000**.

currencies direct

Although changes in the economic climate may be beyond your control, protecting your capital against the effect of these changes isn't.

There are a number of options available to you:

- **Spot Transactions** are ideal for anyone who needs their currency straight away as the currency is purchased today at the current rate. However, if you have time to spare before your payments are due, it may be wiser to consider a Forward Transaction.
- **Forward Transactions** allow you to secure a rate for up to a year in advance to protect yourself against any movements in the market. A small deposit holds the rate until the balance becomes due when the currency contract matures.
- **Limit Orders** allow you to place an order in the market for a desired exchange rate. This has the advantage of protecting you against negative exchange movements whilst still allowing you to gain from a positive movement. Your request is entered into the system and an automatic currency purchase is triggered once the market hits your specified rate.

If you haven't had to deal with this kind of transaction before, this can all seem a little daunting. But that's where a reputable currency company can really come into its own. With specialists in the field ready to explain all the pitfalls and possibilities to you in layman's terms and guide you through each stage of the transaction, you can be sure that your currency solutions will be perfectly tailored to your needs.

Currencies Direct has been helping people to understand the overseas property markets since 1996. Specialising in providing foreign exchange solutions tailored to clients' individual financial situations, it offers a cost-effective and user-friendly alternative to the high-street banks.

With offices in the UK and Spain, Currencies Direct is always on hand to help you. For more information on how you can benefit from their commercial rates of exchange and friendly, professional service, call the Currencies Direct office in London on 020 7813 0332 or visit their website at www.currenciesdirect.com.

FINANCE

CHAPTER SUMMARY

- **Banks**. Banks in Spain are divided into clearing banks and savings banks and there are also a number of foreign banks operating throughout the country.
  - ATMs in Spain now allow you to carry out transactions such as renewing your mobile phone card or making theatre seat reservations.
  - Spanish tax residents pay tax on their worldwide income, including gains or income from trusts and offshore companies, trusts, accounts, shares, etc.
- **Mortgages**. Although a euro mortgage (*hipoteca*) on a Spanish property provides better security against fluctuations in currency values, fluctuation in interest rates may serve to counteract this advantage.
  - With Spanish mortgages, the mortgage repayment period tends to be shorter that in the UK – usually about fifteen to twenty years.
- **Importing Currency.** You can save thousands of pounds by using the services of a currency dealer rather than going through a high street bank.
- **Tax.** Anyone spending 183 days or more in Spain during the Spanish tax year (ending 31 December) is deemed to be a resident and will be liable to pay Spanish tax.
- **Real Estate Taxes**. These payments (taxes, stamp duties, lawyers' fees, notary fees) are likely to add another 10% onto the purchase price of your chosen property.
  - In the Canary Islands, Ceuta and Melilla there is no VAT (IVA). Inheritance Tax is paid by the persons inheriting, and not on the value of the estate of the deceased.
  - After buying any property in Spain, the purchaser should be sure to draw up a Spanish will with a Spanish lawyer witnessed by a notary.

- **Insurance**. Insuring through a company back home with representatives in Spain will mean that claims will be processed in English rather than Spanish and this can be a great help and mean that reading the small print will present no problems.

Buying a property abroad is going to involve, apart from a fair amount of money, getting to grips with a whole new culture of doing business. You will have to learn about Spanish taxes; the Spanish banking system; how you can use your money to bring increased dividends and protect your assets from the tax authorities; the best way to finance and insure the property. What follows is a brief outline of these facets of Spanish life, which will help you to familiarise yourself with the kind of financial bureaucracy and possibilities you will encounter in Spain. Much of what follows will be explained to you by your lawyers and agents at home or once in Spain and you will learn a great deal about the financial side of life in Spain through just being there and learning 'on the spot'. However complicated tax systems seem, however convoluted and impossible these systems appear, if you find yourself a good *gestor* (local fixers who are well worth the money; see the *Residence* chapter), accountant and lawyer, you should find your introduction to Spanish bureaucracy if not exactly a breeze, at least manageable. After all, 300,000 or so foreigners live on the Costa del Sol alone, all filing their tax returns, paying off their mortgages and investing their savings as wisely as possible.

BANKS

All banking activity in Spain is controlled by the Banco de España, which has its headquarters in Madrid and branches in all provincial capitals. Banks in Spain are divided into clearing banks and savings banks and there are also a number of foreign banks operating throughout the country.

To open an account in Spain you will be required to present your passport or some other means of proof of identification, proof of address, and an NIE number (tax identification number: see under *Tax* below). It is advisable to open an account in person rather than rely on a *gestor* to do it for you. It is also advisable to open an account with one of the major banks as they are likely to have far more branches.

The two banking giants in Spain at present are the BSCH (*Banco de Santander Central Hispano*), which resulted from the merger of the Santander, Central and Hispano banks, and the BBVA (*Banco Bilbao Vizcaya Argentaria*). Other banks in Spain include the *Banco Atlántico, BankInter, Solbank, Banco de Andalucía* and *Banco Zaragozano.* Most large towns will have at least one branch of these banks and in the cities there will often be several branches, offering all the usual banking facilities, including mortgages and Internet and telephone banking facilities. Standard bank opening times are from 9am to 2pm on weekdays and from 9am to 1pm on Saturdays, although these may vary from bank to bank. Internet banking has become popular in recent years in Spain and Internet-only banks operating in Spain such as *ING*, *Patagon* and *EvolveBank* offer preferential rates of interest on savings accounts. Internet banking is obviously very useful for checking on your account and carrying out banking transactions while abroad.

It is best to open a bank account in Spain immediately on arrival – or even before leaving home. This can easily be arranged through the major UK banks – which all have branches in Spain – or through a branch of the larger Spanish banks that have branches in the UK. This will enable you to settle any bills that you may get for any professional advice and for day-to-day costs taken while on, for example, a reconnaissance trip to Spain.

If you use your property in Spain only as a holiday home you can have all correspondence from your bank in Spain sent to your main home address abroad. When choosing a bank, it's also a good idea to ask friends and acquaintances for recommendations. Banks in resort areas and cities usually have at least one member of staff who speaks English, however, those in rural areas generally don't. Service in small local branches is often more personalised than in larger branches and the staff less harried. However, smaller branches may not offer such a choice of banking services and are less likely to have English-speaking staff.

ATMs

There are now ATMs (automated teller machines) all over Spain and you can usually even find them in the larger villages. Three ATM networks operate in Spain – 4B (the most common), ServiRed and 6000 and you can generally use any ATM to draw money from your account, although there may be a fee charged. As well as cash withdrawals, paying cash into your account and consulting your balance, some ATMs now allow you to carry out other transactions such as renewing your mobile phone card or making theatre seat reservations. Spanish ATMs offer you a choice of language of instruction.

Bank Accounts

Those who are resident in Spain for tax purposes may open the type of current account (*cuenta corriente*) and savings account available to all Spanish citizens. Non-residents may only open the current and savings accounts available to foreigners, which will still allow you to set up direct debits to pay utility bills while you are away from your property and keep a steady amount of money in the country.

The *Cajas de Ahorro* saving banks have branches throughout Spain which, apart from the *Catalan La Caixa* and *Caja Madrid*, tend to be regional. Many of the savings banks actually started out as agricultural co-operatives and many still act as charitable institutions – investing part of their profits each year in social and cultural causes. The savings banks all issue a bank card enabling the holder to withdraw money from the ATMs that they operate.

For a short-term savings account you can open a deposit account (*libreta de ahorro*), from which withdrawals can be made at any time. Interest will also be added twice yearly to the average credit balance, but this is likely to be negligible unless the account balance is £1,000 or more. For larger amounts of money, long-term savings accounts (*cuentas de plazo*) and investment accounts are also available and will earn more interest, as the money has to be left in the account for an agreed period of time – perhaps six months, perhaps several years. Obviously, the longer the set period the money remains untouched the better the interest earned. Interest rates vary and the best rates are obtained from accounts linked to stocks and shares although, of course, there are associated risks of losing some or all of your investment.

Spanish bank charges cover just about every banking transaction imaginable and are notoriously high. Particularly high are charges made for the payment of cheques into your account and for transferring money between accounts and/or banks. Before opening an account be sure to ask for a breakdown of any charges that may be forthcoming, including annual fees. If you plan to make a lot of transfers between banks and accounts you may be able to negotiate more favourable terms. The Spanish are less hidebound than the British.

Banking Procedures

Bank statements are usually sent out to all customers every month and are available on request at any time. Do not expect to get anything free from the bank. Unlike in the UK, charges are levied on day-to-day banking procedures in Spain, including on all credit card and cheque transactions. Note that cheques are generally not accepted as a form of payment in shops and businesses though credit and debit cards are. Overdrafts and loans are available on request and all the usual services, such as standing orders and direct debit are available from the banks in Spain.

Most Spanish banks will provide cash on presentation of an international credit card (e.g. Access, Visa, American Express). Cardholders are able to withdraw up to their credit limit, which only takes a few minutes, but it is an expensive way of buying euros and it is cheaper, although not as quick, to pay in a Sterling cheque to the Spanish bank where commission charges will usually be less. Even if you are moving permanently to Spain it is a good idea to keep your bank account at home open. This will allow you to transfer money (from a pension, or income accrued from property rentals or business) between accounts if you wish and will be useful when visiting friends and family in 'the old country'.

If you plan to keep most of your money outside Spain, and instead to periodically transfer money from your account back home to your account in Spain, you will need to enquire how long it will take to clear before you can access it and what the bank charges are for this service. Banks tend to like to take their time transferring money as the longer it swills around in their system the more profit they make. Specialist currency exchange companies can make regular payments for mortgages, salaries and pensions faster and more cheeaply than banks: see *Importing Currency* below. If you are a resident for tax purposes in Spain remember that 25% of any interest earned on your account will be retained and paid to the Spanish tax office on your behalf.

Opening a Spanish Bank Account from the UK

Although some people may be more confident opening an account with a Spanish branch of a UK bank, they will find that the Spanish branches of British banks function in just the same way as the Spanish national banks. HSBC and Barclays Bank are the most widely represented of the British banks in Spain with branches throughout the country. Those who wish to open an account with one of the branches in Spain should contact their local branch in the UK, which will provide the relevant forms to complete. Alternatively, the London offices of the largest Spanish banks are also able to provide the forms necessary to open an account with their Spanish branches. The banks which will provide such a service include Banco De Santander Central Hispano (Santander House, 100 Ludgate Hill, London EC4M 7NJ; ☎ 020-7332 7451; www.bsch.es) and Banco Bilbao Vizcaya Argentaria (100 Cannon Street, London EC4N 6EH; ☎ 020-7623 3060).

Offshore Banking

Offshore banking is a favourite topic of conversation all over the world among expats looking for high returns on their savings. Offshore banks offer tax-free interest on deposit accounts and investment portfolios through banking centres in tax havens such as Gibraltar, the Cayman Islands, the Isle of Man and the Channel Islands. More and more high street banks and building societies along with the merchant banks are setting up offshore banking facilities and the list given below offers only a handful of the most widely-known offering such services. Deposit account interest rates work on the basis that the more inaccessible one's money is, the higher the rate of interest paid.

Banks and financial institutions in Spain also offer offshore banking services. In return for a tax-free interest, clients are generally expected to maintain minimum deposit levels, which can be very high, and restrictive terms and conditions often apply. The minimum deposit required by each bank will vary, the norm being between £1,000 and £5,000. Usually, a minimum of £10,000 is needed for year-long deposit accounts, while the lower end of the minimum deposit range applies to 90-day deposits. Instant access accounts are also available.

For the expat living along the southern coast of Spain the banks in Gibraltar offer a convenient place to stash cash in a tax-free account. However, sound financial advice should be sought regarding one's financial and tax position before placing one's life savings in an offshore account. Buying property through an 'offshore' company is sometimes practiced in Spain, although you should be aware that the Spanish Tax Office charges such companies even higher taxes than usual. (see *Offshore Mortgages* below).

Trusts

If you have reasonably substantial assets, then a trust of one kind or another may be an effective way of reducing Spanish taxes, but this can only be done with expert advice. The concept of a 'trust' only exists in countries with common-law legal systems, e.g. the UK, USA, Canada and British colonies. However, there are also moves by the government in the UK to make trusts less effective as a way of evading taxes.

The concept of a trust is simple enough: you give away or lend your money to a trustee; the money is then treated by the taxman as though it were not yours anymore. The trustees appointed to run the trust invest the money as they see fit, or as you specified when making the initial gift. Income generated by the trust is taxed under a special regime in the UK depending on the type of trust.

The two basic categories of trust are:

- *Interest-in-possession trust:* this gives a person or persons the right to income from the trust or the equivalent of income (e.g. the right to live in a rent-free property). The trustees have to hand over the income to the beneficiaries stated in the trust.

- *Discretionary trust*: the trustees decide which beneficiaries should receive income or capital from the trust. Where no money is paid out until the end of the trust, this is known as an *accumulation trust.* If money is paid out for the education, maintenance or benefit of beneficiaries until they get an *interest-in-possession,* then the trust is an *accumulation-and-maintenance* trust.

Spanish tax residents pay tax on their worldwide income, including gains or income from trusts. They also have to pay taxes on any income from offshore companies, trusts, accounts, shares and so on. The income from trusts may be used as decided by the trustees, which means that though you may receive some income from the trust (which will be subject to taxation) other income may be invested or spent by the trustees as they wish. If the trust company is based in a place where taxes are low or non-existent then the income from the investments will have low or no tax payable on them. Additionally, on death, the money put into a trust will not be subject to inheritance tax as it is not 'yours' anymore.

Useful Addresses

Abbey National Offshore: PO Box 150, Carrick House, Circular Road, Douglas, Isle of Man IM99 1NH; ☎ 01624 644505; fax 01624 644550; www.anoffshore.com.

Abbey National (Gibraltar) Ltd: 237 Main Street, PO Box 824, Gibraltar; ☎ 76090; fax 72028.

Bank of Scotland International (Jersey) Ltd: PO Box 664, Halifax House, 31/33 New Street, St Helier, Jersey, Channel Islands JE4 8YW; ☎ 01534-613 500; fax 01534-759 280.

Bank of Scotland International (Isle of Man) Ltd: PO Box 19, Prospect Hill, Douglas, Isle of Man IM99 1AT; ☎ 01624-612323; fax 01624-644090; www.bankofscotland-international.com.

BDO Stoy Hayward: 8 Baker Street, London W1U 3LL; ☎ 020-7486 5888; www.bdo.co.uk. Fifth biggest accountancy firm in the world providing tax advice from offices throughout Europe and overseas.

Bradford and Bingley International Ltd: 30 Ridgeway Street, Douglas, Isle of Man IMI ITA; ☎ 01624-695000; fax 01624-661962; www.bradford-bingley-int.co.im.

Brewin Dolphin Securities Ltd Stockbrokers: 5 Giltspur Street, London EC1A 9BD; ☎ 020-7248 4400; www.brewindolphin.co.uk.

Ex-Pat Tax Consultants Ltd: Suite 2, 2nd Floor, Shakespeare House, 18 Shakespeare Street, Newcastle upon Tyne NE1 6AQ; ☎ 0191-230 3141; www.expattax.co.uk.

HSBC Bank International Limited: PO Box 26, 28/34 Hill Street, St Helier, Jersey JE4 8NR, Channel Islands; ☎ 01534 616111; www.hsbc.com.

Lloyds TSB: Isle of Man Offshore Centre. PO Box 12, Peveril Square, Douglas, Isle of Man IM99 1SS; ☎ 08705 301641; fax 01624 670929; www.lloydstsb-offshore.com. One of their services is the *Lloyds Bank Overseas Club.*

Wilfred T. Fry Limited: Crescent House, Crescent Road, Worthing, West Sussex BN11 1RN; ☎ 01903-231545; fax 01903-200868; www.wtfry.com. A comprehensive tax and compliance service. They may send a copy of their useful free guide *The British Expatriate*.

MORTGAGES

Although a euro mortgage (*hipoteca*) on a Spanish property provides better security against fluctuations in currency values, fluctuation in interest rates may serve to counteract this advantage. One of the main and uncomfortable aspects of Spanish-based mortgages in the recent past is that interest rates have been maintained at a higher rate than other comparable European countries. Sometimes a fixed UK mortgage will be a better bet, and is usually quite easy to organise. Among those who can arrange a mortgage are UK banks like the *Halifax* (Head Office: Trinity Road, Halifax, West Yorkshire HX1 2RG). International and Spanish specialists include *Alexander Watson* (28-30 High Street, Pinner, Middlesex HA5 5PW; ☎020-8866 0127; fax 020-8868 5159; www.alexanderwatson.co.uk.) who offer mortgage, financial and valuing services and are also specialists in property on the Costa del Sol; *Conti Financial Services*, (204 Church Road, Hove, Sussex BN3 2DJ; ☎01273-772 811; fax 01273-321 269; www.mortgage

soverseas.com) and *Philip Lockwood*, (71 Coventry Street, Kidderminster, Worcs. DY1 2BS; ☎01562-745 082; fax 01562-740 202) who can arrange both euro and sterling mortgages and advise on the benefits and risks of each.

It is easier to borrow money at home and be a cash buyer abroad. If you use your home as equity to fund buying a property in Spain you won't have to deal with overseas lenders and brokers and won't have to worry about the mortgage increasing should the euro appreciate against the pound. If you borrow in euros then when currencies move (which they will do), your asset (the home in Spain) will move in the same direction as the mortgage. It also makes sense to keep your debts in the same currency as your income.

If you are thinking of taking a mortgage with a lender in Spain remember that there are fewer fixed, capped and discounted schemes operated on the Continent and terms can be more restrictive than those offered in the UK – a high deposit and a maximum repayment term of 20 years is standard. Euro mortgage rates are about 5% in Spain, sterling mortgages about 5.75%. You will find that the cheaper interest rates and special deals on offer usually only apply to more high-value properties of between £100,000 and £200,000 and not to the more modest end of the property market.

UK Mortgages

A number of people planning to buy second homes in Spain arrange loans in the UK – taking out a second mortgage on their UK property and then buying with cash in Spain. Alternatively, it is now also possible to approach the banks for a sterling loan secured on the property in Spain. If you are considering borrowing in the UK, then the method of calculating the amount that may be borrowed is worked out at between two and a half, or three and a half, times your primary income plus any secondary income you may have, less any capital amount already borrowed on the mortgage. Your credit history will also be checked to assess whether you will be able to manage increased mortgage payments. It is most usual for buyers to pay for their second home with a combination of savings and equity from re-mortgaging an existing property.

> Naturally, the mortgage will be subject to a valuation on any UK property, and you can expect to borrow, subject to equity, up to a maximum of 80% of the purchase price of the overseas property (compared with the availability of 100% mortgages for UK properties). If you are going to take out a second mortgage with your existing mortgage lender then a second charge would be taken by the mortgage company.

Note that some lending institutions charge a higher rate for a loan to cover a second property. You should ensure that if a loan is arranged in the UK then all of the details of this are included in the Spanish property contract deeds (*escritura*).

The Norwich and Peterborough Building Society (www.npbs.co.uk) lends a minimum of £40,000 to people wanting to use a sterling-dominated mortgage to buy on the Costa del Sol – along the stretch of land from Gibraltar in the west to Motril in the East. *Norwich and Peterborough* has reduced the rate on its Spanish two-year fixed rate mortgage from 5.04% to 4.49% and it also offers a base rate tracker mortgage. The *Society* can lend up to 75% for a new property on the stretch of the Costa del Sol mentioned above but will only lend 65% for an old house in the mountains.

Hove-based *Conti Financial Services* (see address above) also deals with overseas property mortgages and at the time of writing offers euro mortgages from 3.83% on repayment and interest-only mortgages. The *Abbey National's* offshore mortgage service (www.anoffshore.com) offers a variable rate deal. The rate is currently 5.75% for a sterling loan and 5% for a euro mortgage. To those who would rather pay the extra to have the choice of being able to repay in sterling the difference in rates may not seem a great deal. However, 0.75% may not seem a lot but it will cream off a tidy sum from a house costing £250,000 or so.

Spanish Mortgages

Many Spanish banks offer euro mortgages both within Spain and through branches in the UK. The conditions relating to Spanish mortgages differ from those in the UK in that a deposit of at least 30% is usually required, with a maximum of 70% of the property value being provided as a loan, unlike the 95% or even 100% available from UK lenders. Those deemed to be non-resident in Spain usually have a lower limit of borrowing of 50% imposed by the lender, and the mortgage repayment period also tends to be shorter – usually about fifteen to twenty years. The buyer must be less than 70 years old by the completion date of the mortgage repayment. Fixed rate loans usually run for periods of up to 20 years (10-12 year deals are commonplace) and early redemption penalties may apply. These loans also carry introductory commissions of between 1% and 2.5%. Spanish mortgage companies peg their rates to a number of different indexes, offering an index-linked rate plus the company's percentage. You will need to provide the mortgage company with an identification card, a fiscal identification number, evidence of income and details of your financial situation and, if married, your spouse's consent may be required.

In Spain the method used to assess your mortgage is also a little different from that in the UK. You will have to put all your UK and, if you have any, your Spanish earnings and income forward, and get references from your UK bank. Any other borrowing you have will also be assessed. Although repayment mortgages still predominate, there are endowment and pension-linked options as well. The self-employed must have held such status for a minimum of three years and be able to show fully audited accounts of earnings.

Spanish mortgages generally offer fixed or variable interest rate mortgages, mixed interest rate mortgages and fixed repayment instalment mortgages. Interest rates may be lower than at home but there will be additional costs incurred, related to the registering charge on property in Spain. Acquisition, construction and renovation mortgages are available. Mortgages are on a capital and interest repayment basis, and security will be taken on the property. Most Spanish mortgage lenders work on the basis of repayments being made at a third of the borrower's net income.

Remember that if you take out a Spanish mortgage you will need to have the currency available in your Spanish bank account to meet the monthly mortgage repayments. There are likely to be tax implications and you will need to ensure that your lawyer explains the legalities in both countries to you. Mortgage lenders deciding how much to advance a potential buyer, both in the UK and in Spain, will not take into consideration any possible

MORTGAGE COMPARISON TABLE

	UK Mortgage	**Spanish Mortgage**
Types available:	Repayment, endowment or pension mortgages etc.	Mostly repayment
Maximum % of value:	100% (can remortgage, i.e. clear existing loan and the new advance becomes a 1st charge or second mortgage)	70% of valuation
Max compared to income:	2.5 x joint or 3.5 x 1	30% of deposable income
Period of mortgage:	5 to 25 years	5 to max. 20 years
Interest rate:	fixed, discounted, variable or capped	4%-5% above UK base
Repayments made:	Monthly	Monthly or quarterly

income derived from renting out the property. However, in truth it may be possible to offset the cost of the mortgage against the income received from renting out a property and so reducing tax demands. And in effect the rental value on a property should repay the mortgage if problems occur.

Barclays offers euro mortgages through its Spanish subsidiary and other overseas mortgage companies include *Banco Banesto; Banco Halifax; Citibank Espana, Deutsche Bank, Caja Madrid* and *Banco Atlantico.* Spanish banks are not interested whether you have an existing mortgage in the UK.

Offshore Mortgages

The principle of offshore companies involves turning a property into a company, the shares of which are held as collateral against a mortgage of up to 75% for a repayment term of up to 20 years by an offshore bank based in a tax haven such as Gibraltar or the Channel Islands. The property owner's name is confidential and the property company is administered on the owner's behalf by the offshore trustees. Previously, the advantage of offshore property purchase was that it reduced tax liability in the country of purchase, as, if and when the property was resold, it merely became a question of transferring the shares confidentially to a new owner, thus avoiding transfer taxes and VAT in the country in question.

However there are risks. For example, due to legislation passed in 1991, thousands of Britons who bought property in Spain through offshore companies ended up facing potentially huge tax bills in the eventuality of either their selling the property, or of their death. Although, in the majority of cases, offshore property purchase has resulted in the legitimate avoidance of wealth tax, succession duty, transfer tax and capital gains tax, a minority of cases has clearly crossed the fine line between tax avoidance and tax evasion at the cost of the state coffers. You should certainly not try to enter into such an arrangement without the advice of an accountant, solicitor, or other professional adviser.

Clampdown on Tax Avoidance. The Spanish government has always been relatively powerless to trace tax evasion carried out in this way, as the confidentiality of the ownership of offshore companies is protected by law. Now, however, even if they are unable to meet this problem directly, the authorities have opted to at least make the avoidance of tax and death duties a costly business for those involved. Offshore companies which own property in Spain are now subject to an annual 3% tax on the property's rateable value (approximately 70% of its market value) unless the owners are prepared to submit the name of the ultimate beneficial owner and proof as to the source of the money used to buy the property. Once this information has been established and the tax levied – or so it is intended – the owners will then not find it so worthwhile to avoid capital gains and inheritance taxes; and the transfer of ownership of property through sale or death will become obvious.

One of the main reasons for Spain clamping down on its own residents is that many have been using money from unpaid taxes to buy property through offshore companies. There is also evidence that offshore companies have been used to launder the proceeds of crime and drugs, and as a convenient way of buying property anonymously. Although the restrictions on offshore companies have seriously inflated some residents' tax bills, tax consultants who advise foreign property owners in Spain have generally welcomed the legislation. They say that it does nothing to alter some of the legitimate advantages of using an offshore company in order to avoid or reduce some taxes, and is deterring those who wish to operate outside the law.

So, potential property buyers in Spain should be wary of any organisations advertising schemes claiming to be able to circumvent the current legislation or claiming huge tax advantages. In the light of the Spanish authorities' determination to improve tax collection, and considering that all Spanish property is within the territory of the Spanish Tax Authority, which has the right ultimately to seize homes in order to collect the tax which it is owed, it is just as well to take some unbiased professional advice before entering into such an arrangement. In all circumstances, paying for this advice before you make a purchase will almost certainly save you money in the long run; and is the best approach.

All of the above being taken into consideration, offshore property mortgages are now available through many building societies and banks. One such is the *Abbey National* which has offices in Gibraltar (237 Main Street, PO Box 824, Gibraltar; ☎ 76090; fax 72028) and can provide a free booklet *Buying your Home in Spain or Portugal*, and Jersey (PO Box 545, Abbey National House, 41 The Parade, St Helier, Jersey JE4 8XG; ☎ 01534-885 100). Your local high street branch of *Abbey National* should be your first port of call. Another building society offering offshore mortgages is the *Bank of Scotland International (Isle of Man) Ltd.* at PO Box 19, Prospect Hill, Douglas, Isle of Man IM99 1AT; ☎ 01624-612323; fax 01624-644090; www.bankofscotland-international.com. *The Bank of Scotland*, like most high street building societies and banks, has leaflets on offshore mortgages, and other financial matters such as international payments, which will be worth consulting. *Lloyds TSB Bank Overseas*

Club, offers a range of services and is based at the Offshore Centre, PO Box 12, Peveril Buildings, Peveril Square, Douglas, Isle of Man IM99 1SS; ☎ 08705 301641; fax 01624 670929; www.lloydstsb-offshore.com.

Another organisation specialising in Spain is *Conti Financial Services* (www.mortgagesoverseas.com). *Cornish & Co*, solicitors, can help you set up an offshore mortgage or overseas trust in Spain. Their address is: Lex House, 1/7 Hainault Street, Ilford, Essex IG1 4EL; ☎ 020-8478 3300; fax 020-8553 3418/3422; www.cornishco.com). In addition Cornish have an office in Spain (Avda Ricardo Soriano 19, Planta Tercera, 29600 Málaga; ☎ 952 866 830; e-mail cornish@mercuryin.es) and an associate office in Gibraltar (Hadfield House, Library Street); and associate offices in Portugal and the USA. They also publish an information pack which is available on request by calling 0800-163507.

Useful addresses

Banco Halifax Hispania: ☎ 01422-332 466 (UK); 902 310 100 (Spain); www.halifax.es.

Conti Financial Services: 204 Church Road, Hove, Sussex BN3 2DJ; ☎ 01273-772 811; fax 01273-321 269; www.mortgagesoverseas.com.

Kevin Sewell Mortgages & Investments: 37A Market Place, Devizes, Wilts. SN10 1JD; ☎ 01380 739 198; fax 01380 723 249; e-mail ksewell@netcomuk.co.uk. Independent mortgage broker.

Mortgages in Spain: PO Box 146, Ilkley, West Yorkshire LS29 8UL; ☎ 0800 027 7057; fax 0845 345 6586; www.mortgages-in-spain.com. Mortgage brokers dealing with Skipton Building Society and Caja Duero – a Spanish mutual savings bank.

Norwich and Peterborough Spanish Home Loans: Peterborough Business Park, Lynch Wood, Peterborough, Cambs. PE2 6WZ; ☎ 0845 300 2522; www.npbs.co.uk. Also a branch in Gibraltar at 198-200 Main Street; www.npbs-gibraltar.co.uk

Solbank ☎ 020-7321 0020 or in Spain 902 343 888; www.solbank.com. A Spanish bank offering various mortgage and banking services.

IMPORTING CURRENCY

Large amounts of money will need to be imported into Spain to cover the costs involved in buying the property (conveyancing costs, fees and taxes, builders and architects and surveyors fees, utility bills and charges, *comunidad de propietarios,* fees, etc.). When you find a property in Spain to buy, you will of course know the price of the property in euros but until you have bought all of the euros you will need to pay for it you won't know the total costs involved. Depending on the exchange rate fluctuations between the sterling and the euro during the conveyancing procedures the property could eventually cost you more or less than you had originally thought. Importing money into Spain can take time and there are various ways of going about transferring funds.

Another method of transferring funds is to obtain a banker's draft from your home bank. This is a cheque guaranteed by the bank, which can be deposited into your bank account in Spain or anywhere in the world. When making the final payment on the purchase of a property at the notary's office it is advisable to hand over a banker's draft made payable to the vendor. Note that a banker's draft works along the lines of a cheque, and once it is paid into an account there will be a short period of waiting before it is cleared and you are able to access the money. You can also transfer money by SWIFT electronic bank transfer. This procedure can take several days and rates of exchange will vary. Unless you are conversant with Spanish banking procedures transferring money electronically may also lead to red tape problems.

Because of currency fluctuations converting currency from, say, sterling to euros will always be something of a gamble. If the pound falls against the euro you will end up paying far more than you budgeted for on the property. If, as soon as you sign the contract to begin the process of buying, you convert the total cost of the property into Euros you may be happy with the conversion rate but you will lose the use of the money while negotiations take place over the settlement of the property.

To avoid this a specialised company such as Currencies Direct (Hanover House, 73-74 High Holborn, London WC1V 6LR; ☎ 020-7813 0332; fax 020-7419 7753; wwww.currenciesdirect.com) can help in a number of ways, by offering better exchange rates than banks, without charging commission, and giving you the possibility of 'forward buying' – agreeing on the rate that you will pay at a fixed date in the future – or with a limit order – waiting until the rate you want is reached. For those who prefer to know exactly how much money they have available for their property purchase, forward buying is the best solution, since you no longer have to worry about the movement of the pound against the euro working to your detriment. Payments can be made in one lump sum or on a regular basis. It is usual when building new property to pay in four instalments, so-called 'stage payments'.

If you are having a pension paid into your bank account in Spain make sure that it is transferred into euros before being sent, otherwise you will have to pay commission on the exchange. Specialist currency companies can handle regular payments such as pensions as well as salaries and mortgage payments. Also be aware that money left sitting in a Spanish bank account attracts little interest and it is therefore advisable to only take into Spain the money that you need and leave the rest offshore or, if you live on or near the Costa del Sol, perhaps open a non-resident account in Gibraltar.

Remember that if the vendors of the property are non-resident in Spain they are likely to want the purchase price paid in the currency of their home country.

Exchange Control

Spain abolished all its laws on exchange control in 1992 and at present there is no limit on the amount of foreign currency or euros which can be brought into Spain and no limit on the amount of currency and euros which anyone is allowed to take out of the country. However, imports of amounts over €6,000 should be declared to customs within 30 days.

TAX

If you have ever been faced with completing a self-assessment tax form you will be aware that sorting out one's tax affairs is a complicated matter and one that isn't made easier by the pages and pages of notes and explanations provided by the tax authorities. Unless your financial affairs are simple, and consist of one source of income and no investments or savings or interest payments you will be advised to enlist the aid of an accountant versed in international tax laws – at least for your first year as a property owner in Spain. Qualified tax consultants should be members of *The Chartered Institute of Taxation – CIOT* – (12 Upper Belgrave Street, London SW1X 8BB; ☎020-7235 9381; www.tax.org.uk) or *The Association of Taxation Technicians – ATT* – (12 Upper Belgrave Street London SW1X 8BB; ☎020-7235 2544; www.att.org.uk) in the UK, or the *Asociación Españiola de Asesores Fiscales – AEDAF* – (C/Montalbán, 3, 6°, 28014 Madrid; ☎915 325 154; fax 915 323 794; www.aedad.es) in Spain.

Despite what you may have heard to the contrary, Spain is not a tax haven. The Spanish tax authorities have tightened up on foreigners coming to Spain in order to dodge income tax by not declaring certain assets and income in their own country. Currently, foreigners resident in Spain will find that they pay approximately the same amount of tax as they would elsewhere in the EU. There is no special tax relief for foreigners residing in Spain; capital gains and disposable assets are included as part of income and are taxed accordingly; residents are liable to pay Spanish tax on their worldwide income. This means that all income is taxable, be it from a pension, private investments, dividends, or interest.

Non-residents as well as residents of Spain need a tax reference number – *Número de Identificacion Extranjero (NIE)* – and it is useful, though not compulsory by law, to appoint a Spanish fiscal representative (*Representante Fiscal*) who will be able to advise when dealing with the Spanish Tax Agency. A *Número de Identificacion Extranjero (NIE)* is a tax identification number for foreign residents and property owning non-residents. You will need this not only for matters concerning tax but also for other matters like opening a bank account; it is also required when registering an *escritura*. You can obtain an NIE from the foreigners' department of a Spanish police station. You will need to fill out a form and present your passport and passport-size photographs. The NIE is the equivalent of the *Número de Identificacion Fiscal* which is issued to all native Spaniards.

Most taxes are based on self-assessment whereby the individual is responsible for reporting and calculating any taxes due. Depending on how complicated your affairs are you will be able to complete the self-assessment forms yourself or use the services of an accountant versed in the tax laws of both Spain and your country of residence (if you are non-resident in Spain). If you are non-resident in Spain a fiscal representative will be able to notify you of dates when taxes are due. Although you are not required by law to employ a fiscal representative, choosing to use the services of one is an important consideration when strict deadlines are laid down by the Tax Agency and where penalties are imposed for late payments. A fiscal representative could be a lawyer or a *gestor* and will need to be registered with the Tax Agency as acting on your behalf.

The Spanish Tax Agency (*Agencia Estatal de Administración Tributaria* commonly referred to as the *Hacienda*) has a website at www.aeat.es with information on Spanish taxes in general and some pages translated into English. For more information on the Spanish tax system, contact your nearest Spanish embassy or consulate, or the *Ministerio de Hacienda*, C/ Alcalá 9, 28014 Madrid; ☎ 901 335 533. More detailed advice may be forthcoming from the *Direccion General de Tributos*, C/Alcalá 5, 28014 Madrid; ☎ 915 221 000 or your local tax office.

Taxation Status

The Spanish tax authorities work on a residence-based system of taxation. Anyone spending 183 days or more in Spain during the Spanish tax year (ending 31 December) is deemed to be a resident and will be liable to pay Spanish tax. This holds true whether or not one is in possession of a formal residence permit; faking tourist status will not, therefore, exclude unwilling contributors from paying their share of taxes.

If Spain is the principal centre of economic activity of an individual (the principal source of income or place of principal business and/or employment) or is the location of an individual's family home then the Spanish Tax Agency (*Agencia Estatal de Administración Tributaria*) may well decide that an individual will be classified as resident in Spain for tax purposes.

In 1998 the *Ley del Impuesto Sobre la Renta de No Residentes* (Non-residents Income Tax Act) was passed by the Spanish government to tackle the problem of wresting some taxable income from the one million or more non-resident property owners in Spain. Under this ruling, anyone who is not resident in Spain, i.e. who spends less than 183 days in the country each year, is still liable for Spanish tax on income *arising* in Spain, e.g. from renting out property. In this case, the recipient of the income will be taxed in Spain and will have to apply for tax relief when they pay income tax in their own country. Additionally, there is a possibility for EU citizens who are non-resident property owners in Spain to pay Spanish taxes under the Spanish Resident Income Tax Act (*Impuesto Sobre la Renta de las Personals Físicas*). Non-residents must declare any investments in property over €3,005,060.52 to the Tax Agency. This is mainly for statistical purposes.

The Tax System

The Spanish system of personal taxation is based on three kinds of levies: *impuestos* (true taxes); *tasas* (dues and fees); and *contribuciones especiales* (special levies). The last two are much lower, and residents will mainly be concerned with the *impuestos*. Income tax is called the *Impuesto sobre la Renta de las Personas Físicas (IRPF)* or simply *'la renta'*. Central, regional and local governments may all levy taxes, but the key factor concerning the payment of tax is residence in Spain. Non-residents will also be taxed if they are regarded as having a permanent establishment in Spain or are carrying on some kind of business there.

Income Tax (Impuesto Sobre la Renta de las Personas Físicas)

Non-residents

Non-residents must still make an annual tax declaration to the Spanish Tax Agency who will be interested in any income received in Spain deriving from such things as interest on accounts held with a Spanish bank or monies from renting out property, and of course any employment undertaken. Any such income will be taxed at a flat rate of 25% and will also need to be declared to the tax authorities at home.

- Owning property is considered to produce a taxable income of between 1.1% and 2% of the value of the property based on the *Valor Catastral* (the rateable value of the property). The percentage will vary depending on the town council where the property is located, and a 25% tax rate will be levied on that percentage. There are no deductions or allowance on this tax against expenses.
- A non-resident company will be taxed at 3% of the *Valor Catastral* of the property that it owns in Spain. This tax is not levied if the company and shareholders are resident in a country that has a double taxation agreement with Spain.
- If you are buying a property to let the taxes applicable on income received will vary depending on circumstances.
- Any non-resident letting a Spanish property will be subject to a Spanish withholding income tax of 25% on the gross rental income. VAT (IVA) will need to be accounted for when letting to businesses or commercial enterprises.
- Any income received outside Spain from the letting of a Spanish property will need to be declared in the country where the owner of the property is resident for tax purposes.
- Mortgage interest costs and other expenses incurred through the rental of property in Spain cannot be offset against the rental income by a non-resident unless the owner is operating a rental business registered in Spain and is subject to Spanish corporation taxes.
- Any other income received from business activity in Spain will generally be charged at 25% although some taxes may be affected by a double taxation agreement with the non-residents country of domicile.

Residents

Those who live in Spain for more than 183 days in any tax year are deemed to be resident in the country for tax purposes. In most cases you will have to pay tax on your worldwide income.

- If you are running a business, self-employed or all your income comes from investments you will need to file a tax return.
- If your income comes to less than €7,800 a year you do not need to file a tax return.
- Income tax is generally assessed on the household. If you are married

then the joint income of husband and wife will be assessed. The income of dependent children in the household will also be included in the tax assessment. If you are a cohabiting common-law couple then the sole income of the individuals will be assessed.

- There are a number of allowances, deductions and tax credits available on income tax. Your accountant or tax adviser will be able to give you the latest rates of these.
- If you own two properties in Spain you will be charged a property tax on the second (non-principal) residence.
- You will need to present several documents along with the tax return. These are: passport and residence permit; copies of any document relating to tax relief, deductions, allowances, payment of tax in a country with a double taxation agreement with Spain; end of year bank statement; statements relating to investments; if you are in receipt of a pension you will need to show your pension slips.

Double Taxation Agreements

> Spain has reciprocal tax agreements with a number of countries around the world, which avoids the possibility of someone being taxed twice on their income from renting property, pensions, gifts, inheritance, etc. – once by the Spanish and once by the tax authorities in their home country.

However, there may be a slight hitch during the initial period of Spanish residency because, for instance, the UK and Spanish tax years run from April to April and from January to January respectively and therefore UK nationals in Spain may be taxed by both the Spanish and UK authorities in the overlapping months of their first year in the new country.

In this case, you would be able to claim a refund of UK tax by applying to the Inland Revenue through your local UK tax office. They will supply you with an SPA/Individual form (which offers relief at source for tax refunds concerning interest, royalties and pensions) or with the SPA/Individual/Credit form (which provides repayment on dividend income for anyone who has suffered double taxation on moving to Spain). Once the form has been filled out, take it to the *hacienda* (tax office) in Spain. They will stamp it and then you can return it to the British tax authorities as proof that you have paid Spanish tax and are therefore no longer liable for British tax. It is a procedure that should be carried out while you are in Spain and not after your return to the UK. It is important to keep accounts of your income, expenditure etc., while in Spain to meet any problems should these arise.

Double taxation agreements will differ depending on the country involved and the circumstances of the individual. If a pension is taxed in the UK it won't be taxed in Spain, although it may be more beneficial to be taxed in Spain rather than in the UK and financial advice should be sought on this.

COUNTRIES WITH A DOUBLE TAXATION AGREEMENT WITH SPAIN					
Argentina	Austria	Australia	Belgium	Bolivia	Brazil
Bulgaria	Canada	China	Cuba	Czech Republic	Equador
Denmark	Finland	France	Germany	Holland	Hungary
India	Indonesia	Ireland	Israel	Italy	Japan
Korea	Luxembourg	Mexico	Morocco	Norway	Philipinnes
Poland	Portugal	Rep. of Slovakia	Romania	Russia & Former USSR	
Sweden	Switzerland	Thailand	Tunisia	UK	USA

Tax Returns

Those whose financial situation is relatively uncomplicated can draw up their own tax return and advice on how to do this is available from the local *hacienda*. Tax returns should be made between 1 May and 20 June (or June 30 for those who are expecting a tax refund). The Spanish tax year runs from 1 January to 31 December. To do this, you will need to have your most recent receipt for the payment of your *Contribucíon Urbana (IBI)* – if you are a property owner – as a percentage of the official value of your property is calculated as if it were income and then added to your income tax total. You will also need your end-of-year bank statement, which will show any interest you have been paid and your average balance over the tax year. The interest is counted as part of your income and the average balance is counted as an asset for the Wealth Tax. You must also take documents pertaining to any other property you own, or any other shares, stocks, investments, insurance policies or bonds you have, as well as copies of your passport and residence permit. Any other major assets in Spain will also need to be declared as well as any tax paid in another country. You will always need to state your NIE reference when dealing with the tax agency.

Various deductions are available from income tax totals for those who are married and/or whose children, parents or grandparents live with them. Invalids also receive a deduction. Additionally, if you have bought a house in the current tax year or if you are making payments on one, you can deduct 15% of that amount from your income tax total.

Rates of income tax have been going down in Spain in the last decade and now compare favourably with most European countries. The system has also been reorganised and a vital minimum (*mínimo vital*) introduced. Before you become liable for tax you deduct the vital minimum from your gross income and also deduct various other allowances depending on your circumstances. If your income is less than a certain amount per year (amounts vary according to the category (over 65, under 65, etc.) you do not have to pay income tax or complete a tax declaration.

DEDUCTIONS ALLOWABLE FROM GROSS INCOME	
Vital Minimum	approx. 3,305 euros (under 65s)
Vital Minimum	approx. 3,907 euros (over 65s)
Vital Minimum	approx. 6,611 euros (married couple
Disability Allowance	approx. 6,912 euros

There are also allowances for professional and trade union fees, Spanish company pension schemes, child support that you may be paying etc. Up to date information about the minimum earnings before tax is liable can be obtained on the Spanish Tax Office website www.aeat.es. Local provincial tax offices (*oficina de informacíon al contribuyente*) in areas where there are many expatriates may be able to deal with your questions in English. Further information about tax or any changes in rates can be found in a leaflet entitled *Taxation Regulations for Foreigners*, available from any *hacienda* in Spain.

Unlike in Britain where accountants, solicitors and bank officials all have some knowledge of tax matters, in Spain the *aesor fiscal* deals with all tax business. For those with complex tax returns or those for whom the word 'tax' succeeds only in producing blind panic and a feeling of deep nausea, the *aesor fiscal* offers invaluable assistance. For fees beginning at around £50 for relatively straightforward tax returns, this god-sent official will complete the form on your behalf and frequently save you a lot of money by virtue of his or her wisdom and general expertise.

REAL ESTATE TAXES

Buying property is an expensive business. Rather than simply being a deal struck between two individuals, where someone hands over a sum of money to someone else in return for a flat or a house or a plot of land, there are all sorts of additional payments that have to be made to various individuals and institutions. These payments (taxes, stamp duties, lawyers' fees, notary fees) are likely to add another 10% onto the purchase price of your chosen property. The fees payable on a brand new property in Spain will be slightly (1.5%) higher than those for a resale property. The figures for the individual services involved in buying property in Spain break down as follows:

- Transfer tax on a resale property: 6%
- *or* IVA (VAT) on a new property: 7%
- Stamp duty (if buying a new property): 0.5%
- Plus valia (local municipal) tax: 0.5%
- Legal (lawyers') fees: 1%
- Notary fees: 0.5%
- Property Registry fees: 0.5%

In addition there may be extra fees payable for the services of a surveyor, for the connection of utilities (electricity, telephone, water, gas, etc.) and for the property agent.

Most of these fees (with the possible exception of the *plus valia* tax) will be paid by the purchaser. Make sure that you are clear on which fees are payable by the buyer and which are payable by the vendor. There is no law in Spain that states one or other of the parties must pay a particular tax or fee, however, the majority of contracts will state that the buyer is liable for *todos los gastos* (all expenses). These fees and taxes are calculated as a percentage of the value of the property as declared in the *escritura*.

Traditionally the price declared in the *escritura* was often much lower than the actual price paid for a property (the difference being discreetly handed over to the vendor in a brown envelope). However, these days the local councils value properties in their area and therefore have accounts of the rateable value (*valor catastral*) of properties. If it is found that the declared value of a property is far below the *valor catastral* a surcharge of 6% (plus costs) on the difference will be levied on the buyer by the authorities, and if the declared value if ridiculously under-valued, by say 50%, then the authorities have the right to buy the property from the new owner at the declared value within a period of two years. Under-declaring the price of a property is illegal. Doing so will also mean that if you decide to sell the property at a later date the increase in value of the property will be disproportionately large and you will then have to pay a large Capital Gains Tax bill. Capital Gains Tax is charged at 35% for non-residents and a maximum of 18% for residents. The majority of the fees and taxes (with the exception of the *plus valia* tax) listed above must be paid within 28 days of the signing of the *escritura* at the notary's office. Penalties will be incurred for late payment.

It is quite common for a prospective buyer to deposit 10% of the purchase price declared in the *escritura* with the lawyers dealing with the conveyancing so that they can make the payments on the buyer's behalf. The lawyers must give you the receipts of payment for these costs and should not charge you extra for this service. It may be in your favour to find out how much the total cost involved in the sale is likely to be before handing over a deposit and signed a contract of sale.

At the time of going to press any UK citizen who owns a house through a company, rather than owning it in their own name, may be liable to a new property tax. The situation has arisen after a ruling in the House of Lords declaring that 'shadow directors' (i.e. anyone who gives instructions or orders to a company director) must pay tax on benefits in kind. Company directors are already taxed on such benefits (such as use of a company car or use of property). What this may mean in effect is that whether a property is a full-time residence or a holiday home, owners may be liable to pay tax on the market rental value of the property, plus an extra charge should the property be worth over £75,000.

Impuesto Sobre Transmisiones Patrimoniales (ITP). This is a transfer tax payable on the purchase, from a private owner, of property or land. (If you buy a new property from a developer you will be liable for IVA (VAT) instead – see below). The ITP is usually charged at a rate of 6% of the value of a property as declared on the *escritura*.

Impuesto sobre el Valor Añadido (IVA). IVA is the equivalent of Value Added Tax (VAT) and is paid instead of ITP (see above) if you buy a new property from a development company rather than a resale property from an individual. IVA on the construction of a building is charged at a rate of 7% of the purchase price. If you buy a house *and* a plot of land at the same time you will be charged the 7% IVA on both purchases. At the time of going to press IVA on building plots, commercial property and on additions to existing buildings (such as the building of a garage or workshop), is charged at a rate of 16%.

Note that in the Canary Islands, Ceuta and Melilla there is no IVA. In the Canaries a regional tax (Canarian Indirect General Tax – IGIC) is charged instead at a rate of 5%.

Impuesto sobre Actos Jurídicos Documentados (AJD). Stamp duty is paid at a rate of 0.5% of the purchase price of a new property (property bought from a developer). If you are buying a resale property stamp duty is included in the transfer tax (ITP). In some *Comunidades Autónomas* the rate of stamp duty is 1% of the purchase price.

Impuesto sobre el Incremento de Valor le los Terrenos de Naturaleza Urbana (Plus Valia Tax). This is a municipal Capital Gains Tax based on the value of urban land. It is a tax on the increased value of the land since the last sale, and is not a tax on the increase in value of any *buildings* on the land. It is only payable on urban land, not on rural land. The tax is payable on both new and resale property and will vary depending on how long the property has been in the hands of the vendor, the amount of land being sold and its value as a building plot. Although this tax should, in theory, be paid by the vendor (who has, after all, made the profit) it is more than likely that the purchaser will pay this tax unless a clause is added to the contract of sale and a sum is withheld for the payment of the tax. If and when you come to sell you will need to make sure that the purchaser of your property also pays this tax or you will end up paying it twice over. The local municipal tax office will be able to tell you before you sign a contract of sale what the *plus valia* tax will be on the property concerned.

Legal Fees. These will depend on the amount of work carried out by the lawyer (or *abogado*) on the buyer's behalf, though there will be a minimum charge imposed. Expect to be billed for about 1% of the purchase price. Each party will pay the fees of the legal representatives acting on their behalf.

Notary Fees. These are dependent on the declared value of the property and the number of pages of the *escritura*, but generally amount to around 0.5% of the value of the property and could be anything between €300 and €700. The fee is calculated using an official sliding scale but there may be further fees applicable depending on the amount of work carried out and the number of documents prepared on your behalf by the notary. Note that if you are buying a plot of land and then having a dwelling constructed on the land you will have to visit the notary (*notario*), and pay his fees, twice. The costs of granting the first copy of the *escritura* are payable by the vendor while the costs for the second copy are payable by the buyer.

Property Registry Fees. Fees for registering a new property with the Spanish authorities in the Property Register (*Registro de la Propriedad*) vary depending on the size, value and locality of a property. The cost is likely to amount to the same as that payable to the notary (around 0.5% of the purchase price of a property). The initial fee payable is a deposit, and you may get a refund should it be discovered that you have been charged too much.

Other fees and charges likely to be applicable.

- The agent's fee will almost certainly be included in the purchase price and will be between 5% and 10%. If there have been negotiations carried out by an agent's representative back home the fee for this should be included in the agent's fee. Check the contract.
- Surveyors' fees will vary depending on the type of survey carried out (valuation only, or full structural survey, etc).
- Utility fees will need to be paid if a new property is without water, electricity or telephone and gas connections. There may also be charges incurred when changing the names in utility bill contracts from the previous owner's to your own.
- Mortgage and mortgage arrangement costs.
- Insurance – both contents and building insurance will need to be paid for.
- If you have hired a tax consultant, their fees will depend on the complexity of your tax affairs. It is worth finding out the most advantageous way to manage your tax affairs in the matter of buying a property abroad.
- Bank charges relating to the transfer of funds from your bank account at home to your bank account in Spain.
- A 5% tax deposit. If the property is bought from a non-resident then 5% of the declared purchase price is deposited with the Tax Agency as a guarantee against Capital Gains Tax payable on the sale of a property in Spain. In such cases the buyer pays the vendor 95% of the purchase price and the other 5% to the Tax Agency. A notary will need to see proof that the 5% has been received by the tax authorities. This 5% will be included in the purchase price and is not an additional cost – the vendor therefore receives 95% of the agreed purchase price of the property.

Tasas y Cargas.

Some, though not all municipalities charge a certain amount for services such as rubbish collection and street maintenance etc. Day to day running costs of property in Spain will include local council taxes, rates, the annual Wealth Tax, tax relating to the letting of property, community fees if you are part of a *comunidad de proprietarios*, garden and pool maintenance, fees for a financial consultant or fiscal representative, standing charges for utilities, and caretaker or property management fees.

The average running costs per year for a property amount to around 3%-4% of the cost of the property, but will depend on size and opulence. Savings will be made on heating costs of course, but charges for water are higher than in many northern European countries. Expect to pay about €3,500 a year on the upkeep and running costs of a property in Spain.

Local Taxes

Impuesto sobre Bienes Inmeubles – IBI. The *Impuesto sobre Bienes Inmeubles* is an annual local property tax calculated on the official rateable value of a property (*valor catastral*). It is payable by both residents and non-residents. The percentage of the property value charged as tax will vary depending on the region/province and takes into consideration such things as the level of local leisure facilities provided, emergency services, population and local services and infrastructure. IBI is raised annually in line with inflation and will be higher in a resort town or city than in a small inland village. Make sure before buying a resale property that all IBI taxes due on the property have been paid to date. Ask to see IBI receipts for the preceding five years if possible. If these charges have not been paid you will inherit any back taxes and penalties liable on the property. If the property that you are buying is new, it is up to you to register it with the town hall. Failure to do so, and late payment, will incur a penalty charge. Payment deadlines of IBI will vary from region to region and from year to year and your fiscal representative should keep you informed of pertinent dates so that you can arrange to pay by standing order.

The IBI receipt will show the *catastral* reference number as well as the *valor catastral* of the property – both of which will be asked for by the notary before a sale of property can go through. The *catastral* reference number refers to details of the property kept at the *Catastro* office.

CAPITAL GAINS TAX (IMPUESTO SOBRE EL PATRIMONIO)

Every time a property changes hands in Spain, taxes and fees are incurred. Capital Gains Tax is calculated on the net gain in the declared (as shown in the *escritura*) purchase price of a property when bought, and the price that it fetches when it is subsequently sold. There are certain allowances available on this tax for the cost of conveyancing and any improvements made to the property. Those resident for tax purposes in Spain will need to include the Capital Gains in the tax return of the year in which the gain occurred. Capital Gains Tax for non-residents on the sale of a property is 35%. Capital Gains Tax is calculated at a maximum of 18% for residents.

It is always best to declare in the *escritura* the full purchase price when you buy in order not to have to pay a high Capital Gains Tax when you sell. If you own a property through a company and the property has not risen in value when you come to sell it is possible to change the ownership structure without incurring a large Capital Gains Tax bill.

Capital Gains is generally paid via the buyer of the property, who retains 5% of the agreed purchase price and pays this to the Tax Agency on account of the vendor's Capital Gains Tax liability. The purchaser therefore only pays 95% of the purchase price to the vendor. Depending on the amount of tax due, the vendor may request a tax refund from the Tax Agency once the sale has gone through. There are several circumstances where the vendor of a property in Spain is exempt from paying Capital Gains Tax and is not subject to the 5% tax deposit:

- Those 65 years of age or over, who are resident in Spain and whose property has been the principal residence of the individual for at least three years pay no Capital Gains Tax on the sale of the property.
- If a resident of Spain sells his or her principal residence in Spain of at least three years and reinvests all of the proceeds of the sale into another property that will become his or her principal residence, s/he is exempt from paying Capital Gains Tax.
- Residents and non-residents who bought the property which they are selling before 31 December 1986 will not have to pay Capital Gains Tax.
- If a resident is 65 years old or over and sells his or her principal residence to a company in exchange for the right to reside in the property till death and a monthly payment there will be no Capital Gains Tax to pay.

There are several circumstances where the vendor of a property in Spain has partial exemption from paying Capital Gains Tax:

- If a resident of Spain sells his or her principal residence in Spain of at least three years, and reinvests part of the proceeds of the sale into another property that will become his or her principal residence s/he will be entitled to tax relief on a proportion of the proceeds.
- Anyone who bought a property in Spain between 1987 and 1994 has the right to a reduction of 11.11% per year, beginning from two years after the purchase up until 1996.
- Those who bought property after 1996 can apply an inflation correction factor that saves them a certain amount of money on Capital Gains Tax liabilities.

INHERITANCE TAX (IMPUESTO SOBRE SUCESIONES Y DONACIONES)

Gifts on the death of an individual can still bring high rates of taxation in Spain – sometimes at a rate of well over 70% on inherited wealth. The

Spanish Inheritance Tax is paid by the persons inheriting, and not on the value of the estate of the deceased. If the deceased was resident in Spain for tax purposes then all his or her assets worldwide will be subject to Spanish Inheritance Tax; if the deceased was a non-tax resident then only the property in Spain will be subject to tax – the rest of the assets being subject to the tax in the country of residence. If the beneficiary is a resident of a country that has a double taxation agreement with Spain then he or she will not be taxed twice.

Property is valued by the Tax Agency at the market rate, or the *valor catastral* depending on which is the higher. Furnishings etc. are usually valued at 3% of the value of the property. Outstanding debts are deducted from the value of the assets, and stocks and shares and bank balances are valued at the date of death. Another point to recognise is that under Spanish law life insurance policies written in trust in the UK are not binding should the policyholder die while a resident of Spain. The policy proceeds will be taxable.

The Spanish tax authorities impose penalties if matters are not cleared up quickly. For example, there is a window of six months in which to pay taxes on the Spanish estate after death. If taxes are not paid within this time limit a surcharge of 20% will be applied, and further, additional interest on the original demand will be charged.

If a joint owner of a property in Spain dies, there is no automatic inheritance by the other owner/s of the property. Even if the property is left to a beneficiary in the owner's will, there will be a tax payable. Because the tax is based on the size of the gift, the more you inherit the more you will be taxed. However, the nearer the relative is to the deceased, the less tax payable on inherited gifts. Near relatives are also entitled to receive a proportion tax-free. One way of making sure that a beneficiary of a will is not liable for crippling taxes is to register a newly purchased property in the name of the person/s who will eventually inherit. Because the property will stay in the name of the original named owner on the death of the buyer of the property, the taxes and fees usually incurred on transference of title deeds will be minimal.

The tax payment is calculated on the degree of kinship between the deceased and the person inheriting. Allowances (at differing rates) are given to direct descendants less than 21 years of age, direct descendants (spouse, parents, children, siblings) over 21 years of age and other relatives (uncles/aunts, cousins, nieces/nephews). The rate of tax payable after the allowances on kinship is then multiplied by a rate ranging from 1%-1.4% dependent on the existing wealth in Spain of the person inheriting. However, if the recipient is not resident in Spain then they will pay no added tax if they have no wealth in Spain. There is also tax relief available on family homes and businesses and 95% of the net value of such properties if the recipients are either the children or spouse of the deceased. However, the property will need to remain in the hands of such recipients for ten years – and continue to be used as a family home or business – if inheritance tax is to be avoided.

Spanish Wills. After buying any property in Spain, the purchaser should be sure to draw up a Spanish will with a Spanish lawyer witnessed by a notary. This is essential as under Spanish law if the foreign resident dies intestate (leaving no will) or without having made a Spanish will the estate may end up being claimed by the Spanish state, as it is a difficult and lengthy process for a British will to be recognised in Spain. When making a Spanish will it is unwise to include any property held outside Spain as this could lead to further complications. In other words, British and Spanish property should be kept entirely separate with two wills being made; one to deal with assets in Spain and another dealing with assets in the UK. To validate a Spanish will you need to obtain a certificate of law (*certificado de ley*) from your consulate which states that the will is being made under the terms of UK national law, which includes a provision for the free disposition of property. Any lawyer will be able to organise this for you.

As a foreign national the Spanish civil code allows you to leave your Spanish assets in accordance with the national law of your country of origin. Once a will has been made you should ask for a copy, known as a *copia simple* from the *notario* who will keep the original. A further copy will be sent to the Central Wills Registry in Madrid.

One company which works with property, wills etc. in Spain is *Bennett & Co. Solicitors*, (144 Knutsford Road, Wilmslow, Cheshire SK9 6JP; ☎ 01625-586 937; fax 01625-585 362; www.bennett-and-co.com). Other firms in the UK include *Cornish & Co.* (Lex House, 1/7 Hainault House, Ilford, Essex IG1 4EL; ☎ 020-8478 3300; www.cornishco.com), *John Howell & Co* (17 Maiden Lane, London WC2E 7NL; ☎ 020-7420 0400; www.europelaw.com), *Fernando Scornik Gerstein* (32 St. James's Street, London SW1A 1HD; email ce dillo@fscornik.co.uk), and *Florez Valcarvel* (130 King Street, London W6 0QU; ☎ 020-8741 4867).

If you are a part-time resident in Spain it is a good idea to appoint a fiscal representative – who will need to be resident in Spain and through whom the tax authorities in Spain can deal with your tax liabilities. A fiscal representative can be a lawyer, a bank, accountant or a *gestor*. The

Institute of Foreign Property Owners (*Fundación Instituto de Propietarios Extranjeros – FIPE*) is a membership organisation providing a support service and newsletter for a small yearly subscription. FIPE can be contacted at Apartado 418, 03590 Altea, Alicante, Spain (☎ 965 842 312; fax 965 841 589; www.fipe.org).

VAT (IMPUESTO SOBRE EL VALOR AÑADIDO (IVA)

The rate of VAT in Spain is normally 16%, though commodities such as food products used for human or animal consumption, water, veterinary products or products to be used in the production of food, seeds and fertilisers carry a rate of 7%. There is a reduced super-reduced IVA of 4% on standard bread, flours and cereals used for the production of bread, milk (in different forms), cheese, eggs, fruit and vegetables, books, periodicals, pharmaceutical products, vehicles for handicapped people and prothesis (artificial arms, teeth, etc.) to be used by handicapped people. Health, education, insurance and financial services are all exempt from VAT as is the transfer of any business, providing the buyer continues the existing business concern, rental of private property etc. IVA does not apply in the Canary Islands, Ceuta or Melilla. In the Canaries a regional tax (Canarian Indirect General Tax – IGIC) is charged instead at a rate of 5%.

INSURANCE

Some considerations that need to be taken into account while looking for an insurance policy on your new property include:

- Is your villa or flat covered by insurance in the event of your letting the property to someone who accidentally burns the place to the ground/floods the bathroom/steals all the electrical appliances and locks a dog in before vacating the premises?
- Is the property covered for insurance purposes even if it remains empty for part of the year?
- Does the insurance policy allow for new-for-old replacements or are their deductions for wear-and-tear?

It is always a good idea to shop around to see what options and premiums are available. Ask neighbours in Spain for recommendations and remember to always, *always*, read the small print on any contract before signing. Do not underinsure property and remember that insurance will also be needed if a property is being built to order by a developer or builder.

It may be better to go with a large insurance company than a small independent company that may be less amenable when it comes to paying out on a claim. Most companies will anyway demand that any claim must be backed by a police report, which may need to be made within a specific time limit after the accident or burglary. If such an event takes place while the house is empty this may be impossible, which is one of the reasons why you should check the small print carefully on all contracts.

In areas where there are earthquakes or heavy flooding or forest fires each year premiums will be much higher than back home, and also may not be as comprehensive as those offered back home. Additionally, buying cover from a Spanish company while in Spain is likely to cost a lot more than taking it from an insurance company back home. Insurance premiums will be cheaper in rural areas than in the larger towns and cities and, wherever your property, you may be required by the company to install certain security arrangements which will need to have been in place should a claim be made.

Insurance premium tax in the UK for instance is about 5% while in Spain it is around 6.5%. Some high street companies will ensure a second home abroad if you are already insured with them. *Norwich Union* (www.norwichunion.co.uk), for instance, place a premium on the value of a prospective client's main home, while Saga (www.saga.co.uk) has special premiums for those over 50 (£2 million liability for property, loss of rent provision, full cover of 60 days for untenanted properties, emergency accommodation cover, etc.). Other companies, such as *Schofields* (www.schofields.ltd.uk) include public liability of up to £3 million. *Towergate Holiday Homes Underwriting Agency Ltd*, Towergate House, St. Edward's Court, London Road, Romford, Essex RM7 9QD; ☎ 0870-242 2470; fax 01708-777 721; www.towergate.co.uk), and *Ketteridge Group Ltd*, 1st Floor, 130A Western Road, Brighton BN1 2LA; ☎ 01273-720 222; fax 01273-722 799 also offer a wide range of travel-related policies and schemes as well as dealing with general insurance, private cars, commercial insurance and homes insurance. The head office addresses of several major British insurance companies that have operations in Spain are given below; these may be worth contacting on arrival.

Insuring through a company back home with representatives in Spain will mean that claims will be processed in English rather than Spanish which can be a great help and will also mean that reading the small print will present no problems. Premiums vary depending on the size, location and age of the property, in addition to other factors such as security arrangements, the amount of time it will be occupied over a period of a year, the value of the contents, distance from emergency services, etc.

If you are going to let your property to holidaymakers getting good insurance cover is a necessity that you mustn't overlook and you must inform your insurers, otherwise the policy may be void or an extra premium may be payable. As well as covering the villa or apartment and its contents, you will need to cover your own liability in the event of the unforeseen occurring. It also makes sense to try and find a policy that will cover you for loss of earnings from rentals if your house becomes impossible to rent through problems arising from floods, earthquakes, fires and Acts of God. Policies will also need to be updated should your property rise substantially in value. Note that your property will not be covered for theft by a tenant unless you take out a policy which covers larceny. Additionally, the policy will only pay out on theft it there are signs of forced entry. Furthermore if the property is to be only used as a holiday home, where the property will be left empty for months at a time you will need to inform the insurance company to ensure that you are covered throughout the year whether in residence or not. It is also useful to get emergency travel cover so that if there is an emergency concerning your property your travelling costs to Spain will be covered.

With long-term rental agreements either the owner or tenant should always arrange appropriate insurance for a property to cover the cost of rebuilding should it be necessary, contents insurance and third party liability. Apart from being a sensible precaution, third party insurance for property is also a legal requirement. Most insurers prefer a multi-risk policy covering theft, damage by fire, vandalism, etc. If the insurer has bought into a development, it may well turn out that the building as a whole is already covered. It is advisable to check this before taking out an individual policy. In any event, it is unlikely that the existing cover will include the private property of individual inhabitants.

Anyone who has purchased a resale property may find that the seller's insurance may be carried on by the next owner. However, the new owner will have to check whether the policy is transferable.

Useful Addresses

Axa Aurora: Paseo de La Castellana 79, 28046, Madrid; ☎ 915 551 700. Mortgages and insurance.

Commercial Union Assurance Co: Via Augusta 281-283, 08017 Barcelona; ☎ 932 534 700. Mortgages and insurance.

Direct Seguros: Ronda de Poniente 14, 28760, Tres Cantos, Madrid; ☎ 902 404 025. Insurance.

Eagle Star Insurance Company: Via Augusta 200, 08017 Barcelona; ☎ 934 140 070.

Knight Insurance: Ed. Lance del Sol, Pta.I, 1ª, Avda. Jesus Santos Rein s/n. Los Boliches, Apartado 113, 29640 Fuengirola, Málaga; ☎952 660 535; fax 952 660 202; www.knight-insurance.com.

Ocaso Insurance Services Ltd: 3rd Floor, 110 Middlesex Street, London E1 7HY; ☎ 020-7377 6465; www.ocaso.co.uk. Spanish company specialising in holiday home insurance.

Plus Ultra Compaña Anonima de Seguras y Resuguras: Plaza de Cortes 8, 28014, Madrid; ☎ 915 899 292; www.plusaltra.es.

La Unión Española de Entidades Aseguradoras y Reaseguradoras (Spanish Union of Insurance and Reinsurance Companies): Calle Núñez de Balboa 101, 28006 Madrid; ☎ 917 451 530; www.unespa.es.

Saga ☎ 020-8282 0330/0800-015 0751; www.saga.co.uk/finance/holidayhome/

IMPUESTO EXTRAORDINARIO SOBRE EL PATRIMONIO (WEALTH TAX)

Wealth Tax is calculated on the value of an individual's assets in Spain on 31 December every year and is imposed on those who are non-resident or resident in Spain for ordinary tax purposes. A non-resident pays Wealth Tax at the same rate as a resident and must declare the value of the property owned in Spain (calculated on the *valor catastral* and declared on the *escritura*), vehicles and investments (if applicable) and the average cleared balance of a Spanish bank account over the previous year. Deductions are available against debts on a property or mortgage.

While a non-resident need only declare assets and property in Spain, residents must declare their worldwide assets when assessing their payment of the Wealth Tax (though a resident pays nothing on the first €150,253 of the valuation). Because the tax is on the individual, unless you are a resident and you have considerable business interests and valuable property in Spain it is unlikely that you will be eligible to pay Wealth Tax. The Wealth Tax is collected every June; the rate beginning at 0.2% for assets valuing €167,129 or over held in Spain. The upper bracket of tax payable is 2.5% on assets over €10,695,996.

LEGAL AND OTHER ADVICE

A useful contact for information concerning the Spanish property market is the *Federation of Overseas Property Developers, Agents and Consultants – FOPDAC –* (Lacey House, St, Clare Business Park, Holly Road, Hampton Hill, Middlesex, TW12 1QQ; ☎ 020-8941 5588; fax 020-8941 0202; www.fopdac.com). *Bennett and Co. solicitors,* (144 Knutsford

Road, Wilmslow, Cheshire SK9 6JP, ☎ 01625-586 937, fax 01625-585 362, www.bennett-and-co.com) also handle property purchasing and finance legalities. Another firm of solicitors specialising in Spain is *John Howell & Co*, (17 Maiden Lane, Covent Garden, London WC2E 7NL; ☎ 020-7420 0400; fax 020-7836 3626; e-mail info@europelaw.com; www.europelaw.com). They have independent associates in Alicante, Barcelona, Benidorm, Madrid, Menorca, Tenerife and many other locations and will answer your enquiry on all aspects of buying property in Spain.

Cornish & Co. Solicitors (Lex House, 1/7 Hainault Street, Ilford, Essex IG1 4EL; ☎ 020-8478 3300; fax 020-8553 3418/3422; e-mail interlex@cornishco.com; www.cornishco.com in Spain ☎ 95-286-6830; e-mail cornish@mercuryin.es; e-mail cornish@gibnet.gi in Gibraltar) can also offer a variety of advice on everything from setting up home to retirement to legal and business structures. They have a range of legal services for expats and residents in Spain – from advice on forming trusts and companies to tax planning and wills and probates as well as property; you can request their information pack by dialling 0800-163507. The publication, *Buying and Selling Your Home in Spain* by Per Svensson (Longman) also contains some useful tips.

Other Useful Addresses

Blevins Franks Financial Management: Barbican House, 26-34 Old Street, London EC1V 9QQ; ☎ 020-7336 1116; fax 020-7336 1100; www.blevinsfranks.com. Offices throughout the Spanish coastal regions and in the Balearic and Canary Islands. Advise on tax planning, offshore trusts and investments, overseas and UK pensions and mortgages.

First Class Investments: Centro Comercial La Cornisa, Local 5, Calle Jaen, Sitio de Calahonda, Mijas Costa, 29649 Málaga; ☎ 952 932 519; www.firstclassinvest.com. UK ☎ 0121 359 5994. Financial planning.

Siddalls: Lothian House, 22 High Street, Fareham, Hampshire PO16 7AE; ☎ 01329 288 641; fax 01329 281 157; www.siddalls.net. Independent financial advisers and investment brokers.

Windram Miller & Co: Jacinto Benavente, 17-2 A, 29600 Marbella, Málaga; ☎ 952 820 779; fax 952 778 468; www.windrammiller.com.

FINDING PROPERTIES FOR SALE

CHAPTER SUMMARY

- **Estate Agents**. If you buy through a Spanish estate agent it is essential that the company be properly licensed. Their official status will be indicated on their stationery and their licence should be displayed on the premises.
  - Spanish estate agents often concentrate on the area around where their office is based. They will have a good knowledge of the possible problems or otherwise associated with planning regulations, utility provision etc., in their locality.
  - Estate agents dealing with properties on the costas are very likely to speak English, and may even be British.
  - The commission rate charged by estate agencies can vary from 5% to 15%.
- If you know the type of property you want to buy and where you want to buy it some property firms can arrange inspection flights to Spain.
- Daily and weekend newspapers all carry adverts for property abroad.

ESTATE AGENTS

Estate agents dealing in properties in Spain and other second-home hotspots such as Portugal, Italy and France are becoming more and more widespread. These agents will be more than willing to offer advice on the costs involved and to help handle the property buying transaction for you.

Discuss your requirements with the estate agent; sound them out about whether what you want is available or whether your ideas are unrealistic. Although the agents will be looking to sell properties already on their books, if they are bona fide they may well tell you honestly that you might do better by going to see their sister company or another estate agency

which will be more likely to offer what you want. Giving an agency a clear idea of what you are looking for will hopefully save both you and them time and money. You don't want to end up traipsing around being shown totally unsuitable properties. On the other hand discussing your requirements with an agency will also allow you to find out about what alternatives there are. You may think you want a particular kind of property but the agency may come up with other suggestions, or localities that you hadn't considered previously.

Agents can take you to view properties in Spain, but you will need to make sure that you arrange an appointment to view far enough in advance of your trip out there. If you are going to Spain on a house-hunting trip and will be viewing a number of properties it is a good idea to take a camera and a map of the area along with you. Take photographs to help you remember salient points about each property that you view and mark the property on a detailed map of the area so that you can then scout around and get to know whether a particular location is right for you. If an agent is showing you the wrong kind of properties let them know so that you, and they, can get back on to the right track. If you are on a house-hunting trip your time will be precious, though in many cases the right property turns up on the last day of such trips ('Well, there is this other property, but we didn't think it would suit you!') necessitating an extension of your trip, or a return to Spain as rapidly as possible.

The bigger international outfits can lay on every service you can think of once you have invested in one of their properties – from an initial inspection trip to sorting out moving your furnishings to Spain, money matters, residency, etc. However, such large companies sometimes deal mainly with large developments (which they may own and manage) in the main resort areas rather than selling more individual properties. If you buy through a Spanish estate agent it is essential that the company is properly licensed. Their official status will be indicated on their stationery and their licence should be displayed on the premises.

Estate agent's websites and advertisements can give you a rough idea of the types and prices of property dealt with by a certain agent but will often not be bang up to date and will only show a small proportion of the properties on the books.

Depending on the time scale you have allowed yourself to find and buy a property in Spain, before dealing with estate agents you should decide first on the area where you want to buy. By all means look in estate agents' shop windows, check out price ranges and property on offer in different parts of the country through property magazines, local English-language newspapers, the Internet, property

exhibitions, etc., but don't tie yourself immediately to one or several estate agencies before you are sure about where you are hoping to buy. It will also be far more productive for those looking for an individual property rather than a new build to research properties (and estate agents) on the ground in Spain. Once there, you will be able to get a feel for the reliability and efficiency or otherwise of a particular agent as well as being able to see the most recent properties that have come onto the market.

There have been horror stories on TV consumer programmes telling of people who have bought property from 'estate agents' in Spain only to be faced with myriad problems with the property – faulty building work, reneged promises, not being told that a development was planned that would cut off that sea view. These 'estate agents' are not officially registered – British agents do not need to register with the official estate agent body, API, or have achieved any professional qualifications in order to operate.

UK Estate Agents

Because estate agents in the UK do not need to be qualified or members of a professional body anyone can set up and call themselves estate agents. They can work from home, or have an office on a high street. They may market their services through advertisements in the local free press, through English-language newspapers and magazines in Spain, and on the Internet. They may act as agents or middlemen for Spanish estate agents who do not have the contacts, the marketing know-how, reach or the fluency in English that a British estate agent has. Because they may well have an office in the UK, contacting such agents is a good starting place for sounding out the prices and property available, above all if they deal with the region/s where you are interested in buying.

Because these agents have experience of dealing with Spanish property law, regulations and red tape they can be very helpful for anyone who is wary of dealing with Spanish estate agents direct. The initial (let's be honest here) suspicion and worry that comes when doing business in a foreign country where you do not know the rules and regulations and way of doing things can be circumvented by dealing with UK-based agents.

Prospective buyers of property should make sure that they are aware of and very clear about everything that is taking place 'on their behalf' during negotiations and to be in control of proceedings. Before entering into a contract through one of these agents check to see what charges for services are going to be levied and ask for a breakdown of costs and commission. It may work out to be far more expensive going through an agent back home than dealing with a Spanish-based estate agent direct.

Spanish Estate Agents – Inmobiliaria

In Spain dealing with a registered estate agent means dealing with an agency belonging to either the *Agente de Propiedad Inmobiliaria* (API) or the *Gestor Intermediario de Promociones y Edificaciones* (GIPE). These agencies display their certificate of registration and identification number on the premises and seeing these should give you some confidence in moving forward with that agency. Any API registered estate agency employs an API accredited lawyer and has paid a bond. They are then bound to act in accordance with regulations of the API and can be sued if they don't.

As in the UK estate agents in Spain often concentrate on the area around which their office is based. They deal with local properties and have a good knowledge of the possible problems or otherwise associated with planning regulations, utility provision etc., in their locality. Estate agents dealing with properties on the *costas* are very likely to speak English, and may even *be* British. *Inmobiliarias* out in the wilds may not be used to dealing with English-speakers, though agents will want to bend over backwards in order to make a sale. Agencies may be one-office outfits, or part of a large chain, or only deal specifically with the selling of their own developments and properties.

Spanish estate agents in general provide far less detailed descriptions of property than those which we are used to at home. Photographs of properties and details will be of varying quality, though in general the more expensive the property the better the marketing will be.

> In 2000 a new law was passed in Spain which relaxed the need for Spanish estate agents to be qualified and members of a professional body of estate agents. This has led to an unrestricted market and any potential buyer of property in Spain should be careful about with whom they deal. Make sure that all staff, or at least those representatives that you are dealing with, are API members.

Some but not all estate agents carry professional indemnity insurance. It is also worth asking whether the estate agent has a bonded client bank account where any monies can be put into until the sale of a property has gone through with the *escritura* signed in front of the notary. This will guard against paying a deposit straight to the vendor who, if the worst-case scenario is evoked, could take the deposit and then sell to another buyer.

The chief role of the *inmobiliarias* is to sell any property that has been placed with them, and they will mostly sell resale properties. Their allegiance is to the vendor from whom they draw their commission, and not to you the buyer. They may well be able to advise on aspects such as mortgages, residency, the Spanish tax system etc, but such services will of course come at a cost. Once a deal has gone through, any issues that arise over the property will have nothing to do with the agents. It is therefore imperative to get a lawyer (an independent lawyer, rather than one recommended by the estate agency or the vendor) to check all contracts thoroughly before buying a property.

When dealing with Spanish estate agents, because of the sometimes 'cash in hand' nature of things in Spain, you may be asked to sign a *nota de encargo* before being shown a property or properties. This document protects the agent's interests, and ensures that he will be paid the commission should you go ahead and buy one of the properties on his books. This is because a property may be placed with several agents all of whom are after making their commission from the sale.

Commission. The commission rate charged by estate agencies can vary from 5% to 15%, with property deposits averaging 10%. A higher commission is payable on cheap properties than on more expensive ones, and the rate will also vary from region to region – higher rates being charged in more popular resort areas, though the commission recommended by the API is, in most regions, 3%.

In Spain the commission on a property sale is not always paid by the vendor and so you will need to check whether the purchase price is inclusive of the agent's commission or whether you, as the buyer, have to pay extra to cover the agent's commission. Theoretically, if you are dealing with an agent based in the UK who works as an intermediary for a Spanish estate agent then the commission charged on the sale of a property should be shared between the two of them, rather than you being charged commission twice.

Inspection Flights

If you know the type of property you want to buy and where you want to buy it some property firms can arrange inspection flights to Spain. A typical deal involves the estate agency booking the flight to Spain, collecting you from and returning you to the airport and providing free accommodation for the duration of your trip. A consultant will take you round various properties on a one-to-one basis, showing you the area and the facilities on offer. Normally you will only have to pay for your flights (prices will depend on whether you are booked with a budget airline, or a more expensive scheduled flight) and these will be refundable if you eventually decide to buy a property with the agents.

Although there will be no obligation to buy on these inspection trips obviously the agency is hoping that they aren't wasting everyone's time by showing properties to someone who has no intention of buying with them. An inspection trip is not a free tour of Spain, but is intended for those seriously wanting to purchase at the time of the inspection.

Before booking a special inspection visit, it is a good idea to have a clear idea of the location/s you would like to buy in and the kind of prices property sells for in that location. You will also need to have talked through the ways in which you can finance your purchase – and the estate agent will want to know that you have the financial backing to be able to pay a deposit there and then should you find a suitable property on the inspection trip.

If you are sure of the area where you wish to buy, a three- or four-day visit is often adequate, though a longer trip leaves room for the unexpected to turn up. To begin with you will be shown the various locations that you are interested in – be able to examine the infrastructures, school and medical facilities, leisure facilities, etc on offer. You will get a good idea of the type of properties available in these locations and be shown round a number of them. Towards the end of an inspection trip you will have time to review any properties that you think might be suitable. If you decide to buy a property that you have seen then the agency will be able to introduce you to a local lawyer who will be able to advise on the contracts etc. should you decide to ask them to act on your behalf. Once back home the estate agency will continue to liaise between your lawyer, the vendor and yourself.

WHEN ON AN ARRANGED INSPECTION TRIP:

- Don't be rushed around by the agent, but take your time and get a measured response to all properties that you view.
- Try and get some time away from the consultants to go off and explore on your own. Some companies may insist that you spend all of your visit under their direction and frankly these are to be avoided as a certain amount of pressure may be brought to bear. You need to be able to hear your own intuitive thoughts about a property and location without the interruptions of a salesman.
- Avoid mass inspections where you are shown a whole load of unsuitable properties. Such an inspection will be a waste of your time and money. Don't waste time looking at properties you have no interest in buying.
- Have a clear notion of what you are looking for in a property in terms of size, location and price and let the agents know.
- If you decided to buy a property while on an inspection trip it may

be difficult to ask to use (or to find) a lawyer other than the one that the agent offers you. You will be under a time limit, and a certain amount of pressure, to close the deal on the property before your return flight leaves.

- Inspection trips take the business relationship between a prospective buyer and an agent into a more complex area. Rather than being able to walk away should you decide that an agent hasn't got what you are looking for, going on an inspection trip means that the agent is investing time and money in you as a client and you therefore become more important to the agent. They will want a return on their investment.

Estate Agent Addresses

A.C.D. Spanish Properties: 125 Summerhouse Drive, Bexley, Kent DA5 2ER; tel/fax 01322-550 409; www.acdsp.co.uk. Specialises in freehold property on the Costa Blanca and Costa Calida. Also legal, financial and insurance services.

Alexander Watson: 28-30 High Street, Pinner, Middlesex HA5 5PW; ☎ 020-8866 0127; fax 020-8868 5159; www.alexanderwatson.co.uk. Specialists in property on the Costa del Sol; also offer mortgage, financial and valuing services.

Anglo Continental Properties: 55 Coten End, Warwick, CV34 4NU; ☎ 01926-401 274; fax 01926-411 198; www.anglocontinental.co.uk.

Atlas International: Atlas House, Station Road, Dorking, Surrey RH4 1EB; ☎ 01306 879 899; fax 01306 877 441; www.atlasinternational.com. Offices throughout Europe. Specialists in Costa Blanca.

Bay of Roses: Apartados de Correos 133, 17480 Girona; ☎ 972 154 358; fax 972 150 452; www.bayofroses.com. Properties for sale and to let on the Costa Brava.

Beaches International: 3/4 Hagley Mews, Hagley Hall, West Midlands DY9 9LQ; ☎ 01562-885181; fax 01562-886724; www.beachesint.co.uk. They can send their guidelines to purchasing property in Spain. Costa Blanca and Costa Calida specialists with over 23 years experience.

Blue Sky Homes: Ansteads Farm, Stancombe, Glos; ☎ 01452-770177; fax 01452-770199; www.blueskyhomes.co.uk. Costa Blanca specialists.

Bravo Spanish Estates Ltd: Crossley House, 423 Wellington Road North, Heaton Chapel, Stockport, Cheshire SK4 5BA; ☎ 0161-431 8111; fax 0161-431 8333; www.bravo-spanish-estates.com. New and resale properties on Costa Blanca South.

Casa Blanca Properties: 19/21 East Bridge Street, Falkirk, Scotland FK1 1YD; ☎ 01324 612 333; fax 01324 638 191; www.casablancascotland.co.uk.

Casa Del Sol Properties: 51 High Street, Emsworth, Hampshire PO10 7AN; ☎ 01243-397797; fax 01234-379737; www.casadelsol.co.uk. Properties on the costas, Canary Islands and Balearic Islands.

Connections Business Consultancy S.L.: Cuesta Molino 1, Arboleas, 04660, Almería; tel/fax 950 449 428. Andalucian farmhouses and new villas in the Almanzora Valley in Almería.

Costa Blanca Choice: Hersal House, 77 Springfield Road, Chelmsford, Essex, CM2 6JG; ☎ 01245-496644; fax 01245-495454.

Courciers: 4-6 Station Road, South Norwood, London SE25 5AJ; ☎ 020-8653 6333. Country homes as well as coastal properties on the Costa Blanca.

Country-Estate España S.L.: C/Amargura 13, Riogordo, 29180 Málaga; ☎ 952 506 268; http://andalucia-fincas.com/. Also have offices in the UK: Omega House, 6 Buckingham Place, Bellfield Road West, High Wycombe, Bucks. HP13 5HW; ☎ 01494-435 309.

David Scott International: Deerhurst House, Epping Road, Roydon, Harlow, Essex CH15 5DA; ☎ 01279-792 162; fax 01279 792 318; www.nerjapro

perties.co.uk. Specialises in inland and coastal properties around Nerja.

Diamond Sun Resorts: Diamond House, Main Street, Markfield, Leics. LE67 9UT; ☎ 015302-241 241; fax 015302-241 242; www.diamondsunresorts.com. Offer a one-to-one specialist service.

Diana Morales Properties: Avda Ricardo Soriano, 72B-1°, 29600 Marbella, Málaga; ☎ 952 765 138; fax 952 771 871; www.dmproperties.com.

Eden Villas: Springfield, 33 Tranent Grove, Dundee DD4 0XP; ☎ 01382-505101; fax 01382-502 082; www.edenvillas.com. Properties along the coast from Valnecia to Marbella.

Elite Spanish Properties: 8 Abbey Court, High Street, Newport, Shropshire TF10 7BW; ☎ 01952-814 741; fax 01952-825 573; www.elite-spanish.co.uk. New developments, urbanizaciónes and luxury villas on the Costa del Sol, Costa Blanca North, the Balearics and Fuerteventura.

Ellington International Ltd: ☎ 023 92 639 638; fax 023 92 639 039; www.ellingtononline.com. All types of property in Fuerteventura.

Escapes 2 Ltd: Hamilton House, 205 Bury New Road, Whitefield, Manchester M45 6GE; ☎ 0161-280 7375; fax 0161-959 5680; www.escape2spain.com. Properties on the Mediterranean coastline.

European Villa Solutions: 618 Newmarket Road, Cambridge CB5 8LP; ☎ 01223 514 241; fax 01223 562 713; www.europeanvs.com. Properties along the Mediterranean coastline and on the Balearics.

G & R Properties: 5 Chings Alley, Launceston, Cornwall; ☎ 01566-774 499; fax 01566-776 767; www.chilcott-villas.com. Properties on Costa Blanca North.

Garrison Resorts: Marlborough Court, Pickford Street, Macclesfield SK11 6JD; ☎ 01625-613 681/0800-975 7198; fax 01625-613 737.

Gibsons Overseas: 10 Fairfield Avenue, Upminster, Essex RM14 3AY; tel/fax 01708 502 270; www.gibsons-overseas.com. Properties in Menorca, Mallorca, Nerja and Málaga and the Costa Blanca.

Gran Sol Properties (Europe) Ltd: Summerville House, Heatley Street, Preston, Lancs.; ☎ 01772 825 587; fax 01772 251 902; www.gransol properties.com. Spanish office: Edificio Apolo 1, Calle Corbeta, Calpe, 03710 Alicante; tel/fax 96-583-5468. Specialise in Costa Blanca North, Madrid and Barcelona.

Greenbox Properties: Wansbeck Business Centre, Rotary Parkway, Ashington, Northumberland NE63 8QZ; ☎ 01670-528 258; fax 01670-528 259; www.greenbox.co.uk. Residential rural property on the Costa del Sol, Costa Blanca, Costa Calida and Tenerife.

Grupo Si Real Estate Services: Edificio Perla 1, Ctra. de Málaga, 107 Alhaurín el Grande; 29120 Málaga; ☎ 952 596 261; www.inmogruposi.com.

Villas and fincas in inland Costa del Sol.

Homes in Fuerteventura: 15 The Triangle, Bournemouth, Dorset BH2 5RY; ☎ 0800 783 9637; www.homesinfuerteventura.com.

Horizon Property Group S.L.: Tenerife office CC Don Antonio Local 25, Calle Juan XXIII, Los Cristianos, 38650 Arona, Tenerife; ☎ 922 792 651; Birmingham office ☎ 01384 866 000; www.horizonpropertygrou p.com. Produces a free guide to property in Tenerife.

Iberian International: Century House, 26 Bridge Street, Leatherhead, Surrey KT22 8BZ; ☎ 0870 770 5202; www.iberianinternational.net. Apartments, villas, bungalows, townhouses etc.

Images of Andalucia (Spain): Tara, Cortijo del Roble, Carboneras, 29312 Villanueva del Rosario, Málaga; tel/fax 952 111 178; www.imagesofan dalucia.com.

Interealty Canary Islands: B15 Vista Sur, Avda Rafael Puig, 38660 Playa de las Americas, Tenerife; ☎ 922 789 600; fax 922 789 614; www.interea ltycanaryislands.com.

IPC Property Consultants: 38 Church Street, Seaford, East Sussex BN25 1LD; ☎ 01323 899 204; fax 01323 899 210; www.ipc-homes.com. Villas, apartments and townhouses; Costa Blanca and in Tenerife.

John Taylor: Raval Inferior 17, 17200 Palafrugell, Girona; ☎ 972 307 827; fax 972 307 829; www.johntaylorspain.com. Properties in Barcelona and on the Costa Brava.

Kensington Properties International: Calle Sant Joan 4a, La Lonja, 07012 Palma de Mallorca; ☎ 971 713 951; fax 971 711 872; www.kensington.nu. Top end of the market with villas, mansions and estates.

Larrosa UK Ltd: 3 Newcastle Avenue, Worksop, Notts S80 1EY; ☎ 01909-509 099; fax 01909-509 029; www.larrosa.co.uk. New properties on the Costa Blanca.

LEC Estate Agents S.L.: Edifico Hibiscus, Calle Manuel Bello 76, 38670 Adeje, Tenerife; ☎ 922 710 096; fax 922 781 513; www.lec-tenerife.com.

Leiner: Avda. Los Boliches 36, 29640 Fuengirola, Málaga; tel/fax 952 460 603; www.leiner.net.

McCallum S.L. UK: Paseo Anglada Camarasa 65, Puerto Pollensa, Mallorca; ☎ 971 866 615; fax 971 866 814; www.puertopollensa.com/mccallum/index.html. Specialists in Mallorca.

Marja's Euro Residencias S.L.: Villamartin Plaza, Local 45, 03189 Orihuela Costa, Alicante; ☎ 966 765 112; fax 966 764 009; www.costablancaim mobilien.com. Costa Blanca South properties.

Martin's Property Service Ltd: Scottish Mutual House, Ground Floor Suite,

27-29 North Street, Hornchurch, Essex RM11 1RS; ☎ 01708 437 744; fax 01708 446 238. Organises inspection flights to properties on Costa Blanca, Costa Calida and the Costa del Sol.

MASA International: Airport House, Purley Way, Croydon CR0 0XZ; ☎ 020-8781 1995; fax 020-8781 1922; www.masainter.com. Specialise in the southern Costa Blanca.

Nyrae Propeties (Overseas): Old Bank House, 1 High Street, Arundel, West Sussex BN18 9AD; ☎ 01903-884663; fax 01903-732554. Deals with agencies throughout the world including Spain.

Oranges and Lemons: Alcalde Francisco Llorca 15, 1° , C, Oliva, 46780 Valencia; ☎ 962 853 112; www.orangesandlemons.com. Specialise in resale properties in the Oliva/Gandia region.

Parador Properties Ltd.: Property House, 55 Station Road, Redhill, Surrey RH1 1QH; ☎ 01737 770 137; fax 01737 770 177; www.paradorprop erties.com.

Parasio Estates: 51 Station Road, Cheadle Hulme, Stockport, Cheshire SK8 7AA; ☎ 0161-482 8866; fax 0161-482 8868; www.villashop.com. New build properties; Costa del Sol, Costa Blanca and Costa Calida.

Phoenix Overseas Properties: Windmill Oast, Benenden, Kent TN17 4PF; ☎ 0870-241 4108; fax 0870-074 1410; www.phoenix-overseas,com. Holiday and permanent homes and property for investment on the Costa Blanca, Calida and Almeria.

Philip Lockwood: 71 Coventry Street, Kidderminster DY1 2BS; ☎ 01562-745082; fax 01562-740202. Arranges both euro and Sterling mortgages and advises on the benefits and risks.

Pilgrim Homes UK: 9 High Street, Oakham, Rutland LE15 6AH; ☎ 01572-756 577; fax 01572-722 977; www.pilgrimhomes.com. Licensed credit and mortgage brokers.

Prestige Homes International: 37 East Street, Havant, Hampshire PO9 1AA; ☎ 02392-452 545; www.prestigehomesinternational.com. Properties on the Costa Blanca South.

Propertunities: 13/17 Newbury Street, Wantage OX12 8BU; ☎ 01235-772345; fax 01235-770018; www.propertunities.co.uk. Specialists in villas on the Costa Blanca and Costa Calida.

Rusticas del Noroeste: Ctra de la Lanzada 36, Portonovo 36970, Sanxenxo, Pontevedra; tel/fax 986 690 524; www.rusticas.com. Specialists in rural property in Galicia.

Solymar Estates S.L: Urb. El Saladillo, Oficina Solymar Estates S.L., Estepona 29680, Malaga; ☎ 952 904 020; email solymarestates@hotmail.com.

Spain Direct Ltd: 22 Poole Hill, Bournemouth, Dorset BH2 5PS; ☎ 01202-299 499; fax 01202-298 299; www.buyahouseinspain.com.

Properties on Costa Blanca South.

Spain on Show Ltd: 15 The Triangle, Bournemouth, Dorset BH2 5RY; ☎ 0800-783 9637; fax 01202-291 211; www.spainonshow.com. Costa del Sol and Costa Blanca.

Spanish Properties Direct: Centro Comercial 'Aguamarina' local 16B, Cabo Roig, Apdo Correos. 529, Orihuela Costa, Alicante; ☎ 965 322 901; fax 965 321 165; www.spanishonlineproperties.com. Costa Blanca Properties.

Spanish Property Investments: 7 Sussex Place, Claverton Street, Bath BA2 4LA; ☎ 01225 446 567; www.spaininvest.co.uk. Properties all along the Mediterranean coastline.

Swan International: 505 Pensby Road, Thingwall, Wirral CH61 7UQ; ☎ 0151-658 3597; fax 0151-648 5514; www.swanint.co.uk. Property between Marbella and Estepona.

Talinto Group: Gran Via 3, Fuerte Alamo, 30320, Murcia; ☎ 968 597 947; fax 654 261 131; www.talinto-costacalida.com. Coastal, rural, restoration projects, land and new builds on the Costa Calida.

Tara European Property Consultants: C/Roque Nublo 3, Centro Comercial La Hoya, 35510 Puerto del Carmen, Tias, Lanzarote; ☎ 928 514 094; fax 928 512 383; www.realestatelanzarote.com. Properties in Lanzarote.

Town & Country South West: 6 Fore Street, Trowbridge, Wiltshire B14 8HD; ☎ 01225-755811; fax 01225-755886; www.spanishproperty.uk.com. Specialise in the Costa del Sol, north Costa Blanca and south Costa Blanca.

Ultra Villas Ltd: Clarendon House, 42 Clarence Street, Cheltenham, Gloucestershire GL50 3PL; ☎ 01242-221500; fax 01242-226388; www.ultravillas.co.uk. Costa Blanca properties.

Vera Gold: 1 Richmond Gate, 168A Charminster Road, Bournemouth;

☎ 01202 514 477; www.veragold.com. Properties in Almería.
Wessex Homes (Spain): 95B Cavendish Place, Eastbourne, East Sussex BN12 3TZ; ☎ 01323 749 007; www.wessexhomes.net. Resale properties and developments on the Costa Blanca, Costa Calida and Almería.
William H. Emmerson:, Thomas Lane, Liverpool L14 5NR; ☎ 0151-228 0679; fax 0151-259 4136; ww.emmersoninternational.com. Properties in Costa Blanca, Costa del Sol, Menorca and the Canaries.
Winkworth Gesinar: 126 Wigmore Street, London W1U 3RZ; ☎ 020-7486 4666; www.winkworth-gesinar.co.uk. Provide a range of services for the homebuyer. Also have real estate offices throughout Spain.
World Class Homes: 22 High Street, Wheathampstead, Herts. AL4 8AA; ☎ 01582-832 001; fax 01582-831071; www.worldclasshome s.co.uk., plus offices overseas. Properties throughout Spain including the Costa Brava, Costa Blanca, Costa Orihuela, Costa del Sol, Gibraltar and Ibiza.
www.torrevieja.uk.com: 18 Rheingold Way, Wallington, Surrey SM6 9NA; ☎ 020-8669 7920; fax 020-8669 3208; www.torrevieja.uk.com. Commercial and residential properties on the Costa Blanca and Costa Calida.

Names of other agents dealing in Spanish property can be obtained from the *National Association of Estate Agents*, Arbon House, 21 Jury Street, Warwick CV34 4EH; ☎01926-496 800; www.naea.co.uk (select the international section). They can send a list (ask for their `Homelink' department) of members specialising in Spain. Or contact the *Royal Institute of Chartered Surveyors,* 12 Great George Street, Parliament Square, London SW1 3AD; ☎020-7222 7000; www.rics.org.

The CEI (*Confédération Européenne de l'Immobilier*: European Confederation of Real Estate Agents) is one of Europe's largest professional organisation of estate agents, now with well over 25,000 members from hundreds of cities in thirteen European countries, Austria, France, Germany, Greece, Hungary, Ireland, Italy, the Netherlands, Portugal, Romania, Spain, the United Kingdom and the Slovak Republic, representing a total of over 60,000 operators in real estate. The CEI website (www.web-cei.com) has a search facility.

The Federation of Overseas Property Developers, Agents & Consultants (FOPDAC) is a membership organisation restricted to agents, developers and consultants active in the international property markets whose probity is beyond reasonable question. They can be contacted at Lacey House, St.

Clare Business Park, Holly Road, Hampton Hill, Middlesex, TW12 1QQ; ☎020-8941 5588; fax 020-8941 0202; www.fopdac.com.

ADVERTS

When you begin looking into the possibilities of buying a property in Spain you will very quickly become aware of the vast number of companies out there who are looking to persuade you to do business with them. Take out a subscription to one of the property or lifestyle magazines such as *Spanish Homes Magazine* or *Spain* and you will find their pages rammed with advertisements placed by property developers, estate agents, removals firms, lawyers and insurers and accountants. The property pages of the weekend national newspapers frequently have articles on buying property abroad and these pieces will include sample prices of properties and details of the companies featured. Note that many property advertisements will include the size of the property (and/or land) in square metres, which allows those interested to compare prices regionally or nationally. Another invaluable resource for both prospective property buyers and service companies is the Internet.

The Internet

Although you won't be able (and won't want) to buy properties over the Internet there is a growing number of websites that deal with property, from estate agents' home pages to those of property developers, mortgage lenders, letting agencies, plus websites aimed at the expatriate and the house-hunter. Estate agents and property developers are increasingly using the World Wide Web as a marketing tool, as a relatively cheap way to get their name known internationally. There are now Internet portals (websites dedicated to one area of information and/or commerce), which deal exclusively with properties for sale from thousands of leading agents and developers. Using a search engine such as www.google.com or a web directory such as www.yahoo.com will lead you into a selection of websites dealing solely with Spanish property for sale.

> Because of the vast amount of information (as well as misinformation and downright junk) that is posted on the Internet you will need to narrow down any search that you make using a web directory or search engine. Rather than just typing in for example, 'property, Spain' or 'villas for sale, Costa del Sol' name the specific area or town you are looking to buy in. If you have the name of a property developer or estate agent that you are thinking of doing business with, then use the web as a research tool. Find out as much as you can about their company. You can make initial contact with vendors of property which interests you by using

e-mail (you can get a free e-mail address at such places as www.hotmail.com, or yahoo.co.uk) but be very wary of any company or individual who asks for payment of any kind over the Internet. Although e-commerce has come a long way and although those who have the money to invest in Internet security have made it virtually impossible for a 'hacker' to get hold of clients' credit card details that are given over the web, smaller operators may not have the latest security systems. If you decide to continue with negotiations after initial contact over the Internet it is best to set up a face to face meeting as soon as possible. Anyone can be anybody they want in cyberspace.

The Internet can be a great marketing tool – the Hamptons website for example has reported getting 150,000 hits (visitors to its website) in one month alone. A few sites worth looking at, especially for those looking to buy at the top end of the property market, are Knight Frank (www.knightfrank.com), Hamptons (www.hamptons.co.uk), www.primelocation.com (which includes property from 250 estate agents), www.propertyfinder.com (property from 900 agencies), www.altea.com and newskys.co.uk. The best of these websites will allow you to search for suitable properties by specifying search criteria such as whether you want a villa with or without a swimming pool, its proximity to the beach, hospitals etc., as well as the desired region in Spain, and of course purchase price. Increasingly, agencies are linking up to property portals. There is also an Internet 'forum' website (www.spanishforum.org/spain) which has features and advice on buying property and living in Spain.

The Press

Daily and weekend newspapers all carry adverts for property abroad – mostly in their property sections, but also sometimes at the back of the travel pages. You may want to take out a subscription to some of the English-language newspapers published in Spain, many of which are regional rather than national in scope. There are also a number of free sheets available from establishments such as bars, estate agents and tourist offices, which carry property advertisements. Another place to look for both property advertisements and articles on living, working and buying property in Spain is in the rising number of glossy magazines published both in the UK and in Spain. Below is a list of some of the newspapers and magazines dealing with property in Spain:

Absolute Marbella: Office 21, Edificio Tembo, c/ Rotary Internacional s/n 29660 Puerto Banús, Málaga; ☎ 902 301 130; fax 952 908 743; www.absolutemarbella.com.

Costa Blanca News: c/ Alicante 9, Poligono Ind. La Cala, Finestrat,

Alicante; ☎ 965 855 286/87; fax 965 858 361; www.costablanca-news.com.

Costa del Sol News: C.C. Las Moriscas, Local 10, Avda. Juan Luis Peralta s/n, 29639 Benalmádena Pueblo, Málaga; ☎ 952 448 730; fax 952 568 712; http://costadelsolnews.es.

Diario Sur: Avda. Doctor Marañón 48, 29009 Málaga; ☎ 952 649 600; fax 952 279 508; www.diariosur.es.

Homes Overseas Magazine: Blendon Communications Ltd., 207 Providence Square, Mill Street, London SE1 2EW; ☎ 020-7939-9888 fax 020-7939-9889; www.blendoncommunications.co.uk.

International Homes Magazine: 3 St. Johns Court, Moulsham Street, Chelmsford, Essex CM2 0JD; ☎ 01245-358 877; fax 01245-357 767; www.international-homes.com.

Living Spain: Albany Publishing Ltd, 9 High Street, Bucks MK46 4EB; ☎ 01234-710 992; fax 01234-240 578; www.livingspain.co.uk.

Lookout: Urb. Molino de Viento, Calle Rio Darro, Portal 1, 29650 Mijas, Málaga; ☎ 952 473 090; 952 473 757.

Mallorca Daily Bulletin: Palau de la Prensa, P° Mallorca 9° A, 07011 Palma de Mallorca; ☎ 971 788 410; fax 971 719 706; www.majorcadailybulletin.es.

123 Property News: Unit 36, Harbours Deck, The New Harbours, Rosia Road, Gibraltar; ☎ 350-47123; fax 350-78300; www.123propertynews.com.

Property World Magazine: Calle Espana 1, Edificio Buendia 1-A, Fuengirola, 29640 Málaga; ☎ 952 666 234; www.propertyworldmagazine.com.

Spain Magazine: Media Company Publications Ltd., 21 Royal Circus, Edinburgh EH1 6TL; ☎ 0131-226 7766; fax 0131-225 4567; www.spainmagazine.info.

Spanish Homes Magazine: 116 Greenwich South Street, London SE10 8UN; ☎ 020-8469 4381; www.spanishhomesmagazine.com.

Spain Property Pages: Cariñena 3B, 18690 Almuñécar, Granada, Spain; ☎ 958 639 447; fax 958 634 105; www.sppgo.com. 100s of properties and independent agents in Andalucía.

Sur in English: Avda Dr Marañón 48, 29009 Málaga; ☎ 952 649 677; fax 952 611 256; www.surinenglish.com.

Tenerife News: Apartado de Correos 11, Los Realejos, Tenerife; ☎ 922 346 000; fax 922 344 967; www.tennews.com.

The Broadsheet: Gran Vía 22 dpdo, 4° D, 28013 Madrid; ☎ 911 310 180; fax 911 310 186; www.spainalive.com.

The Entertainer: Costa del Sol Edition, Avda. Condes San Isidro, 59 – 1°, 29640 Fuengirola; ☎ 952 561 245; 952 440 887; www.theentertainer.net.

The Reporter: Avda Alcalde Clemente Díaz Ruiz (Avda Suel) 37, Pueblo López, 29640, Fuengirola; ☎ 952 468 645; fax 952 467 104.
World of Property: Outbound Publishing, 1 Commercial Road, Eastbourne, East Sussex, BN21 3XQ; ☎ 01323-726 040; fax 01323-649 249; www.outboundpublishing.com.

A full list of all English-language press in Spain can be found on the UK government run official website, www.ukinspain.com.

What Type of Property to Buy

CHAPTER SUMMARY

- **Types of Property.** Classic old houses in the country are highly sought after and harder to find.
  - *Finca* is a generic term used in Spain to describe a large estate or plot of land in the countryside.
  - Many developers sell 'off-plan' homes – homes that have yet to be built, or are now being built.
  - Finding a site for self-build projects can be difficult.
  - Flats in Spain are often large, airy and spacious.
  - Some *urbanizaciónes* are part of towns or villages, others may adjoin a marina or golf course.
  - The timeshare market is expanding at around 10% a year.

OLD HOUSES

Many people looking for their dream holiday home in Spain would love to buy a classic old house in the country. However, such properties are, understandably, highly sought after and depending on their state of disrepair will be harder to find than more modern properties. Many estate agents are looking to make a good commission on a straightforward property that won't require the added hassle of getting structural surveys, finding out about boundaries, rights of way over the land etc., etc.

Renovation costs for such properties can be exorbitant and many old houses don't have (and never have had) adequate sanitation, power provision, access to telephone lines and water etc., which is often why the former owners abandoned them. Before deciding on buying a crumbling palace with loads of potential you should ask yourself some straight questions: How much will it cost to install all the mod cons deemed necessary for 21st century living? Will it actually be feasible to install them? And what will be the estimated waiting time before you can move into your renovated palace? The British especially seem to have something of a reputation for buying up old crocks and spending vast amounts of time and money turning them into habitable dwellings once more.

Without some experience of renovating property, what may have seemed like a bargain can end up just being a burden, both financially and mentally. A relatively small initial financial outlay to buy a tumbledown property will be augmented by the need to hire builders and architects and sort out planning permissions. Time, patience, perseverance and, above all, money will be needed to create or recreate the house and grounds of your dreams and without a generous supply of all these the project may falter and the dream die.

Precautions to Take. Before buying such a property you will need to get a structural survey done to judge whether there is actually scope for renovation or whether the rot is so bad that demolition and rebuilding is the only option available. If this is the case then you will need to know whether changes/additions to the property are allowed by the planning authorities.

Look to get a survey of the property done before signing any contract. Make sure that boundaries are clearly marked on the property but more importantly on the *escritura*. Boundary disputes can turn particularly nasty, and sour relations between neighbours. If there is an orchard, or an olive grove, on the property find out it you have the right of harvest. Do you have water rights over any river or well that may be on the land? Is there a right of way over the land that you aren't aware of? Are there plans afoot to built roads/drainage systems/reservoirs or irrigation canals/factories/mines etc., close to the property? Are there any debts on the property? Your lawyer should check this. Remember that under Spain's *Law of Subrogation* any unpaid monies due – such as defaulting on mortgage repayments, locals taxes etc. – are on the property and therefore will be inherited by a new owner leaving the debtor vendor scot-free.

Find out from the town hall what the planning regulations in the area are. What will you be allowed to do with the property? Will you be allowed to demolish and rebuild, to extend beyond the existing structure, or only to renovate the house to the original design? Are there restrictions on size and height, and the type of any building work that you plan to do? In a town or village you are likely to be more severely restricted in what you can do with a property than in the countryside. You will also need to obtain a *Permiso de Obra* from the town hall that will allow you to rebuild.

Another point to consider is that if you buy a tumbling down bargain and then renovate it to sell on, you will have to pay a hefty sum in Capital

Gains Tax on the resale value of the house. You may also find that such a property does not come with an *escritura* – perhaps it was not registered by a former owner, or the original owner died. If this is the case, and your lawyer will find out and let you know, a court decision will need to be taken to establish who the rightful owner of the house is. This action, called *expediente de dominio* could take up to two years to complete. Another procedure that you may come across if a property has no *escritura* is the 205 Procedure which will mean that before handing over the purchase price you will need to get a 'negative certification' from the Land Registry stating that they hold no title deeds for the property and that, given the evidence of ownership by the vendor, the title of ownership now passes to you. This 'negative certification' is then published so that anyone who may have a claim to the house can come forward to state their case. If no one does this, after about a year you will be officially registered as the owner of the property.

THE FINCA

Finca is a generic term used in Spain to describe a large estate or plot of land situated away from centres of population. Included on this land may be a farmhouse, orchards, olive groves, outbuildings, or a modern or derelict detached house. In Catalonia there are large grand farmhouses called *masiás*, in Andalucía such farmhouses are called *cortijos*. In the basque country there are large chalet-type houses among the hills that come with outbuildings and land which have a great deal of potential for development if the owner has the time, money and necessary building permits.

> Due to their relative isolation *fincas* are highly sought after, especially those situated along or near the coast. Increasingly few of them are falling down and in need of serious financial outlay to rebuild. Most have been found and renovated. If you can find one, a rebuild, apart from costing a great deal of money (and always more than you will have budgeted) will need the go ahead from the local council, the granting of planning permission and much paperwork and bureaucracy, which, if you are not fluent in Spanish, will mean a bit of a headache. Unless you can cope both financially and mentally with the uncertainties of renovating a property in a foreign land it may be more sensible to start out buying a newer property and taking the time to find your way in Spain before putting all your energies into reconstructing a semi-derelict ruin into a *palacio*. It is better to look inland for such properties these days though the extremes of climate and topography may put off all but the most adventurous.

For a long time the Spanish had no interest in old properties and were looking to move into modern housing and leave their past behind – leaving foreigners the room to snap up and renovated their cast-offs. Today the tastes and the wealth of Spaniards are changing. Many Spaniards now also own second homes and look for places with character in which to escape at weekends or on their annual summer holiday. The *masiás* around Barcelona are particularly in demand from both Spaniards and foreigners.

NEW HOUSES

There are several options when it comes to purchasing a new property, each with their own set of rules and pros and cons:

Buying Off-Plan (*sobre plano*). Selling off-plan means that less money has to be put into a project from the developers' own pocket. This saves developers from going to the expense of building houses and then waiting for a customer; they sell homes before they are built, or while they are building them.

At property exhibitions and through estate agents and property developers, prospective buyers will come across opportunities to buy villas and apartments off-plan. Clients will be shown the design and plans of a property with specifications, municipal permissions, a model of the development to be built, and perhaps the interior of a show house. Those clients interested in buying one of the homes on offer will be flown out to view the location of the proposed property and, if happy, will be asked to sign a contract. The contract will contain a clear description of the property, the schedule for completion and the dates when down payments on the property will be due.

With apartment and *urbanización* developments it is very likely that the builder or agent will already have a standard contract, together with a statement listing the quality and type of all items used in the building, such as construction materials, floor and wall tiles, kitchen fittings, fixtures and appliances, glazing, quality of internal and external doors, fitted furniture, security measures, etc. Both the buyer and seller should sign the statement to ensure that what is agreed on will be delivered. At this stage in negotiations it may be possible for the client to substitute or modify items included on the statement – perhaps air conditioning doesn't come as standard or the style of tiles and plumbing fixtures lack a certain finesse. If such items are added or substituted they will of course be regarded as extras, and any charges in excess of the builder's list price will need to be recorded and signed for by both parties.

Any builders' contract should include a 10-year insurance policy as a guarantee against any loss incurred by the purchaser due to building defects.

The buyer pays for the house or flat in instalments and will pay an initial – often hefty – deposit, and the final payment once the home is completed.

> There are pitfalls with this type of property purchase in that delays can occur in the building process, and clients may not be given information on any further development planned on the *urbanización* or the surrounding land. It is therefore essential that as much information as possible is obtained about the development company's track record, and that an independent lawyer checks the contract before it is signed. Landscaping of the property, access, utility provision, and additional maintenance charges are all matters that may need to be clarified in the contract. If they are not, it may come as a shock after paying the final instalment to find that such things have been left in abeyance. It is vital to get a termination agreement backed up by insurance guaranteeing that every aspect of the property will be professionally finished before you move in.

When buying off-plan you may have to wait for anything from a year to 18 months for a property to be completed. Instalments may be 10% on signing of the contract with two subsequent instalments followed by the final payment on completion. If a property has been partially completed on the signing of the contract, a higher initial payment may be required. It is advisable to stipulate that any payments made before the completion of the property be paid into an escrow account – money paid into such accounts cannot be touched by the developer until the property is completed. An extra charge will be made for the use of such an option but the bank will then guarantee your money should the developer go bust or, God forbid, be a rogue. It is in any case a legal requirement for property developers to have a bank guarantee to ensure that, should they become bankrupt before the completion of a project, the buyer who has paid instalments will not lose his or her investment.

Useful Addresses

Country Estate: 30-32 Teville Road, Worthing, West Sussex BN11 1UG; ☎ 01903 235 333; http://sp.country-estatenewbuild.com. In Spain: C/Amargura, 13. CP. 29810 Riogordo; ☎ 952 732 597.

Joshua Jacob: 15 Wheelergate, Nottingham NG1 2NA; ☎ 0115-852 4013;www.joshua-jacob.co.uk. Inland from Moraira and Javea.

Secret Spain: ☎ 020-8551 5405; www.secretspain.com. Costa de la Luz.

Spain Direct Ltd: 22 Poole Hill, Bournemouth BH2 5PS; ☎ 01202-299 499; www.freeholdspanishproperty.com.

Taylor Woodrow de España S.A.: Heyford Park House, Upper Heyford, Bicester, Oxon. OX25 5HD; ☎ 01869 238 295; fax 01869 233 530, or

Taylor Woodrow de España, S.A., Calle Aragon 223-223A, 07008 Palma de Mallorca; ☎ 971706 570; www.taylorwoodrow.com. New builds in Costa del Sol, Mallorca, Costa Blanca.

SELF-BUILD

Self-build entails buying a plot of land and then building a house on it yourself. Unfortunately, it isn't as simple as that and there are bureaucratic hoops to be jumped through in order to erect that edifice. Potential builders can spend a year or more waiting for the necessary licences to be granted before being given the go-ahead to start building. Finding a site can also be very difficult, and finding land to buy is practically impossible in the Balearic Islands since an embargo on the erection of new property has come into force.

The ratio of build (the size of the house to be built) to plot is determined by local planning authorities and it therefore makes sense to check this ratio with the authorities before going ahead and buying a plot. Before buying a plot you should run checks on the general status of the land – is it in a conservation area where there will be tight regulations on planning permission? Are there public rights of way over it, by-laws pertaining to water, hunting, grazing, harvesting rights? Are there likely to be objections to the building schemes that you may have? How costly will it be to install services such as sewerage, a telephone, electricity, or a water supply? Are the ground and resources suitable should you want to put in a swimming pool or tennis court? Get a lawyer, an architect and a surveyor to check over the plot before you buy and get price ranges for the area in which you are interested. If you are buying the plot through an estate agent then he or she should already know what type and size of property would be allowable.

You will want to consult the town plan (*plan general de ordenación urbana*) at the local town hall. This plan outlines the areas that have already been given over to development where planning permission should be relatively easy and straightforward to obtain. Furthermore, the town plan will tell you at a glance whether the piece of land you are interested in developing has major restrictions imposed on the size or height of proposed building projects. If your grasp of Spanish is not great then take along a lawyer or surveyor who will be able to explain the technical jargon on the plan. Also check the details of the separate plots around the one that you are interested in. Are they set for further development? Find out what types of regulations pertain to the surrounding land. These will give you a good idea of what regulations relate to your piece of land. Is the planned view of the sea or spectacular mountain scenery from your planned home liable to being blocked by an *urbanización* planned for completion a few years down the line?

The First Steps. Wherever you are proposing to buy land, changes to planning restrictions can and often are made by local councils in return for a share of a developer's profits, or a disagreement between the municipal and regional governments. Once you have checked out that planning permission for what you intend building is definitely likely to be forthcoming you can go ahead and buy the plot of land. The vendor must be in possession of an *escritura* or other officially recognised deed of title. It is at this stage that you will need to firm up descriptions of the land bordering neighbouring property. A casually waved arm pointing over towards a row of olive trees and the words 'Your land stops over there' really isn't good enough and is likely to lead to problems in the future. Get boundaries sorted out and marked on the *escritura* if they aren't already. You will also need to get your land surveyed either by an independent surveyor or through the *Catastro* (Land Registry) which holds plans marking boundaries of plots (*parcelas*) of land. When you are happy that all these points have been cleared up to your satisfaction you can sign the *escritura* for the land at the *notario's* office and hand over the money.

You will then need to apply for a building permit (*Permiso de Obra*). To obtain this you have to submit the plans for the building to the Town Hall. It is likely to take at least two months for plans of the building project to be ready for submission to the authorities.

Building Plans. To get a plan for your house you will need to get in touch with a firm of builders or an architect. If you are buying a plot on an *urbanización* then the developers will be able to give you details of local builders, or you can enquire locally. A builder will be able to provide you with details of the type of houses he could build for you and together you can work out any variations you may want, interior designs etc.

Alternatively you can find an architect and work together to come up with an original design that will answer your needs and pass the building regulations. An architect's fee is typically 6% but may run to as much as 9% of the total cost of the build – which means that they will be in no hurry to design you a cheap house. Once you and the architect have finalised the plans building specifications (*memoria*) are prepared. These include such things as the type of materials to be used, the specification of window- and door-frames, guttering, tiles etc., and are submitted to the Town Hall. Once approved, a building licence will be issued and a fee will be due (around 3-4% of the total cost of the project, depending on the region).

Builders. With planning permission granted you can now look for a builder to take on the contract to build your house. Get several estimates. The builders will look at the plans, the *memoria* and tell you how much they think it'll cost them to complete the job. Estimates will vary – both for the time it will take to complete the job and the price they will ask to do the job. You will need to weigh up the prices as well as the individual builders' reputations. Having decided upon a builder get your lawyer to look over the contract and make sure that any changes and amendments that arise over the course of the building work (they may be quite a few) are added to the contract and signed by both parties. This will avoid any problems when it comes to the reappraisal of the initial estimate and the final demand for payment. Changes to the initial specifications will also prolong the build time and delay the completion of the work. This will need to be taken into consideration, as the original completion date clause in the contract will have to be changed.

As with all purchases it is advisable to use the services of a solicitor who speaks fluent English and get all documentation completely translated into English. Don't just settle for a précis or summary of contracts. The process of buying a plot of land will involve obtaining one *escritura* while the building of a property on that land will necessitate obtaining a second.

The Building Process. Once building starts it is advisable to be on site as often as possible. If you can't be there to oversee the building process personally then try and find someone who you trust to keep an eye on things, or employ a professional to supervise and troubleshoot. Builders everywhere can occasionally be unreliable, or decide not to turn up for work if something more lucrative can be had that day by doing a spot of building elsewhere. You should also check the plans, make sure that the footings are laid correctly – it would be a great shame if your house ended up facing the wrong way for example – and check on type and costings of materials. Do you want cheap, chic, expensive, or flash? This is your house that is being built and you will want to be on hand to choose materials and fixtures and fittings. Keep in mind that things rarely go exactly to plan – for instance there may be rock where the footings should go and blasting this out of the way will increase the labour cost, or you may decide that you want changes made to the original designs. It is therefore a good idea to factor in at least 10%-30% on top of the original estimate. Building costs are likely to come in at £1,000 per square metre of build but remember that land is likely to increase in value before the building work is complete.

Stagger payment to the builder (for example make payments on: the signing of the contract, the completion of the exterior walls and roof, the completion of the interior, the completion of plumbing, installation of electricity and other services, on completion of exterior landscaping) and negotiate to hold back a final payment until a certain period has passed once the house has been completed so that should cracks in walls appear, or there be problems with drainage, plumbing, electrics, etc., you will have some clout should you need to call the builders back in to repair defects.

Depending on the size and design of the house expect a wait of about a year before being able to gaze upon your dream house. Even after the completion of the house it could take an additional year or two to knock the garden and surrounding land into shape.

On Completion. After the house has been built the final instalment of the architect's fees will need to be paid once he has signed the completion of construction certificate (*certificado final de obra*). You will need to make a Declaration of the New Building (*declaración de la obra nueva*), which will allow you to add the new building to the original *escritura* relating to the purchase of the land. You will also need to take the *permiso de obra* (building licence), the *certificado final de obra* (completion of construction certificate) issued by the architect and the *licencia de primera ocupación* (licence of first occupation) to the local town hall. To register the building for real estate taxes (*Impuesto sobre Bienes Inmeubles* – IBI) refer to the chapter on finance.

Because so many foreigners are interested in self-builds there are a lot more clued up agents and developers than previously buying up plots of land, often with services and *permiso de obra* already obtained, to sell on to clients. Property developers also sell plots on their housing schemes (*parcelas*) for buyers to build their own house on. For example, in 2002 there were plots ranging from 1,500 square metres to 4,600 square metres for sale at £75-£160 per square metre available in Sotogrande on the Costa del Sol.

A prospective self-builder should look into ways to minimise the amount that will need to be paid in VAT and municipal taxes over the period of the project from its inception to its completion and the registration of the property. There may also be tax saving ways to finance the building project, whether through funds held in Spain, at home or in an offshore account. Be aware that IVA (Spain's equivalent to VAT) will need to be paid on building land at 16 percent; IVA at a rate of 7% will be added on to building costs.

Useful Addresses

Househam Henderson Architects: 3 Charlecote Mews, Staple Gardens, Winchester SO23 8SR; ☎ 01962 835 500, or in Madrid – Fernando el Santo 25, 1-D, 28010 Madrid; ☎ 913 081 555 (Spain); www.hharchitects.co.uk. UK architectural practice with a Spanish office.

Punta de Lanza: C/ Compañá, 30, 1° , 29008 Málaga; ☎ 619 641 635; fax 952 603 629; www.puntadelanza.com. One stop shop architectural service in Andalucía.

APARTMENTS (PISOS)

Spaniards, especially urbanites, are traditionally apartment-dwellers, and flats in Spain are often large, airy and spacious. A great many holiday flats have been built since the arrival of the tourist hordes in the 1960s, especially around the coastal areas frequented by summer visitors. These flats, though often coming onto the market at a reasonable price, tend to be smaller and less soundproof than other apartments because they were built for short-let holidays and not designed to be lived in on a full-time basis. Older apartments may well be in need of some repair, either cosmetic or structural.

Apartments offer a cheap way to move on to the property owning ladder in Spain and often come with a balcony as standard, and in addition some top floor flats have access to roof gardens. As in any apartment, it is important to try and gauge the thickness of the walls and degree of protection from the sound of your potential neighbours. Flats in the middle of town may be great in terms of location but very noisy during the evenings and long into the night as the populace enjoys its *paseo*. In the areas of greatest tourist density, flats along the seafront with great views of the sea may be marred by the noise of those next door taking their hedonistic two-week break in the sun. Choice of location will depend on your predilection. One man's heaven is another man's hell. Flats are generally easy to sell on, and are cheap to maintain. In the cities almost all available property will be apartments; detached villas and townhouses are rare in the inner city areas.

La Comunidad de Propietarios (The Community of Owners)

Buying an apartment in a block or a villa in an *urbanización* will involve you joining a *comunidad de propietarios* whereby you will be involved in the running of the apartment block. This involves attending meetings to discuss the communal aspects of the block – such matters as provision of garbage collection, the lighting of communal areas (the stairwell, entrance hall, etc.) the maintenance of the lift, entrance hall, gardens, swimming pool, etc. If you are living on an *urbanización* the *comunidad* will also be responsible for street lighting, roads and communal areas on or around the *urbanización*. In effect, as well as buying your flat or villa you are buying into those elements that are common to all the owners in the block or *urbanización*. This system of co-operative maintenance is similar to the condominiums in America, though there is nothing analogous in the UK.

Some *urbanizaciónes* do not have a *comunidad de propietarios* – a commitee may never have been established by the original developers, or as the *urbanización* is not yet complete a *comunidad* has not been set up – and one should be wary of buying a property in such places. The *comunidad de propietarios* are run on the principal set up in the Law of Horizontal Property (*La Ley de Propiedad Horizontal*) originally instated in 1960 and amended in 1999. You cannot opt out of joining a *comunidad* and you are legally bound to become a member when buying a property.

You will need to read the regulations and statutes pertaining to the *comunidad* before you buy the apartment, as they will be binding after your purchase. If they are only available in Spanish – and by law they must be set out in Spanish – you must get them translated into English and have them explained in detail. Note that changes or additions to the statutes of the *comunidad* can only be made if there is a unanimous agreement among members at the AGM. Not being clear on the community's statutes and the Law of Horizontal Property could lead to problems – for example if you intend keeping a dog in your flat then find out that there is a ban on keeping dogs in the block, or that there are restrictions on noise being made during certain periods of the day or night, or if the *comunidad* is in debt after having to pay for repair work and will be trying to claw back some of the money it owes by increasing the community charges.

Ask to see the minutes of the last annual general meeting (AGM) to find out where any recurring problems within the community and apartment block lie, to help you locate what problems, if any, you are likely to face in the future once ensconced in your flat.

Depending on the location of your property the communal facilities will vary. For example if you are living in an upmarket *urbanización* which is built around a golf course or a marina with free or discounted access or membership to owners, there are likely to be some very high community fees to pay for the privilege of the great view and extensive leisure facilities, restaurants and bars etc. Such places will hire security, catering and other staff whose salary will be paid for, if not in full then in some part, by the Community of Owners.

> Properties that are part of a *comunidad de propietarios* pay less property tax than detached villas or houses as the tax is on the *urbanización* or apartment block as a whole rather than on individuals. Maintenance of the communal areas will be taken care of for you. However, there will be rules and regulations that you may well feel to be intrusive and unnecessary and being part of a community of strangers may not suit everyone. Talk to other owners before committing to buy a community property. Try and get a feel of any infighting or power struggles that may be ongoing among the community. Meet the neighbours. Are they your kind of people?

If you are buying in one of the main cities or towns away from the *costas* your neighbours are more than likely going to be Spanish and, depending on your reasons for buying in Spain, being part of a community is a great way to meet the locals and improve your command of the language. However, it is as well to remember that to the locals you will always be a foreigner, however long you live among them, and this will lessen any influence that you might like to have when it comes to the AGM and trying to change or have an affect on the running of the community. Voting rights at these meetings are also affected by the proportion of the community fees the individual owner pays – the more you pay the more clout you have in these meetings.

Meetings. At the AGM an elected President presides over the proceedings, often aided by an elected secretary, treasurer and/or an elected committee depending on the size of the *comunidad*. You should be notified well in advance of the date of these meetings and are advised to attend them as all decisions taken will affect every member of the *comunidad*. Complaints and suggestions will be dealt with and voted on at the meetings so your vote will count. If you cannot attend a meeting, then choose another of the owners to vote for you by proxy. Just like any other meeting where people's lives can and are affected by forces beyond their control these AGMs can be heated affairs. Disagreements and arguments can break out over the necessity of paying for things that a minority don't want or, in the case of non-residents, having to pay the full yearly fees when the property may only be used for a fraction of a year.

Charges. Depending on the size of the community an Administrator of Properties (*Administrador de Fincas*) may be appointed to deal with the necessary payments for communal services within the complex or apartment block and to prepare the annual accounts to be presented at the AGM.

The community charges (*cuotas*) payable by the individual owners will vary depending on the services used, amenities taken advantage of, together with the size of the individual's apartment or villa. It may be as little as €50 a month but is likely to be more. The community fees are not affected by whether an owner is a full-time or part-time resident in Spain and the amount payable will be stated in the *escritura*, though the annual fees will obviously change year by year. You will need to find out when such payments are due and if you are not resident in Spain, set up a standing order to pay them. Failure to pay community fees by one or more of the owners can lead to all sorts of problems within the *comunidad*, such as being unable to pay its debts or provide some services. The actions of such debtors led to a new law being introduced in 1999 whereby action can be taken against debtors and, in extreme cases, the debtor's property may be auctioned off to reclaim fees due on it. This law can see owners in the dock within 3 months for non-payment of community fees. Because rulings on fees are passed on a majority vote during the AGM, you will have to pay whatever the majority decides upon.

When entering into a contract of sale on a community property ask to see the former owner's community fee receipts for the last few years to make sure that they have been paid and that you won't be inheriting any debts on the property, and also to give you some idea of the fee increase over the years. Occurrences such as a repaint job on the whole block or structural repairs, though rare, will call for an additional payment should they occur during your ownership of the property.

Those who buy a house in the country or, say, a detached house in a town street, will not have to get involved in a *comunidad de propietarios*.

VILLAS

There are plenty of villas along the Spanish coastline that are purpose-built for holiday use. A detached villa will sell for more than an equivalent-sized ordinary house in town but will give more privacy as villas tend to be set in their own grounds. Buying a villa is usually a straightforward business as long as the Land Registry has details of any alterations or additions that have been made to the property since the last *escritura* was signed. If such changes have not been registered then delays are likely to occur while negotiations take place between your lawyers and the Town Hall. If extensive alterations have been made to the villa and not registered (say a large conservatory added, or an outhouse converted into a dwelling) then there may be fines to pay and, in the worst-case scenario, even a demand by the authorities for the property to be returned to the state as declared in the *escritura*.

Villas, though they offer a great deal of privacy – depending on location of course, and whether they are set back from the road – lack the security of a flat or a detached house on an *urbanización*. Many of the things to take into consideration when looking to buy a villa are similar to those when looking at old houses (see above). Check out the location of any prospective purchase carefully. Is the villa situated in an area where seasonal tempests or sand storms may cover the house, your car, swimming pool and tennis court in layers of dust? Most villas are relatively modern and you are unlikely to have much problem with access to water, electricity and telephone connections and drainage.

Buying a villa will not involve you becoming a member of a *comunidad de propietarios* unless the villa is part of a resort complex.

TOWN HOUSES

Town Houses in the towns and villages can be a good buy and an excellent way to get absorbed into Spanish life instead of peering at it through binoculars from a detached villa in the hills. Houses in villages and towns tend to have shady, rather dark rooms with small patio areas at the back of the property. Properties in the centre of villages are generally joined together in rows along the streets and lanes and may come with roof terraces – especially in the south of Spain. It is advisable to get a surveyor to check these houses as they are often of quite an age and may need rewiring, or to have the old water pipes replaced, or have some structural work done to the supporting walls or the roof. These houses in the villages and towns can have a great deal of character, far more than the modern developments and bring the added bonus of placing you right in the heart of Spanish life.

URBANIZACIÓNES

If you visit any property exhibition you will come across a number of different *urbanizaciónes*, with a wide variety of properties on offer – from studio and duplex apartments to semi-detached houses and detached villas on huge landscaped estates. You will also come across a number of different purchasing options available to the prospective buyer – timeshare, leaseback and outright sale.

Urbanizaciónes are akin to housing estates – rows of housing (often of an attractive design) running along the crest of a hill or along a beach, or on the outskirts of town. Some are beautifully designed and well run while others may appear bland to the discerning buyer. Because beach frontage property is now at a premium in Spain it may well be worth investing in an *urbanización* further inland. If you decide to buy into an *urbanización* away from the beaches or without a sea view you are going to get a lot more for you money in terms of the size of the property and the amount of surrounding land.

Some *urbanizaciónes* are part of towns and villages while others may have been developed around a marina or golf course (which may mean that they are away from communication centres and correspondingly may become rather desolate places out of season – beware). You may find developments that appear to be entirely populated by one nationality, or are very insular, or where everyone clusters around the communal swimming pool and makes for the local bar every evening – giving a feeling of homely community where you will meet and become life-long friends with people like yourself. Owners of properties on *urbanizaciónes* may be mainly retirees, or the majority may only visit for a few weeks a year leaving the place a bit of a ghost-town for much of the rest of the time. All things appeal to all people and it will be difficult to be certain of what the particular atmosphere of a place will be without spending some time there first. Life is a gamble, but it pays to try and stack the odds as much in your favour as possible.

The advantages of *urbanizaciónes* are that they can make for a ready made social circle, security will be less of a problem if there are friendly neighbours always milling around, and through them cheaper properties can be found in otherwise expensive areas. It is also likely to be easier to sell on such properties. The disadvantages of *urbanizaciónes* are the possibility of higher community charges for maintenance of the estate (you will be part of a *comunidad de propietarios* – see above), a lack of privacy and space, and the worry of difficult or noisy or boring neighbours.

Urbanizaciónes have sprung up all over Spain since the beginning of the tourist invasion of the 1960s. These developments grew up to cater not only for foreigners looking to buy holiday homes but also for Spaniards, many of whom own second homes where they go at weekends and during holidays to escape the confines of an apartment in the city. *Urbanizaciónes* vary considerably in the size of the development, the grandiosity of the flats or villas built on it, the infrastructure (lighting, roads, gardens, pools etc.) and the way the *comunidad de propietarios* is run.

Many, though not all, of the *urbanizaciónes* built along the *costas* are marketed to attract foreign buyers. As the prime beach frontage along the Costa del Sol, the Costa Brava and the Costa Blanca has run out, new developments, with all the associated marketing and promotional activity, have been built along the Costa Calida in Almería and the Costa de la Luz in south-west Spain – areas previously overlooked due to lacking the natural beauty and closeness to the 'action' of the more celebrated *costas*. These newly developed *costas* are at present good places to look for property.

TIME SHARE

If you, like many others, are looking for a low cost alternative to purchasing property outright, then timeshare is well worth looking into but get the advice of an independent lawyer before signing anything or handing over any money. Timeshares have had a very bad reputation in the past, with touts practically kidnapping tourists off the streets and dragging them along to presentations where they have been subjected to very high-pressure sales tactics. Cunning psychological tricks have been played on the 'punters' where they have been unable to think rationally and have come away from presentations having parted with far too much money for overpriced and low quality properties. Insult has then been added to injury when further tranches of cash have been demanded for annual maintenance costs. The punter is stuck in a binding contract of ten years or so with a timeshare virtually impossible to swap or sell. However, it must be stressed that only the bad stories about timeshare come to light, and many people are very satisfied with the deal they've got on a timeshare. In addition, figures show that the timeshare market is expanding at around 10% a year.

Timeshare involves paying a sum of money over an agreed number of years for the use of a property for a certain number of weeks at a certain time of the year. The buyer must also pay an annual maintenance fee. The benefit to the buyers of a timeshare is that they gain the use of a self-catering property for a reasonable rate, as well as having the upkeep and maintenance of the property looked after by the management company. The timeshare operators also benefit because if they can find enough people willing to take up the offer of the use of an apartment or villa every week of the year, and pay a certain amount of money for the privilege, they will recoup the cost of building and development many times over during the course of a 15-20 year contract. On top of this they will also charge management and maintenance fees (expect to pay up to £500 annually).

There are risks involved with timeshare, but then there are risks involved in buying any property. The property may not even be built yet, or the photographs you are shown of a property may be totally misleading. You will be shown an apartment or building and promised that you will have access to it if you sign up. One scam is to sign up far more customers than there are properties, and then to disappear once the customers start to complain.

Timeshare is still a popular and relatively cheap way of acquiring (admittedly only the use of) a property in areas that would otherwise be too expensive to buy into, for a few weeks of the year. However, because other people will be using the property for most of the year, it will never feel like it is yours. The average timeshare costs from £3,000 to £12,000.

Since 1998 timeshare operators have been subject to EU regulations which demand that should you agree to a timeshare purchase you are given a 'cooling off' period of ten days allowing you to pull out of a contract before any monies are paid. There are also restrictions on 'touting' in public areas, and contracts and publicity material must be printed in the mother tongue of the prospective purchaser. The contract should give the identity and address of the sellers, and all the costs involved, the location and description of the property, and the number of weeks a year you can use it. Be aware that if you pay a non-returnable deposit this will be lost if you walk away from the deal. It is important to be fully informed of management fees payable on a property as these can add considerably to the initial outlay, and it is a good idea to talk to other timeshare owners before committing yourself.

Timeshare apartments and villas are often part of a large development or resort rather than detached. Because you will not, as a timeshare holder, be eligible to join the *comunidad de propietarios* you will have no say in the running of the property or any control over the community fees charged, or those charged by the management company. Unfortunately, the resale value on timeshare is not very high and unless you have bought into a property in a sought-after area you are unlikely to recoup the price that you initially paid.

Checking up on Timeshare Dealers. Because of the low resale value, a timeshare can be bought for less than half the original asking price, so there is little purpose in buying a new one. Resale timeshares are sometimes advertised in *Dalton's Weekly* and *Exchange & Mart*. There are also professional dealers who take timeshares off your hands at a low price to resell. You should not agree to pay any fees to such dealers up-front – they could be thousands of miles away by the time you try to catch up with them. Dealers that resell timeshares should be members of the *Organisation for Timeshare in Europe (OTE)*, the official trade association for the industry in Europe, which has a website at www.ote-info.com. You can look at the *Timeshare Consumers' Association (TCA)* website at www.timeshare.org.uk to see if there have been any complaints about any particular timeshare company. Tenerife resorts at present are alive with some fairly dodgy timeshare operators and the *Office of Fair Trading* (www.oft.gsi.gov.uk) is acting on new EU legal directives to try and combat businesses that are harmful to consumer interests; timeshare companies are included in this.

Other Timeshare Options. Once timeshare became popular in Spain and Florida, many people decided they would like to exchange their timeshare with someone else, so timeshare exchange clubs such as *Resort Condominiums International* (www.rci.com) came about. There are membership fees for these clubs, and costs involved with arranging an exchange. Timeshare weeks are graded as 'low', 'medium' and 'high' season; a week in 'low' season cannot be exchanged for one in 'high' season without extra payment.

Some timeshare operators now run options where holidays can be taken in various properties owned by the management group around the world. Depending on the value of the property (based on points given for type of contract and the value of the property) it is also possible to swap properties.

If you are interested in looking into timeshare properties it is a good idea to make contact with the *Timeshare User's Group* (www.tug2.net) whose website provides information on the possible pitfalls as well as the benefits of buying into a timeshare.

HOLIDAY PROPERTY BONDS AND HOLIDAY CLUBS

Given the bad reputation of timeshare, other similar schemes have been thought up which claim not to be timeshare. One of these is HPBs – Holiday Property Bonds. You pay a sum of money, of which most (around 75%) is invested into a portfolio of properties, and the rest in management fees. In return for your investment you are allocated points. Provided you have accrued enough points you can stay in one of the properties offered by the bond company. The positive side of the HPB is that you will be staying in well-managed properties, though you will still have to pay a user's fee for cleaning and maintenance. The downside is much the same as with timeshare – the property is never yours and you may make a loss if you decide to sell your HPB. These are suitable schemes if you take several short holidays a year and are prepared to take potluck about where you go.

More downmarket are Holiday Clubs or Travel Clubs, which promise holidays for life for a lump sum payment, with even bigger risks than timeshare. The most common scam is to tell thousands of people that they have won a free holiday, and charge them to attend a presentation. There are endless horror stories about holiday clubs and they should be treated with extreme caution.

SALE AND LEASEBACK

Leaseback is a certain type of contract whereby you can buy a property from a developer at a reduced price, which may be as much as a third off the cost price of a similar property. In return for this saving the property is leased back to the developer for a set number of years. The developer then takes up the cost of furnishing, managing and the maintenance of the property over the lease period and rents out the property to holidaymakers as self-catering accommodation. The purchaser retains the right to use the property over a certain number of weeks during the year, and is the registered owner of the property – named as such on the *escritura*.

This scheme is more likely to be found in upmarket, rather than bargain basement, properties and is an option worth considering should you only want the use of a holiday home, without the complications of maintenance or having to find tenants when the property is empty. It may be a good option for someone deep into a career at home but hoping to eventually retire to Spain. As with all schemes it is necessary to get a lawyer to check contracts for hidden charges or grey areas that may cause problems later on when the leaseback period comes to an end and you gain the full possession of you property. Leaseback makes sense if you have the initial capital to put into a property and are not in a rush to become a full-time resident of Spain.

CO-OWNERSHIP

If you cannot afford to buy a property (or have found a property that is far beyond your means) an option worth considering is getting friends or family to come in on the deal with you. You will be able to buy a larger property in a location that otherwise would have been far too expensive and, because of the reduced cost, there may be no need to enter into mortgage agreements. Or if you are more interested in saving money, you could first buy the property yourself and then offer shares or part-ownership to relatives, friends and perhaps even friends of friends. Shares in such arrangements do not necessarily even have to be equal.

> Buying a property between several people can be beneficial to all those involved as long as everyone is happy with the contract and the periods of use of the property are settled well in advance. Use of the property by the investors/owners will need to be sorted out amicably as there will be times, such as at the height of the high season and/or over the Christmas or Easter holidays, when everyone will want to use the property.

If the owners want to live in the property full-time then, depending on the size and the possibilities of the property it may be possible for several families to live in a house that has been divided into individual apartments. If you and your potential co-owners decide to buy a cheaper property it could work out very well and be a very cheap holiday home when you take into consideration the low cost of flights to Spain.

Some of those who decide to co-own a property in Spain buy through a company set up in Spain for this purpose. The names of all the co-owners will appear on the *escritura*. However, one of the main stumbling blocks of this kind of ownership is the question of what would happen in the eventuality of one of the consortium wishing to sell their share of the property. A good lawyer will be able to draw up a contract that should be acceptable to all parties. When one of the consortium wishes to sell, it is usual for the others to have first refusal of the share of the property, however, how this is worked out will depend on the contract drawn up between the group. Another problem that may be encountered is if one of the owners wishes to sub-let or rent out their portion of the property, or the time allotted for their use of the property. These factors and possible areas of friction will much depend on the dynamics of the group of owners.

Some property developers offer schemes whereby four co-owners buy a property with the right for each owner to use it for three months a year, with the developer continuing to manage the property. However, such schemes are invariably more expensive that buying privately and the total cost of the 'package' will benefit the developer rather than the buyers, who will be charged a higher price for the property than would a single buyer.

RETIREMENT VILLAGES

The over-55 age group make up over 50% of the total number of foreign owners of property in Spain. However, this fact, so far, is not reflected in the number of retirement homes being built in the country, perhaps because Spaniards tend to look after their aged relatives in the family home and there is a fear of the costs involved in staffing such places. Although medical provision for the elderly in Spain is good and often free to those over 65, the lack of residential care leads many retirees to eventually return home when they become less capable of living an independent life. This gap in the market has led some developers to build top-end retirement homes and sheltered housing with 24-hour medical facilities on site, particularly along the Costa del Sol around Marbella and along the Costa Blanca. These properties have much the same features as similar outfits back home – swimming pools, restaurants, medical block, shopping centre, gym etc., and as with *urbanizaciónes* there are additional service charges payable (around €30-€80 per month) on top of the purchase price of the flat.

Depending of what you are looking for – whether you are happy to live out your last years away from your family back home – nursing costs in Spain are likely to be lower and residential nursing homes far more appealing than those in, for instance, the UK. If you are only a temporarily resident in Spain you may even be able to generate some income by renting out a sheltered property to senior citizens back home in need of a bit of sun.

One such residential resort home, with 24-hour medical service, being advertised at the time of going to press was *Sol Andalusí* (C/Don Cristian 2-4, Edificio Málaga Plaza, Oficina 101, 29007 Málaga; ☎ 952 640 642; fax 952 070 750; www.solandalusi.com). Another is *Sanyres* (www.sanyres.com), part of the Prasa Property Group (avd. Gran Capitan No. 2, 14008 Córdoba; ☎ 957 475 676; www.grupoprasa.es), with residential homes in Puerto Banús, Córdoba, A Coruña, Madrid and Logroño, and others being developed along the Costa del Sol, Valencia, Huelva and Alicante. *Palazzo Vivaldi* (www.overseashomesearch.co.uk) is a purpose built retirement development at Roquetas de Mar on the Costa Almería. One or two bedroom flats in the 132 flat complex are available with medical cover to UK buyers over the age of 55. There is a swimming pool, sauna, gym, bar and restaurant attached to the complex. Service charges are approximated £65/€100 per month while the medical cover costs an additional £19/€30 per month. A one bedroom flat costs around £58,250, while a two bedroom apartment starts at £78,700.

APARTMENTS IN HOTELS

Another option for those looking to sink capital into property in Spain is buying a flat in a hotel. For those with a fair amount of disposable income a luxury apartment in a top-end hotel can be had, normally under a 100-day a year letting scheme which, if your flat is occupied by tenants over that period, should more than cover running costs. These hotels arrange to rent out the apartment during periods when you are abroad or living elsewhere. In this way, the responsibility of the flat is left with the hotel meaning that there is no need to worry about security, the payment of utility bills etc. This option might appeal to older people looking for the 24-hour amenities that a hotel offers, or those looking to get into the rental market.

Maintenance fees will need to be paid on such properties but these generally also cover the use of all the hotel's facilities. Because you can use the property whenever you want this option, though much more expensive, is far more appealing than timeshare, and some of the initial investment can be offset by income generated from letting the property. The one caveat is that if the hotel goes bust things could get tricky. You should still own the freehold of the flat, but if the services were cut off then you would be left with an unrentable and uninhabitable property. As with all the various property options available make sure that you are happy with the contracts and have them checked by an independent lawyer.

RENTING A HOME IN SPAIN

CHAPTER SUMMARY

- Rents on short-term accommodation will be at their highest in July and August (and often over Christmas and Easter), and at their lowest in late autumn and over the winter.
- Advertisements in Spanish newspapers for property to let are listed under *Alquileres*.
- Spanish renting and letting laws were extensively updated with the enforcement of regulations passed in 1985. These were further revised in the Rent Law of January 1995.
- Short-term leases (for a period of six months or less) are known as *por temporada*, while long lets, which generally give tenants more rights than a short-term let, are known as *viviendas*.
- When you sign a contract for a long-term let you will usually need to pay between one and three month's rent as a deposit or bond to cover damages to the property.
- When renting a property within a 'community of owners' it is important to get a copy of the deed establishing this communal ownership and to become familiar with the rules of the community.
- Short-term lets differ from longer lets in that the rental price will usually include all utilities such as electricity, gas and water.

RENTING PROPERTY

There are thousands of apartments and villas for rent in Spain, available both through commercial agents and through private owners. For those hunting around for property to buy and who intend to live in Spain permanently it is always a good idea to initially rent for a while just in case you find that the reality of Spanish life doesn't quite meet up to your expectations. Renting property means a less permanent commitment and will allow you time to make up your mind about where you want to live, to see if you like the area, the climate and the amenities and decide what kind of property will suit your needs. If you are thinking about buying a holiday villa or apartment remember that such properties are mainly purpose-built for summer only residence, and that even in the south of Spain winter can still be a bit chilly. Marble floors can be unpleasantly frigid on the feet over the winter months, the walls not particularly thick, and anyone considering buying one of these holiday properties with an idea to moving in permanently should spend a winter renting such a property first before buying.

The disadvantage of Spanish rentals generally is that, price-wise, they can be fairly exorbitant, with prices in sought-after locations such as Mallorca starting at a minimum of €800 per month. Rents in Madrid and San Sebastián are uniformly expensive, and to live in one of the more affluent suburbs of Barcelona you would be looking at about €4,500 a month or more for a spacious two or three-bedroom house. Prices in these places are comparable to London. Prices will depend on the size of the property, the time of year, and the location – beach and golf properties command premium rates and as elsewhere the cheapest rents are to be found in the smaller towns and villages inland away from the coasts. Rents on short-term accommodation will be at their highest in July and August (and often over Christmas and Easter), and at their lowest in late autumn and over the winter.

RENTAL AGENTS

Major tour operators like *Thomson* (www.thomson-holidays.com) and *First Choice* (www.firstchoice.co.uk) offer many such longer-term stays, and in particular cater for older people. The *Spanish Tourist Office* (22-23 Manchester Square, London W1U 3PX; ☎ 020-7486 8077; www.tourspain.co.uk) can supply on request a list of many companies which offer self-catering holidays in villas, apartments and rural houses. In some resort areas it can be harder to find a long-term rental due in part to the high demand for such properties but also because property owners prefer the higher returns they can get from short-term holiday lets.

Rental Agencies will ask for an extra month's rent in advance, plus a commission for the agency service itself (usually of an additional month's rent). This way of searching for an apartment tends be more expensive, but offers more security and is a way to avoid the interminable search for the 'right' place. Many rentals which are part of an apartment block or *urbanización* work on the *comunidad* principle where communal facilities (and some bills) are shared. Tenants pay a monthly fee for the maintenance of services and therefore need to be aware of these charges in advance.

Advertisements

You will find advertisements offering property for rent in the property magazines listed in the *Buying a Home in Spain* chapter, in local area newspapers, and even national newspapers and magazines, both in Spain and at home. Some estate agents handle properties for rent as well as for sale and many estate agents now market themselves through the Internet. A quick search on the web using a search engine such as google (www.google.com) will bring up a number of sites offering short- and long-term rents all over Spain. Websites about a specific area or region often have links to sites offering rental accommodation and many owners of property now have their own website in order to attract customers.

There are many companies offering self-catering holiday lets though these will invariably work out to be more expensive that renting privately as such companies are looking for a high turnover of clients throughout the high season rather than longer-term tenants. Although these companies may offer out of season lets at a cheaper rate, such lets are often impractical for those seeking to remain in one area for some time as the rental period is only as long as the low – winter – season.

As elsewhere when looking for a place to rent, personal recommendation and the 'friend-of-a-friend' approach may be the best way of avoiding unexpected problems, as well as helping you to find the best deal. The locals may well know of someone who has accommodation available for rent. Check the noticeboards of local supermarkets and churches and bars where expats congregate. Clubhouses on golf courses, shops in marinas and kiosks also often have small noticeboards, which may turn up a suitable property.

One of the best places to look is in the small ad sections of local newspapers (both the Spanish papers and the English-language papers), and free sheets. If you find a property that sounds good be prepared to act quickly – buy the newspaper in the morning of that day that it is published and make contact with the person who has placed the advertisement immediately to organise a time to view the property. Advertisements in Spanish newspapers for property to let are listed under *Alquileres.*

TENANCY LAWS

Spanish renting and letting laws were extensively updated with the enforcement of regulations passed in 1985. These were revised in the Rent Law of January 1995. These regulations have ended some very strict forms of tenant protection, which included what was in effect the tenant's right to an indefinitely extendable rental contract. This situation was regarded as unfair to landlords and made many owners think twice about renting out their property. Rents in some circumstances can now be raised by more than the cost of living index. However, there are still some third-generation Spanish families in Madrid paying these low protected rents for downtown apartments.

The new legislation means that the rights of tenants are very similar to those in Britain, with some additional protection that stops landlords raising the rent unfairly. When a rental contract specifies that the rental period ends, for example, in July, it means just that. All tenants now have the right to renew their tenancy for an initial minimum period of five years and if a tenant fails to vacate the property when the temporary contract expires, the owner does not have the right to evict if a renewal has been sought. Therefore, a landlord must offer a tenant a new contract, which can either be temporary or long-term. It used to be that landlords could raise the rent as much as they liked in the process, however, the present situation is that most annual rent rises are in line with inflation and the Consumer Price Index (IPC), which is rarely more than 3% to 4%.

Arrangements are often administered by a rental agency and payments are made to the agency. In Spain as elsewhere all evictions involve the rather time-consuming and costly (for the landlord) process of getting a court order first, but it is the responsibility of a tenant to give one month's clear notice before the end of a contract or he or she may have to pay compensation to the landlord.

There is provision for a tenant to pay a deposit of one month's rent for unfurnished accommodation, or two months for furnished accommodation. This would be lodged with the local Autonomous Community. Additional guarantees may also be negotiated.

THE RENTAL CONTRACT

A rental contract is a prerequisite to renting any kind of property in Spain and you will find that both short- and long-term lets are available. Short-term leases (for a period of six months or less) are known as *por temporada*, while long lets, which generally give tenants more rights than a short-term let, are known as *viviendas*. Longer-term contracts often require tenants living in blocks of flats to pay *comunidad* fees. However, if these charges are not mentioned in the contract then they are wholly the landlord's responsibility and the tenant is under no obligation to pay them or to have them imposed subsequently.

All long-term tenants are legally required to take out house insurance on the property they are renting. The choice of which insurance company to take out a policy with is entirely his or her own decision and cannot be dictated by the landlord.

Contracts are drawn up through the standard, state-sponsored tenant/landlord agreements which are available from street kiosks and *estancos*: it is really your responsibility as the tenant to obtain one of these and to make sure the contract type matches the rent you will be paying, as contracts vary. A contract will include personal details of the tenant and the landlord together with information about the property (location, size, and inventory of furnishings, fittings etc.), the terms of the lease and payment and expenses details. It is advisable to have the contract checked by a solicitor or someone who really knows about rentals before signing. The written contract should clearly state the amount of rent payable and when the tenant should pay it (usually within the first five days of every month). Many rental contracts ask for rent to be paid by direct debit into the landlord's bank account.

> When you sign a contract for a long-term let you will usually need to pay between one and three month's rent as a deposit or bond to cover damages to the property. When the contract is terminated the deposit is returned in full or in part depending on the state of the property. Sometimes the tenant and landlord may agree to use up the deposit in lieu of rent at the end of a lease. You will need to agree on whether the landlord or tenant pays rates, the property tax (IBI) and community fees and you will almost certainly have to pay the bills for electricity, water, gas and the telephone. It is advisable to ask to see previous bills for the property to give you an idea of how much you will need to pay each month and also to make sure that all utility charges have been paid up to date.

The landlord's obligations include maintaining the property in good order and offering the services stated in the contract. Anyone who feels that they have a complaint to make regarding their rental contract can – surprisingly – apply to the local tourist office. This is more suitable for those in short-lets, while semi-permanent and permanent tenants will do better to enquire at the nearest OMIC (*Oficina Municipal de Información al Consumidor*) – the consumer information office run by the local government or Autonomous Community. Although the OMIC's function is primarily to deal with consumer problems, they will be able to put you in contact with the most effective place to register a formal rental complaint.

Communal Apartment Blocks

Many apartments for rent in Spain are part of a block of flats or *urbaniza-*

ción which work on the *comunidad de propietarios* (community of owners) principle, similar to the concept of *copropriété* in France. Both concepts involve the sharing of certain communal facilities (e.g. swimming pool, car park, garden areas), towards the upkeep of which tenants pay a monthly fee. This fee covers such costs as stair cleaning, rubbish disposal, garden maintenance, etc., and the level of the fee varies according to the size of the flat: the smarter and larger the flat, the more you pay. This fee can be as high as £150 (€230) a month for the more upmarket apartment blocks.

When renting a property within a 'community of owners' as it is known, it is important to get a copy of the deed establishing this communal ownership (called the Deed of Horizontal Division) and to become familiar with the rules of the Community. A meeting of all residents (owners *and* tenants) of these communal apartment blocks is usually held once or twice a year to plan the following year's budget, elect representatives, and to discuss maintenance, refurbishment and the like. It is your legal duty to attend these meetings, which are also a useful way to meet the neighbours, or an interminable waste of time, depending to your point of view.

On leaving a property at the end of a lease the landlord will check the inventory of the contents of the property and has the right to charge the tenant from the deposit for any missing items or breakages. Note, however, that the landlord is obliged to replace and repair items such as water heaters, kitchen appliances and washing machines, at a cost to himself, that have broken through general wear and tear. Additionally, when you leave a rented property the landlord may levy a charge for cleaning.

Short-Term Lets

Short-term lets differ from longer lets in that the rental price will usually include all utilities such as electricity, gas and water. Renting for longer than a month may have reduced weekly rates but you may have to pay utility bills separately.

You will usually be required to sign a contract and pay a deposit in order to secure a property. Before you hand over any money or sign the contract, check the terms and conditions of the property rental very carefully. The deposit may be refundable either in whole or in part up to one month before your booking. However, if you cancel within a month of your booking, the deposit is rarely returned. Some travel insurance policies may refund your deposit if you have to cancel your accommodation owing to unforeseen circumstances such as family illness but others may not. Before you can move into a property you are usually required to pay for the rental accommodation in full, although if your rental is for longer than four weeks you may be able to pay in monthly instalments. Depending on how long you will be staying you may also be required to pay a deposit in case of breakages or damage to the property. If the property needs extra cleaning after you have left, the deposit may be used to pay for this otherwise, all being well, the deposit will be returned to you after you have moved out of the property. If you are booking a short-term let from outside Spain check that the company or individual you're planning to book through is reputable before parting with any money/deposits etc. Be wary of parting with large sums of money to unidentifiable individuals.

Useful Addresses

Casa Paraíso: ☎ 616 374 973/0870-128 9000; www.rent-in-spain.com. Rentals in Torrevieja on the Costa Blanca.

Holiday-Rentals.com Ltd: Westpoint, 34 Warple Way, London W3 0RG; ☎ 020-8743 5577; fax 020-8740 3863; www.holiday-rentals.com. Holiday homes booked direct through the owner. Over 1,500 properties.

Interhome Ltd: 383 Richmond Road, Twickenham, Surrey TW1 2EF; ☎ 020-8891 1294; fax 020-8891 5331; www.interhome.co.uk.

Masiarentals: Can Mercé de la Penya, Apartado 82, Calle Can Mercé de la Penya, Can Lloses Can Mercer, 08810 San Pere de Ribes, Barcelona; ☎ 938 964 933; fax 679 900 679; www.masiarentals.com. Restored Masia guesthouse a few miles from inland from Sitges on the Costa Dorada.

Spanish Retreats Ltd: 1-2 Terminus Road, Littlehampton, Sussex BN17 5BS; ☎ 01903 722 234; fax 01903 722 235; www.daydreamvillas.co.u k. Winters lets and B&B in private villas.

Villa Spain: ☎ 01424 420 575; fax 01424 420 576; www.villaspain.co.uk. Selection of privately owned villas and apartments for rent on the Costa Blanca from Calpe to Moraira.

Villas Ferrer: PO Box 39, Carrer del Pont 22, 03700 Denia, Costa Blanca; ☎ 965 780 263; fax 965 788 621; www.villasferrer.com. Winter and spring rentals on the Costa Blanca.

Villas Spain Rentals: 18 Wellright Road, Fairwater, Cardiff; www.villas-spain-rentals.com.

Fees, Contracts and Conveyancing

CHAPTER SUMMARY

- **Conveyancing**. The total overall costs of conveyancing will be around 10% of the cost price of a resale property in mainland Spain, and between 7-9% on such properties in the Canary Islands.
  - For new properties, and property that is less than ten years old, the structure will have been guaranteed by the original builders or developers against major structural defects for a decade.
  - Because of the differences in surveying criteria between the UK and Spanish systems you should make sure that you know what should be checked, and discuss with the surveyor what aspects you want checked.
  - For properties that are still under construction at the time of purchase, stage payments will be required during the construction period.
  - The Land Registry (*Catastro*) contains details of the physical and topographical details of a property as well as a valuation.
  - The Property Registry (*Registro de la Propiedad*) holds details of ownership and title.
  - The *notario* witnesses the signing of the title deeds (*escritura*) in his or her office located in the area where the property is being purchased.
  - After the signing of the *escritura*, the payment of the purchase price and all fees, the notary will pass the purchaser a copy (*copia simple*) of the *escritura* and the keys to the property.
  - Consult the town plan (*plan general de ordenación urbana*) at the local town hall, which outlines

the areas that have already been given over to development and where planning permission should be relatively easy and straightforward to obtain.

- **Lawyers.** Vendors of property in Spain will not necessarily need to hire a lawyer, but buyers most certainly will.
  - An independent lawyer should be either a specialist lawyer from home or an English-speaking Spanish *abogado*.
  - In the major Spanish coastal resorts, finding an *abogado* who speaks English will not be a problem.
  - You should get your lawyer to check everything that is put on the table by the agents before signing anything.
  - The fees charged by a lawyer for their work buying a new or resale property are likely to be about 1% of the price of the property, although there may be a minimum charge.

FEES

Total inclusive costs (lawyers, land registry, *notario*, taxes, bank charges, associates fees etc.) bring the overall costs of conveyancing to around 10% of the cost price of a resale property in mainland Spain, and between 7-9% on such properties in the Canary Islands. Tax on new property in mainland Spain is 7%, to which must be added 4% additional fees; in the Canary Islands tax on new property is 4%, with another 4% to pay in additional fees. The cheaper the property the more the likelihood of that percentage rising due to the minimum charges imposed by lawyers and others involved in the conveyancing.

TYPICAL COSTS INVOLVED IN CONVEYANCING

- Notary Fee: for preparation of the title deed (usually around €300-€600).
- Land Registry Fee: dependent on the value of property (around €300).
- *Plus Valia* Tax: paid to the municipality on the transfer of property. It is dependent on the value of the land on which the property sits. The vendor should pay this, but contracts of sale often try to impose the fee on the buyer. It can come to several thousand pounds and is usually around 0.5% on a property that last changed

hands ten years previously.

- VAT/Transfer Tax/Stamp Duty: depends on the value of the property, the type of property and where the property is situated. Usually around 7% of the purchase price on new property.
- Registration with the Spanish Tax Authorities and obtaining a foreigners' identification number (NIE): This can be done by your solicitor for a fee.

EXAMPLE OF COSTS ON THE PURCHASE OF A €125,000 PROPERTY		
Notary Fees	Preparation of *escritura*, registering of ownership, stamp duty	€1,950
Legal Fees	Making searches on registries, preparation of *escritura*, translation of contracts, etc	€1,250
Plus Valia	Capital Gains Tax levied by the Town Hall on increased value of land since last sold	€120
VAT (IVA) 7%	Payable on the declared value of the property	€8,750
Connection Charges	Water, electricity, gas, drainage, telephone	€425
	TOTAL	€12,495
		Fees exclusive of VAT

LAWYERS

Vendors of property in Spain will not necessarily need to hire a lawyer, but as has been stated elsewhere in this book, buyers most certainly will. It is very important to employ an *abogado* to look after your personal interests. A solicitor should check that the vendor of the property is the legal (and sole) owner of the property and whether there are any outstanding charges or bills on it. They should be able to check that the property has or is being built with proper planning permission and has all the necessary licences. They should check that the terms of the contract are fair and reasonable and prepare a report of their findings for the potential buyer's information. Given the go ahead, the solicitor can then arrange for currency to be transferred to Spain, the title deeds (*escritura*) to be transferred into the buyer's name and registered with the Land Registry and for fees and taxes to be paid.

An independent lawyer should be either a specialist lawyer from home or an English-speaking Spanish *abogado.* Be wary of using the services of a lawyer recommended by the vendor or their estate agent, as their impartiality may be, though probably isn't, questionable. Also, should you use a Spanish lawyer, even if they speak fluent English, they may be unfamiliar with UK law and the ramifications that buying a property overseas may have on your tax or legal situation back home.

Most *abogados* are found through recommendation. If your gasp of Spanish is shaky then you should definitely find a lawyer who speaks English. The lawyer will be able to:

- advise a client whose name should be registered as the owner of a property as ownership will have knock-on effects with regards taxation.
- advise on how to pay for the property – whether through a mortgage, re-mortgaging, forming a company, cash, etc., and how to minimise costs.
- arrange for Power of Attorney should it be necessary (see below).
- arrange for the signing of the *escritura* and making purchase payments, and may also be able to organise currency exchange and the transferral of funds from a buyer's home bank account into Spain.
- check that there are no cases pending against the property with regards to planning permission not having been obtained when the property was originally built.
- draw up the contract for the sale of the property or between a builder, architect and client.
- guide a client through the legal processes involved in buying property in Spain.
- look after the conveyancing procedures.
- make payments for the conveyancing costs, taxes etc, on behalf of the buyer.
- obtain an NIE number on behalf of the client (this number is needed for the payment of taxes and the purchase of property in Spain).
- recommend local tradesmen, surveyors, agents, mortgage brokers and banks that will suit a client's needs.

In the major Spanish coastal resorts, finding an *abogado* who speaks English will not be a problem. Lawyers in these areas will be used to dealing with foreigners looking to buy property in their locality and may well advertise their services in local free sheets and the English-language press. They will be well aware of potential areas of conflicting interests and will be able to smooth your way to the best of their ability within the confines of Spanish law.

Get the best legal advice – Lindy Walsh

We used an abogado for the purchase, but it was still fairly traumatic as he was a city lawyer (there weren't any local gestors who spoke English) and didn't know much about laws affecting property such as ours and what licences we needed. For example we got 'denounced' (the Spanish word is denuncia *and refers to being reported to the police by a neighbour for – generally – a minor infraction such as having a dog that barks all night long, or putting up an unsightly satellite dish that 'lowers the tone' of a neighbourhood, etc) to the river police for having a well dug without their permission. We'd got four licences (local town hall, local ministry of the environment, mines, water authority) and he didn't know that within half a kilometre of a dried up riverbed we needed another permit too. He got the hunting laws wrong which led to lots of trouble and he didn't bother to find out about the Andalucian Tourist laws, which affected us greatly, telling us we only had to keep inside the building regulations. For nearly ten years our business was 'illegal' and I am still unable to develop certain aspects that we had planned for back in 1988 and which he had told us would be 'no problem'.*

If you are hoping to buy property with land attached in a rural part of Spain then your lawyer will be useful in finding out about what the planning restrictions are in the area and if there are local bylaws in force with regards to water, grazing or hunting and access rights on the land. You will also want your lawyer to check out where property boundaries end and begin as these may differ from what has been written in the *escritura*, what the owners of the property believe, and what is registered in the Land Registry. If you are buying into an *urbanización* or an apartment block where you will be part of the *comunidad de propietarios* you will also want the rules and regulations checked by a lawyer.

You should get your lawyer to check everything that is put on the table by the agents before signing anything. Don't rely on a notary to do the work that a lawyer would normally do. Another good reason for getting a lawyer is that they may well be able to advise you on the most financially beneficial way to deal with the conveyancing process, saving you money by guiding you through the taxation systems of Spain and the UK.

It is a good idea to find a lawyer and get their advice before even starting on the house-hunt in Spain. They will be able to give you pointers and tell you about the possible pitfalls. They will also be ready to look at contracts before you sign – you may be able to fax them over while you are in Spain and wait for their appraisal before going ahead and signing and committing yourself to something that you may later regret. Remember that you will need to find either a lawyer from home versed in international law and the laws pertaining to Spanish property in particular, or an English-speaking Spanish lawyer versed in the taxation system of your home country. Without this knowledge a lawyer may not be able to organise your affairs to your best advantage.

Fees. The fees charged by a lawyer for their work on buying a new or resale property are likely to be about 1% of the price of the property, although there may be a minimum charge (perhaps around £1,000). You will need to be aware that apart from the basic fee, should additional negotiations need to be undertaken on your behalf you will be charged. For example there may need to be further clauses added to a contract, or negotiations over the price of a property; if there are irregularities in the *escritura* these will need to be corrected before change of title can take place. There will also be correspondence generated between the solicitors and a mortgage company if you are taking out a mortgage and all these matters will incur further fees.

For properties that have not yet been built, lawyers will generally charge around 1% of the property value plus an hourly rate on work done on your behalf while the construction continues. Because, as in the way of all things, there can never be a 100% definite completion date, more work may need to be done on your behalf as projects and the legalities involved unfold. The solicitor should give you an estimate of the likely charges to be incurred once s/he has seen the existing paperwork relating to the project.

Consulates and embassies in Spain will hold lists of English-speaking lawyers in your locality. In the UK the *Law Society* (113 Chancery Lane, London WC2A 1PL; ☎ 020-7242 1222; www.lawsoc.org.uk) also holds lists of registered English-speaking lawyers in Spain. *The Consejo General de la Abogacia Española* have their headquarters at C/Paseo de Recoletos 13, Madrid 28004; ☎ 915 232 593; fax 915 327 836; www.cgae.es.

Useful Addresses

Altea Lex: Conde de Altea 52, 03590 Altea, Alicante; 966 880 012; fax 966 880 154; www.alteainvest.com/lex/.

Anderson & Asociados Abogados: Centro Dona Pepa Local 1-2 Urb Reserva de Marbella, Ctra. Nac. 340, km. 193,6 Marbella 29600; ☎ 952 932 997; fax 952 934 902; www.andersonabogados.com.

Baily Gibson Solicitors: 5 Station Parade, Beaconsfield, Bucks. HP9 2PG; ☎ 01494 672 661; www.bailygibson.co.uk.

Baker & McKenzie: Paseo de la Castellana 33, Edificio Fenix Planta 6, 28046 Madrid; ☎ 912 304 500. UK Office: 100 New Bridge

Street, London EC4V 6JA; ☎ 020-7919 1000; fax 020-7919 1438; www.bakerinfo.com.

Bennett & Co. Solicitors: 144 Knutsford Road, Wilmslow, Cheshire SK9 6JP; ☎ 01625 586 937; fax 01625 585 362; www.bennett-and-co.com. Associated offices throughout Spain.

Bufete Roca Puig: Avenida Diagonal 506, 5th Floor, 2a, 08006 Barcelona; ☎ 943 158 116; fax 943 151 762.

Champion Miller & Honey Solicitors: 153 High Street, Tenterden, Kent TN30 6JT; ☎ 01580 762 251; fax 01580 764 302.

Cornish & Co.: Lex House, 1/7 Hainault Street, Ilford, Essex IG1 4EL; ☎ 020-8478 3300; fax 020-8552 3418; www.cornishco.com. Spanish office: ☎ 952 866 830; email cornish@mercuryin.es. Gibraltar office: ☎ 41800; email cornish@gibnet.gi.

De Cotta McKenna y Santafé Abogados: Nuñez de Balboa 30, 3rd Floor B, 28001 Madrid; ☎ 914 319 525; fax 915 762 139, also have an office in Málaga. London office: ☎ 020-7353 0998.

De Pinna Notaries: 35 Piccadilly, London W1J 0LJ; ☎ 020-7208 2900; fax 020-7208 0066; www.depinna.co.uk.

Ernst & Young Abogados: Diagonal, 575 L'Illa Diagonal, Barcelona 08029; ☎ 933 663 800; fax 934 397 891.

Euro-Abogados Costa Blanca S.L.: C/Apolo 88-3B, 03180 Torrevieja, Alicante; ☎ 966 703 202; fax 965 712 306. Also has offices in Almería (Urb. Las Buganvillas, local 24, 04620 Vera; ☎ 950 617 017; fax 950 133 342.

Fernando Scornik Gerstein: 32 St. James's Street, 3rd Floor, London SW1A 1HD; ☎ 020-7930 3593; fax 020-7930 3385; www.scornik-gerstein.com. Also has offices in Lanzarote, Madrid, Tenerife and Gran Canaria.

M Florez Valcarcel: 130 King Street, London W6 0QU; tel/fax 020-8741 4867.

Hector Diaz: 14 Old Square, Lincoln's Inn, London WC2A 3UB; ☎ 020-7404 9349; fax 020-7404 9348; www.hectordiaz.co.uk.
Javier de Juan: 36 Greyhound Road, London W6 8NX; ☎ 020-7381 0470; fax 020-7381 4155; www.spanishlaw.org.uk.
Jesús Bello Albertos: N/Sra de García 24, 5B, Marbella, 29600 Málaga; ☎ 952 772 487; fax 952 829 329.
John Howell & Co.: 17 Maiden Lane, London WC2E 7NL; ☎ 020-7420 0400; fax 020-7836 3626; www.europelaw.com.
M Vega Penichet: Alcalá 115, Primera Planta, 28009 Madrid; ☎ 914 315 500; fax 914 315 938; www.mvegapenichet.com.
Ventura Garcés Solicitors: Calle Freixa 26-28 baixos, 08021 Barcelona; ☎ 932 419 740; fax 932 098 391; www.ventura-garces.com. Also have offices in Madrid.

INSPECTIONS AND SURVEYS

It wouldn't be prudent to buy a property in the UK without having it checked over by a qualified surveyor, so it makes sense therefore to get a property that you are interested in buying in Spain surveyed. That said, the surveying of property before purchasing is not a typical Spanish trait and many buy on sight. However, there are always horror stories of people who have bought a flat that looked 'okay' only to find that during the winter months it became flooded; or the hairline crack that they initially noticed but were told wasn't anything structurally damaging worsened year on year. The old adage, 'when in Rome do as the Romans do...' shouldn't apply when it comes to something as financially risky as buying a house. If you are buying a property on a mortgage, the lenders may well require a survey, even if it is only to provide an appraisal of the purchase price.

For new properties, and property that is less than ten years old the structure will have been guaranteed by the original builders or developers as all builders must guarantee their work against major structural defects for a decade. However, should you be buying an older resale property, or even a derelict building that you are hoping to renovate, you would be wise to get a survey done.

When you initially view a property that you are interested in, give it the amateur eye and check for any signs of subsidence, bowing walls, damp patches or strange smells. Check for dry rot (stick a knife into windowsills and other likely areas where damp may have struck), a leaking roof (stains on the ceilings), cracks or fractures in the walls. You will want to make sure that all plumbing, electrics, and water heating systems are in good working order, as well as the drainage and water provision. If there is a well on the land ask the vendor if it has been tested recently. Be on the look out for any signs of rising damp or signs of condensation/humidity. While viewing a property take your time and get the feel of the place – you will usually be able to tell if there are any *major* structural problems.

Expert Opinions. If you are still not sure, you could arrange for a local estate agent (other than the one showing you the property of course) to give their opinion of the place and the price asked. Alternatively a local builder may be able to give their opinion of the structural soundness or otherwise of the property. In any case, should you be looking to buy a derelict property for renovation you will want to get a quote from a few builders as to the likely cost of renovation. A builder will also have local knowledge and be able to comment on the purchase price asked by the vendor. All of these opinions will of course come at a cost but will be worth it to set your mind at rest.

All the above people will be able to give you their 'expert' opinions on whether your desired property is sound or not but they are unlikely to be backed up by a professional report. A trained surveyor on the other hand will be able to cast a professional eye over the property and give you a full and detailed report on it. Such a survey will cost you perhaps £1,000-£1,500 depending on the surveyor and size of property. Spanish surveyors tend to concentrate on different aspects than their British equivalents, although those who are used to dealing with foreigners are likely to provide you with a report similar to what you would expect to get back home. Be sure to get any report that is presented to you in Spanish translated into English. Alternatively, you will find British RICS qualified surveyors such as Andrew Tuckett, (☎ 649 961 630; email atuckett@terra.es.) or *Gibsons* (urb Bahia Azul 75, Estepona, Málaga; ☎ 952 794 628; www.gibsons-spain.com) who may have moved to Spain and are able to carry out professional surveys and valuations. These surveyors will often advertise their services in the local English-language newspapers and property magazines. Although they will be able to give you a sound structural analysis of the property, unless they have the equivalent Spanish chartered surveying training they will be unable to advise on certain aspects such as building regulations.

Because of the differences in surveying criteria between the UK and Spanish systems you should make sure that *you* know what should be checked and discuss with the surveyor what aspects you want checked. Prices, as already stated, are negotiable. Note that most vendors will not sign any contract of sale with a 'subject to survey' clause. They are more likely to demand that you arrange a survey – at your own expense – before they sign anything. Should another interested party come along and sign a contract with the vendor before you have been able to satisfy yourself as to the soundness of the property, you will have lost out on the chance to buy.

CONVEYANCING

Contracts

Once you have found the right property, you will probably have to act swiftly to ensure that you get it, as at present there is a sellers market in Spain – the property market is booming. However, never sign anything without having first sought independent legal advice. If there is for some reason such a pressing time limit that you may lose a property that you are interested in unless you sign NOW, then at least try to fax over a copy of the contract to your legal representatives. Contracts are often short, containing the details of the vendor and purchaser, the purchase price, a legal description of the property, the date set for completion and possession of the property and the type of payment involved in the sale.

Purchase contracts for resale/new properties

When you are satisfied that the property won't be falling down in the near future, having been able to negotiate a structural survey, or you have decided, 'to hell with the expense, it's what I've always wanted…' then you will be ready to sign contracts with the vendor. Note that there may be potential tax advantages as well as other savings at a later stage by registering the property in the joint names of a wife and husband or partner, or in the name of your child or children, or in the name of the person who will stand to inherit the property, or in the name of a limited company.

There are three differing types of contract that you may be asked to sign at this stage:

- **Offer to Buy**: A formal offer to buy the property at a fixed price – the contract being valid for a set period of time. Should the vendor accept your offer then a non-returnable, negotiable, deposit will be payable and the contract will become binding between the two parties.
- **Reservation Contract**: An agreement between the potential buyer of a property and the vendor or estate agent. This type of contract dictates that the property is taken off the market for a set period of time. A reservation fee is paid by the potential buyer, which, if a full contract to buy is signed within the set period, will count toward the full price of the property to be paid. If problems concerning the

property are unearthed during the reservation period (such as the vendor not being the named owner on the *escritura*) and the potential buyer decides to pull out then the reservation fee will be lost. The clauses in this type of contract, therefore, need to be carefully checked.

- **Private Purchase Contract**: A full and binding contract to buy. You will pay a negotiable deposit of around 10% of the purchase price, the balance to be paid on the signing of the *escritura*. Obviously, before signing such a contract you will want to get your lawyer to check it.

The contract will be prepared by either an estate agent or developer or, if you decide to buy privately from an individual, by the vendor's lawyer. Whichever contract is offered to you, have it presented to you in your mother tongue as well as in Spanish, and make sure that you have your lawyer check it before you sign. There may well be clauses that either you or the vendor will not accept and these will need to be negotiated, as will the purchase price and the amount of deposit payable.

There are strict conditions relating to the repayment of deposits, and make sure that you are informed of these by your lawyer. When paying a deposit ensure that the money is kept by the estate agent or legal representative of the vendor in a bonded account until the sale has gone through. This will guard against a crooked vendor, or estate agent, taking your deposit and then deciding to sell the property to another instead. Though they will be acting illegally, should they do such a thing getting your money back through the courts may take quite a time and will certainly leave a nasty taste in your mouth – perhaps putting you off ever buying in Spain.

Purchase contracts for off-plan properties

For properties that are still under construction at the time of purchase, stage payments will be required during the construction period. It may be possible to arrange the payment schedule to suit the purchaser's individual needs and a typical payment schedule could be as follows:

- **On the signing of the contract:** a deposit of 20% payable by bankers draft, personal cheque, cash, traveller's cheques or credit card.
- **After a set period, or on completion of a certain phase in the building work (e.g. completion of the exterior walls and roof):** 25% of the agreed purchase price.
- **After a set period, or on completion of another phase in the building work (e.g. completion of interior, fitting of interior**

furniture and windows and doors): Another 25% of the agreed purchase price – the timing of this payment may vary and is generally dependent upon the building project completion date.

- **On completion or signing of the *escritura*:** Outstanding balance payable.

With such contracts it is advisable to negotiate a clause in the contract that allows you to withhold a certain percentage of the cost price – say 10% – for a certain period after you have moved into the property as a guarantee against possible defects. This will ensure that the builders will come back to rectify any problems that crop up, and a good firm should be happy to provide this type of insurance. You may also want to alter the specifications of fixtures and fittings, type and style of tiles, faucets, etc., that have been specified by the builders/developers. If you do alter specifications there will be changes needing to be made to the price structure and also to the completion date. Make sure that the developer is the legal owner of the land, has obtained the required building regulations and that the required payments are held in a bonded account until completion and your taking possession of the property.

Checks That Should Be Made On A Property Before Completion

Resale Properties

- Are fittings and/or furniture included in the purchase price?
- Are there any planning restrictions pertaining to the property and/or location which will affect your plans should you wish to build on or alter the property?
- Are there community charges to be paid on the property? Do you understand the statutes of the *comunidad de propietarios*, and are you happy to comply with them?
- Are there restrictions on the uses that can be made of the property?
- Boundaries, access, and public right of way bylaws should be clearly defined and understood.
- Check the *Plan General de Ordenación Urbana* at the town hall to see whether there are going to be future developments (e.g. new lines of communication/building projects, etc.) that may affect the value/ view of the property at a later date.
- Check the description of the property in the Land Registry **and** the Property Registry.
- Check the property is free of any debts or charges; that all utility and community bills, and taxes (including the IBI tax) have been paid

up to date. Remember that debts on a property are 'inherited' by the new owner.

- Has there been a completion of a survey to your satisfaction?
- Has there been any alteration done to the property that has not been registered with the authorities?
- How much are the local taxes and charges?
- Is there adequate water, drainage, electricity and telecommunication provision?
- The vendor is the legal registered owner of the property.

Additional checks that should be made on off-plan and new build property

- A full break-down of the materials, fixtures and fittings used in the building of the property.
- Be clear what you are paying for. What are the finishings? Will the surrounding land be landscaped? What will the property look like (have you seen a show home to gauge this)?
- Make sure that all completion licences (*certificado de fin de obra*, *licencia de primera ocupación*, and the *boletin de instalación*) have been obtained.
- Make sure that the developers or builders have obtained the necessary planning permissions to build upon the land.
- Make sure that the payment schedule and completion date are clear.
- Make sure the developers or builders are the legal owners of the land they are developing.
- Protect yourself and insure against the possibility of the developer or builders going bankrupt before completing the property.
- The property has been registered with the local authorities for real estate taxes.

Additional checks that should be made on the purchase of plots of land for self-build projects

- Will you be given a permit to build (*permiso de obra*) from the town hall?
- How much will it cost to build on the land and can you afford the costs – get quotes from architects and builders?

Registries

The Land Registry (*Catastro*) contains details of the physical and topographical details of a property as well as a valuation, while the Property

Registry (*Registro de la Propiedad*) only holds the details of ownership and title. These two registries may have differing details of the same property and a potential buyer should check that the description of a property in the contract tallies with that in both the Property and Land Registries. It may take a month or so for the Land Registry to provide a *certificado catastral* outlining the boundaries and measurements of a property so you should ask for it as soon as you have found the property of your choice.

The Notary

The Spanish Notary Public – the *notario* – although a lawyer, does not give legal advice to either the vendor or the purchaser of a property. The job of the *notario* is to witness the signing of the title deeds (*escritura*) in his or her office located in the area where the property is being purchased and to deal with other administrative matters. Once the *escritura* has been signed, the purchase price of the property is then handed over to the vendor, or the vendor confirms that payment has already been received. Proof of payment is then noted down in the *escritura* which is then registered in the local Property Register. Before preparing the *escritura* a *notario* will ensure that the purchaser has received the property as stated on the contract and that the vendor has received the correct purchase price. The *notario* will also advise on taxes that are due on the property.

Notaries collect their fees from the vendor and the purchaser and these fees are charged in accordance with a sliding scale of charges set by the Spanish government. These will vary depending on the price of a property and the amount of work the *notario* has done on behalf of the two parties in preparing documents. Note that not all notaries will speak English and you may therefore need to be accompanied to meetings by a Spanish speaker.

Power of Attorney

The person buying or selling a property does not necessarily have to be present when the title deeds are signed in front of the *notario* and, for a fee, a Power of Attorney can be granted which will allow another person to attend on the vendor's behalf instead. If a Power of Attorney has been arranged outside Spain, it will need to be witnessed and stamped by a *notario* in Spain.

THE SIGNING OF THE ESCRITURA

The date of the signing of the *escritura* will have been fixed in the contact to buy, though in reality the date may slip a little depending on the status of the checks on the property made by your lawyer. It should normally take place two to three months after signing the contract to buy a resale or new property but will take longer if you are buying off-plan. If there are problems such as sorting out ownership of the property or outstanding taxes on the property then this can obviously hold matters up.

When the *notario* has received all the documentation he or she needs to complete the *escritura* you should receive a draft copy which it is advisable to have scrutinised by your lawyer to check that all is as should be. Though a notary is a trained lawyer who has taken further exams to qualify for the post of notary, it is not a requirement of the job to do the work of a lawyer. Make a last check on the property to see that everything is in order and that what was agreed as included in the purchase price in the contract of sale remains in or with the property (e.g. fixtures and fittings).

Once everything has been settled the vendor and the purchaser (or someone acting on their behalf who has been granted Power of Attorney) meet at the *notario's* office. The notary will read through the *escritura* after which the two parties will sign the document.

For properties that are ready for immediate occupation, full payment is made before signing the *escritura* and taking possession of the property. It may be that the money paid for a property is to be transferred to wherever in the world the vendor wishes to receive it. However, if the purchase price is paid into a Spanish account, then the importation of currency will need to be registered with the Spanish authorities and your solicitor should deal with this for you. Many people hand over a banker's draft at this point as it can be witnessed by the *notario* there and then, but other methods of payment are available (see the chapter on *Finance*). At the same time the notary will collect his fee and inform the purchaser of any taxes payable on the transfer of property. Remember that if the vendor is a non-resident there will be 5% withheld from the purchase price, which will be paid to the Spanish Tax Agency on the vendor's behalf due to Capital Gains Tax liabilities.

After the signing of the *escritura*, the payment of the purchase price and all fees, the notary will pass the purchaser a copy (*copia simple*) of the *escritura* and the keys to the property. The original (*primera copia*) will be sent to the Property Register and the new owner's name registered. It can take several months for the process of registering the change of title deeds as all taxes and fees must be paid before a property can be registered in the new owner's name. Once a certificate has been issued stating that the name of the owner of the property has been registered, the purchaser's lawyer should collect it and forward it on to the new owner.

Part IV

WHAT HAPPENS NEXT

SERVICES

MAKING THE MOVE

BUILDING OR RENOVATING

MAKING MONEY FROM YOUR PROPERTY

SERVICES

CHAPTER SUMMARY

- It is important to give the utility companies notice of a second address should you have one, or set up a standing order from your bank account, so that you remain in credit with the utility service companies at all times.
- Spain uses two-pin plugs in older properties and three-pin plugs in more modern ones. UK appliances should perform quite adequately, if a little more slowly, using an adaptor.
- Owners of new property that isn't already connected to the electricity grid will need to register with their local electricity company and arrange to have a meter installed.
- Gas bottles (*Bombonas*) can be easily re-filled through the butane home delivery service which operates in most areas.
- Spanish water is perfectly safe to drink, however most expats and visitors to Spain follow the example of the Spanish and drink bottled mineral water instead.
- With the notable exception of northern and central areas of Spain, the provision of heating is not of major importance throughout most of the year.
- If you are unlikely to be at home all year round you will need to make sure that someone is employed to come in regularly to tend the garden unless you plan to spend the first week of your holiday gardening.
- If you are intending to rent out your property on a full-time basis, it is a good idea to hire a caretaker/gardener to look after the property and to welcome guests.
- Paying for the services of a property management agency to look after your home while you are away is likely to cost far more than employing a local to do ostensibly the same job.

UTILITIES

It is essential to understand that although all public utility services are widely available in Spain, and that the service in question will always be provided in the end, how long it will take to arrive is far less certain.

Electricity, telephone and water bills have a payment term of between 15 days and a month, after which a reminder notice will be sent to the occupant. If payment is still not made then the telephone line, water supply or electricity supply will be cut off and a reconnection fee charged. It is therefore important to give the utility companies notice of a second address should you have one, or set up a standing order from your bank account so that you remain in credit with the utility service companies at all times. You will also need to notify the local Town Hall (*ayuntamiento*) that you own property within their jurisdiction, and register with the municipality for local rates (*Impuestos sobre los Bienes Inmeubles (IBI)*). Make sure that all bills have been paid up to date before you move into a property. If the previous owner has left without paying them then you will be responsible for clearing the debt.

Electricity

The domestic electricity supply in Spain is mostly 220v or 225v AC, 50Hz and, less commonly in the more remote country areas, 110v or 125v AC. Plugs on electrical appliances in Spain are often two-pin in older properties and three-pin in more modern ones. UK appliances should perform quite adequately, if a little more slowly, using an adaptor while US appliances will need an adaptor plus a 220-110v transformer. Make sure to choose the right socket – flat pins for 220v or 110v. Light bulbs are usually 110v and are of the continental screw-in type. Buy the necessary adaptors in your home country as they will be harder to find, and more expensive to buy, in Spain.

Electricity is supplied by the electricity supply company (*la compañía de electricidad* that operates in your area through the overhead lines of an extensive grid system linking the hydroelectric and atomic power stations with cities, towns and villages throughout the country. It is essential to organise meter installation or reconnection through your regional branch of the electricity company well in advance, as the waiting lists for both services can be very long. New owners of a previously occupied property will need to present to the electricity company the deeds of the property (*escritura*), a Spanish bank account number to pay by standing order, and some form of identification document. The *compañía de electricidad* will come and inspect the electrics on the property and if they need updating you will need to have this done before you can transfer the contract for electricity from the previous owners into your name. Owners of new property that isn't already connected to the electricity grid will need to register with their local electricity company and arrange to have a meter installed.

Electricity is priced on the international system of a small standing charge and a further charge per kilowatt-hour consumed, the rate for which diminishes as consumption increases. Bills are issued bi-monthly and VAT (IVA) at the standard rate is added.

Gas

The use of butane gas (*butano*) is not as common in Spain as in Northern Europe and, except in the larger cities and perhaps on *urbanizaciónes*, there tends to be no piped household supply. However, readily available bottled gas (supplied in cylinders known as *bombonas*) is cheap (a large 12.5kg cylinder will cost approximately £5) and commonly used for cooking and heating in most homes. *Bombonas* can be easily re-filled through the butane home delivery service which operates in most areas. Those in more secluded areas may have to collect their gas supplies from the local depot. As with electricity, if you are in an area where piped gas is provided you will need to sign up with the gas company and arrange to pay the standing charge and gas bills by standing order. The gas companies are likely to come and inspect your appliances for safety every few years. Gas bills (for piped gas) are rendered bi-monthly and VAT (IVA) is added.

Because gas is generally a cheaper form of energy than electricity many properties run as many household appliances as possible on it. There are safety issues when using gas so make sure that the property has adequate ventilation, that pipes are checked regularly to ensure that they haven't perished and regulator valves are in good order. Leaked gas sinks and lingers in a room where a spark or a dropped match will ignite it with disastrous results if there isn't the ventilation to disperse it. Bottled gas has a tendency to run out at the most inopportune times and so it pays to always make sure that you have an adequate supply ready for such eventualities.

Water

Spanish water is perfectly safe to drink in almost all urban areas as government regulations require public water supplies to be treated with anti-pollutants. However, for this same reason the water can have an unpleasant taste and most expats and visitors to Spain follow the example of the Spanish and drink bottled mineral water instead. This is cheap, of good quality and sold at practically every corner shop in Spain – *con gas* means carbonated and *sin gas*, non-carbonated.

Although there is surplus rainfall in the north that provides an adequate natural water supply, water shortages can often occur over the summer months along the Mediterranean coast and in the Balearic Islands. The problem mainly arises because the municipalities individually control the supply of water and plans to lay national pipelines are continually frustrated by local political issues. The provision of desalination plants, purification plants and the sinking of wells are common topics of discussion in local politics. The Canary Islands, in particular, have a problem with sourcing enough water for the local populace.

The mains water piped to private premises is metered, with charges calculated either per cubic metre used, or at a flat rate. To have a water meter installed, you will need to apply to the local water company office with your passport, the *escritura*, a copy of a previous water bill for the property if you have one, and the number of your Spanish bank account. A deposit is payable, and there is a charge made for installing (or repairing) a water meter. Bills are usually issued quarterly. Depending on the hardness of the water it may pay to have filters installed, preferably within the system (as opposed to just on the outlets), to prevent the furring up of pipes, radiators etc.

HEATING AND AIR CONDITIONING

With the notable exception of northern and central areas of Spain, the provision of heating is not of major importance throughout most of the year. Winters – December, January and February – all over Spain will have their cold days, evenings will be cooler after sunset during these months but are as nothing compared to a northern European winter.

> Bear in mind that if you decide to live in a purpose-built summer holiday villa through the winter months your heating bill is going to be substantially higher than if you reside in a well-insulated house. Older properties in Spain may not be too well insulated and it will be well worth the investment to insulate your property as well as possible – it will keep the place cooler in the summer, and warmer in the winter.

Often the cheapest options of heating, if you live near a ready supply of logs, is to install a wood-burning stove, which can also be used as a water heater and from which radiators can be run from. Alternatively portable gas or electric heaters can be used. Surprisingly, solar heating is still relatively uncommon, although becoming less so, in most areas of Spain.

Apartment blocks may have central heating systems running through the building, the cost of which is paid for by the community charges.

Many modern air-conditioning units will also incorporate warm air heating systems. If you can't afford air conditioning then installing either fans on the ceilings or portable fans is a good idea, especially in the hotter parts of Spain such as Almería, and on the Canary Islands.

THE COST OF LIVING

The cost of living in Spain may be as much as 30% less than that in the UK. Running a property such as a two bedroom apartment could cost as little as €750/£500 a year, depending on how much electricity, water etc., is consumed. Electricity is likely to cost between €40-€50/£25-£35 every two months, depending on usage. Water charges can be as little as €20/£12 every quarter. Rates could be as little as £70 a year for a small property, while community charges depend on the size of the property, the number of properties in a *comunidad* and the services provided. These charges could cost around €25/£15 per month in a larger community. In addition, car prices, and car tax and insurance, are lower in Spain than in the UK and petrol at €0.70/£0.46 per litre is far cheaper than back home.

Typical Annual Running Costs of a Property in Spain

Community Fees:	Controlled by the committee of owners (*comunidad de propietarios*) and based on a percentage of the cost to maintain the facilities provided, relative to the size of your property. Will vary but usually 0.5%-1% of property value
Local Rates (IBI)	Typically 0.2% of property value but will vary from region to region
Property Tax	0.2% of rateable value
Insurance	0.5%-1% of value of property
Water, electricity, telephone & gas:	A standing charge and metering slightly higher than in the UK
Fiscal Representative/ Gestor	£100/€150 approx. (dependent on services)

GARDENS, GARDEN CENTRES AND DIY

One thing to bear in mind if you are a keen gardener is the topography of the area in which you are hoping to buy a property. Is the area prone to flooding, or drought or forest fires? If you are hoping to cultivate large gardens with lawns is there adequate water provision? Check the orientation of the house. Which parts are likely to catch the morning and afternoon sun? This will be important when planning various aspects to your garden, where to place certain features, lay a patio, etc. Even a small garden requires a lot of upkeep, regular maintenance to keep the undergrowth trimmed back, to plant and harvest vegetables and pick fruit, water and mow the lawns. If you are unlikely to be at home all year round you will need to make sure that someone is employed to come in regularly to tend the garden unless you plan to spend the first week of your holiday gardening. Property management companies will take on this work for a fee, or you may find a local gardener who will be happy to look after your garden – and keep an eye on the property. Be aware that it is not unknown for a property to include an orchard or olive grove to which the owners have no right of harvest, i.e. the crop is owned by someone else, even though the orchard is on your land.

There are enough builders' merchants and DIY centres around for those who fancy the challenge of doing their own renovating or landscaping of their property. Frequenting such places will certainly improve one's ability to speak Spanish, though to begin with you may need a dictionary of technical terms or a helpful local to guide you through the processes. It is very important to remember that even small alterations to a property must be approved by the town hall before you can begin operations. Many owners do not bother with this procedure and, depending on the size of the modification to an existing property, if the authorities discover the alterations (which they are likely to do when the property comes to be sold) the owners will be fined and the building reverted to its original design. Getting a *licencia de obra* for small changes is usually not a problem and merely involves filling in a form outlining the planned changes and paying a small fee.

SECURITY & HOUSESITTERS

Security

The last thing anyone wants is to leave home for a week or a month only to return to find that their house has been the target of a burglar's grand night out. Apart from buying an adequate insurance policy, fitting quality locks (it may be a good idea to change all the external locks on a property before moving in) and security grills (ironwork bars – *rejas*) over doors and windows (especially on the ground and first floors) and an alarm system, how else can you make sure than your property will remain secure? CCTV, automated gates and a couple of Dobermans may turn your property into a fortress but will also turn it into a potential target for any thieves that may live locally – they will be watching and waiting for when the house is left unoccupied when you and the rest of the family go away on holiday.

While theft from properties in a small village is likely to be rare (everyone will know everyone else's business and it won't be hard to trace the culprits), in some of the areas populated by well-heeled foreigners, as well as in urban and resort areas, theft is likely to be far more of a common occurrence. In such areas of relatively high crime, insurance premiums will also be higher and there will be stipulations in insurance contracts regarding the provision of adequate home security. One of the benefits of buying into an *urbanización* is that security is often regarded as being of a high importance and there are likely to be neighbours milling around at all times.

If you are buying to let it is in many ways foolish to be too opulent in your furnishing of the property. People on holiday often leave some of their commonsense behind, especially the young, and breakages and wear and tear are inevitable for rented accommodation. Never put the address of the house on a key fob and if you are letting the house out to many clients, rather than just friends and family, over the years it might be an idea to install a lock that works by a keypad rather than a key. This will save changing locks should you have suspicions about tenants as codes can be changed after every tenancy if need be. It is also a good idea to only give tenants keys to the front door. Back doors can remain locked for the duration of their stay.

Deadbolt locks such as those manufactured by Chubb are far superior to cylinder Yale-type locks, however, they are also more expensive, and will therefore cost more to replace. Replacement cylinders for Yale-type locks are cheap and easy to find.

A burglar alarm placed in a prominent position at the front of a house is a very effective deterrent and should be linked to a 24-hour monitoring centre. If an alarm is triggered which is not connected to a monitoring centre (especially if the property is in an isolated location) it is of limited benefit. Another good deterrent is the installation of external security lights that use sensors to switch themselves on for a timed period if they sense movement. However, depending on how sensitive they are they can be triggered by a rabbit (*conejo*) or some other non-human night-time prowler.

A determined thief will be able to break into a property whatever deterrents an owner may devise. All you can do is put as many obstacles in his way as possible. Your insurance company will be able to put you in touch with household security experts who will look over your property and advise on the best options. Remember to get at least two different quotes from two independent companies.

Housesitting

Depending on the value of your property and the worth or sentimental value of the contents contained within, it may be a good idea to find either someone willing to keep an eye on the place – a trusted neighbour for instance – or pay the extra and employ a professional housesitter. If you take the latter option make sure that the housesitter's references are in good order. *The Lady* (39-40 Bedford Street, London WC2E 9ER; ☎020-7379 4717; www.lady.co.uk) and other local newspapers carry advertisements of housesitting agencies.

Another option, especially if you are intending to rent out your property on a full-time basis, is to hire a caretaker/gardener to look after the property: to keep the garden orderly and lawn watered, as well as other household chores such as preparing the house for guests and tidying up once they have left, even looking after bills and taking care of any minor repairs that may need to be carried out from time to time. You will of course need to be sure that you can trust the person you employ. Ask your neighbours if they know of or have dealings with anyone suitable. It may be that if there are a number of properties in the vicinity being used solely as holiday homes then a gardener/caretaker could be employed full-time to look after all the properties, ensuring a good wage for the caretaker and a help to all the owners involved.

Paying for the services of a property management agency to look after your home while you are away is likely to cost far more than employing a local to do ostensibly the same job.

Local staff availability – cleaners, cooks, gardeners, etc.

Although Spain isn't as cheap as it once was, it is still reasonably cheap, and many property owners can afford to hire a part-time gardener, handyman, cook or home help. It should not be difficult to find staff, either through employment agencies, property management companies or by asking around and putting up advertisements in the vicinity.

Because the business relationship between the employer and the employee in these circumstances is often cash in hand such dealing are in theory illegal as the employee won't be paying tax on their earnings and the employer won't be making social security payments on the employee's behalf. There are pitfalls in employing on a cash in hand basis. Without a written contract between employer and employee misunderstandings, and grudges, can occur and it is better to be on the side of the law than not, though this is likely to cost you more than paying cash in hand. Should you fall out with your local Spanish handyman whom you have employed for years, and who you have decided to 'let go' you will find that the employee has far more clout when it comes to labour legislation that you as the employer. Whatever you decide, keep a record of all transactions made between yourself and the employee and get a receipt for all wages paid. Another worry is if an accident occurs to an uninsured employee while on your property. You could be sued for negligence and your home insurance will not cover claims made by employees working on your property. In this age of suing for suing's sake it is as well to be safe rather than sorry and make sure than all work on and in your property is carried out by employees who are covered by insurance and are registered as self-employed. The minimum wage in Spain is €451 per month and if an employee works less than 40 hours per week, payment will be in direct proportion to the hours worked.

MAKING THE MOVE

CHAPTER SUMMARY

- **Removals**. When considering what to take with you to Spain and what to leave behind or sell at a car boot sale start with a list of essential items and then try and cut this down again.
  - Any EU citizen intending to take up permanent residence in Spain may import their household effects and personal possessions free of customs duty.
  - The British Association of Removers (BAR) can provide advice on choosing a removal company, and members offer a financial guarantee through BAR if they go out of business.
- **Pets.** Before deciding to take your pet to Spain think carefully about the implications for both yourself and the animal.
  - Passports for pets allow UK citizens to take their animals abroad and to return with them without enduring the compulsory six-month quarantine that was formerly in force.
  - In some regions of Spain, dogs have to be registered and insured and a dog licence required or a tax levied.

Moving house is one of the most stressful times in a person's life. This statement has been stated so often now that it has become a cliché. However, considering that you will not be just moving down the road, or to another location a few hours' distant by car, but to another country with an alien culture, it is as well to plan your move with as much precision as possible. For citizens of the European Union there are now very few restrictions on living and working in the EU, and there are no customs duties to pay on personal effects. However, citizens of non-EU member states will need to check with the nearest Spanish embassy or consulate to find out the current regulations relating to their country. With the cheapness and availability of flights between Spain and most other countries in Europe there is no longer that feeling of great distance between say, Andalucía and Aberdeen that there used to be. These days most of us are used to travelling relatively large distances at least once a year and separation from our family and friends for varying periods of time is a natural part of day-to-day living.

Whether you are moving to your property in Spain for a trial period in order to see whether you wish (and can afford) to live there full-time, or whether you are moving some of your belongings there in order to set up a business, it is advisable to make a trip out to your property first, unencumbered with belongings. Check that all services are connected and that all papers and permits are in order. While you are in Spain you could look into the costs involved in hiring removals men or hire cars or a van from the Spanish end. Organise your financial affairs in Spain, set up direct debits to pay the utility companies, and organise the transferral of funds from your bank account at home to your account in Spain. Then go home, let your house, either privately or through a management company, or sell it, and begin your journey into a new life.

REMOVALS

When considering what to take with you to Spain and what to leave behind or sell at a car boot sale start with a list of essential items and then try and cut this down again. Anything one decides to take must be carefully considered to ensure that it really is practical, and necessary. Electrical items are slightly more expensive in Spain and it may be worth taking yours as long as they are compatible. However, there may be difficulties with electrical repair as some home appliances in Spain are of Spanish design and manufacture so spare parts for other items can be a problem. Anything of substantial weight will be very expensive to ship abroad, and no matter how carefully you or the removals men wrap an item, breakages occur. A good removals company can avoid or deal with most of the disasters, which can coincide with uprooting yourself, your family and all your possessions to a foreign country. The cost of hiring a removals firm to take everything from a home in the UK to a home in Spain will typically cost between £2,000-£3,000/€3,000-€4,500 and take a couple of weeks. Of course, a few brave souls tackle the move themselves, or with help from friends.

Making the move – Stuart Anderson
The move to Spain was well planned and ran smoothly. Thanks to friends who volunteered to drive the furniture van here in a self-drive hired van (the largest that one can drive with an ordinary UK driving

licence) from Cumbria to Portsmouth and then via the St. Malo ferry, through France and finally here, a journey of three days. Simultaneously, our two cars and three dogs travelled via the Channel Tunnel. We met up at Angoulême and travelled the rest of the journey in convoy. I booked overnight accommodation in advance, staying at inexpensive 'Premiere Classe' hotels in France where dogs were made quite welcome.

For the rest of us the *British Association of Removers* (3 Churchill Court, 58 Station Road, North Harrow, London HA2 7SA; ☎ 020-8861 3331; www.bar.co.uk) provides a free and useful leaflet *Now that you're ready to move...* which covers most of the issues you may face and ends with the advice, 'Relax...', which no one moving home will find easy to do. The *British Association of Removers* can also provide the names and telephone numbers of reputable removals companies throughout the country that are members of BAR and specialise in overseas operations. The addresses and phone numbers of some of the companies which deal with Spain, whether directly or by sub-contracting to other agencies, are given below.

General Conditions Of Import

Any EU citizen intending to take up permanent residence in Spain may import their household effects and personal possessions free of customs duty. There are now no customs duties to pay on household effects transported from one member country of the EU to another. All reputable international removals firms should be fully aware of the regulations concerning the transport of personal and household items. Anyone thinking of taking their household effects out to Spain in a private truck or van should first consult their nearest Spanish embassy or consulate for the most up to date regulations and advice. Much of the paperwork involved in importing goods will have to be in Spanish. *The Association of Translation Companies* (Suite 10-11, Kent House, 87 Regent Street, London W1B 4EH; ☎020-7437 0007; fax 020-7439 7701; www.atc.org.uk) will be able to put you in touch with translation services specialising in translating documents relating to removals abroad, property purchase, residence, import/export etc. Translation service companies are also listed in the yellow pages.

If you are moving to Spain permanently you will need to have proof of intended permanent residence in Spain, in the form of a residence permit; if you haven't received this before leaving home the initial *visado de residencia* will suffice, but a deposit may have to be paid. This deposit exempts the holder from customs duties and will be returned once the permit has been produced.

You need an application form (*Cambio de Residencia*) requesting the

Head of Customs to allow the goods free entry into Spain (obtainable from the Consulate) as well as an itemised list of the contents in duplicate, written in Spanish, which shows the estimated value in euros. These should accompany the goods or shipment and should have been legalised – stamped – at the Spanish Consulate. If you are sending the goods with a removals company, they will also need a photocopy of your passport, which has been similarly legalised. To import wedding gifts, you will also need a copy of your marriage certificate; and there are similar special requirements for diplomats' removals; gifts by inheritance and, for example, new furniture whose value is greater than €3,000.

Exemption of duties payable on importing effects for non-EU citizens may be possible if the individual has not been resident in Spain during the two years prior to the importation of the goods; if the goods enter Spain within three months of the individual's arrival, that the goods are for personal use, are at least six months old and will not be sold in Spain for at least two years. However, if the individual decides to leave Spain within two years of arrival, he or she will have to export the goods again (a relatively simple process within the EU) or pay duty on them.

Another form of concession on import duties is available for those who wish to import furniture for a second residence or holiday home; this is known as the *vivienda secundaria*. Entitlement to this exemption does not include taking Spanish residency and involves making a deposit (around 50% of the value of the goods), which will be returned on the expiry of a two-year period.

The Import Procedure

This basically consists of compiling a signed inventory, written in Spanish, of all the goods to be transported to Spain. This list should then be presented to the Spanish Consulate with a completed customs clearance form where the inventory will be stamped for a small fee. The removals company should handle a good deal of the paperwork required, however, the basic procedure is outlined below:

- Make two copies of a complete inventory of all the items to be taken, valuing all of the items at their present value, not cost new, and opting for the low side of the estimate. Even if there are some things you want to take now and others that will not follow for several months, include the latter on the inventory, as once the list is compiled, it cannot be added to later. Remember to include the makes, models and serial numbers of all electrical items on the inventory, plus two copies of a declaration of ownership of the goods in Spanish.
- The customs clearance form, *la Dirección General de Aduanas* must

be completed; this will be available from your nearest Spanish consulate.

- You may also need to present either a copy of the *escritura* to the new Spanish property or, if you have had your own property built, a copy of the habitation certificate from the local authority in Spain that granted the planning permission for building.
- A full passport; and photocopies of the pages which have been stamped at the consulate.

Although it is obviously more economical to transport all of your possessions in one go, new Spanish residents are allowed to import all household goods in as many trips as are required. It is worth remembering that it may be difficult to import goods after the expiry of the one-year period; it can take up to a year to obtain a separate import licence and the duty on the import for non-EU citizens can be astronomical. For those who have bought a second home or holiday residence, the procedure for importing personal effects and furnishings is similar to that for long-term and permanent residents except that the home owner is required to draw up a notarised declaration that he or she will not sell, hire out or otherwise transfer ownership of the property or personal goods within the twelve months following importation.

Finally, it is a commonly-held misunderstanding that if you buy an item in Britain (or another EU country), pay VAT (sales tax) and then subsequently export it to another country in the EU such as Spain, there is an entitlement for a refund of the VAT paid on purchase – this is simply not true. The misunderstanding arises from the fact that if you are buying anything to take with you, such as a fridge or stereo, it can be supplied *VAT free* if the goods are delivered direct to the remover as an export shipment from the dealer.

CHECKLIST FOR MOVING HOUSE

- Confirm dates with removal company.
- Sign and return contract together with payment.
- Book insurance at declared value.
- Arrange a contact number where you can be reached at all times.
- Arrange transport for pets.
- Dispose of anything you don't want to take with you.
- Start running down freezer contents.
- Contact carpet fitters if needed.

- Book disconnection of mains services.
- Cancel all rental agreements.
- Notify dentist, doctor, optician, vet.
- Notify bank and savings/share accounts of change of address.
- Inform telephone company.
- Ask the post office to re-route mail.
- Tell TV licence, car registration, passport offices of change of address.
- Notify hire purchase and credit firms.
- Make local map of new property for friends/removal company.
- Clear the loft/basement.
- Organise your own transport to new home.
- Plan where things will go in new home.
- Cancel the milk/newspapers.
- Clean out the freezer/fridge.
- Find and label keys.
- Send address cards to friends and relatives.
- Separate trinkets, jewellery and small items.
- Sort out linen and clothes.
- Put garage/garden tools together.
- Take down curtains/blinds.
- Collect children's toys.
- Put together basic catering for family at new house.

Removal Companies

The *British Association of Removers* (BAR) can provide advice on choosing a removal company; and members offer a financial guarantee through BAR if they go out of business. Write to *BAR Overseas* at the address above.

Removal companies can take away much of the hassle of moving if you choose the right one; as one successfully-moved expatriate put it:

> *The secret is to use a really good removal company. Ours was superb and handled everything for us – all the paperwork, form filling, everything we could possibly worry about was handled by the firm.*

Although Spanish consulates will supply information concerning the export of household goods and personal effects on receipt of an sae, you may find that their own information is out of date, as more than in any other European country (with the possible exception of Portugal) Spain constantly amends and alters its regulations regarding the importation of personal and household effects. The most up-to-date information will come from a removal company specialising in exports to the Iberian Peninsula. These can provide quotes, and should also be able to give information on Spanish import procedures on request.

It is particularly important to shop around for a wide variety of quotes as removal companies sometimes sub-contract jobs to other companies whose drivers are going to the country in question and charge their client the extra fees picked up along the way. The approximate charge from the UK to Spain is £120 to £150 per cubic metre plus a fixed fee for administration and paperwork. The amount will vary greatly on either side of this estimate however, depending on where in Spain the shipment is going and where it is coming from in the UK. The price per cubic metre should decrease with the volume of goods you are transporting.

It is advisable to take out comprehensive insurance against possible damage to your possessions while in transit. A removals company can advise you about cover and make arrangements on your behalf, and the cost is usually quite modest. Another fact to bear in mind for non-EU citizens is that the customs clearance charges involved in exporting and importing goods can sometimes be more expensive than the shipping charges themselves (also something which a good removal company should advise you of and deal with on your behalf).

Make sure that the removals lorry will be able to reach your Spanish property with ease (check parking restrictions, access etc.). If goods are held up for days at a time at customs in Spain it may be that another removals firm may be subcontracted to deliver to the Spanish address. Check the contract to see what the clauses (and fees) are regarding such delays.

Useful Addresses – Removal Companies

Allied Pickfords: Heritage House, 345 Southbury Road, Enfield, Middlesex EN1 1UP; ☎ 020-8219 8000; www.allied-pickfords.co.uk. A worldwide network with many branches in Britain. In Spain: Calle Calendula 95EDFO, Miniparc II, Soto de la Moraleja, 28109 Madrid; ☎ +34 1 650 4027; fax +34 1 650 6087; www.alliedintl.com.

Ambassador Five Star Movers: Pattenden Lane, Marden, Kent TN12 9QJ; ☎ 01622 832 324; fax 01622 832 325; www.ambassador5star.co.uk.

Andrich Removals: The Shortwoods, Waterfallows Lane, Linton Heath, Derbyshire DE12 6PF; ☎ 01283-761 990; fax 01283-763 965; www.andrichinternationalremovals.com. Associated companies in Spain (Cádiz, and Denia). Regular service to Spain with full and part loads.

Atlantis Overseas Removals: Atlantis House, Bennett Road, Leeds LS6 3HN; ☎ 0113-278 9191; fax 0113-274 4916; www.atlantisltd.co.uk.

Avalon Overseas: Drury Way, Brent Park, London NW10 0JN; ☎ 020-

8451 6336; www.transeuro.com.

Britannia Bradshaw International: Units 2 & 3 Tilson Road, Roundthorn Industrial Estate, Manchester M23 9PH; ☎ 0161-946 0809; fax 0161-946 0442; www.bradshawinternational.com.

Britannia Lanes of Devon: Hennock Road, Marsh Barton, Exeter EX2 8NP; ☎ 01392-494 966. Fortnightly service to Spain and Portugal.

Britannia Pink & Jones Ltd: Britannia House, Riley Road, Telford Way, Kettering, Northants. NN16 8NN; ☎ 01536-512 019.

Clark & Rose Ltd: Barclayhill Place, Portlethen, Aberdeen AB12 4LH; ☎ 01224-782 800; fax 01224-782 822; www.clarkandrose.co.uk. Also have a depot in Biggleswade, Bedfordshire.

Cotswold Carriers: Warehouse 2, The Walk, Hook Norton Road, Chipping Norton, Oxon OX7 5TG; ☎ 01608-730 500; www.cotswoldcarriers.co.uk.

Crown Relocations: Freephone 0800-393 363, with offices in; Birmingham (01827 264100; Glasgow (0123-644 9666); Heathrow (020-8897 1288); Leeds (0113-277 1000); London (020-8591 3388); Montrose (01674-672 155). Branches in Barcelona and Madrid; www.crownrelo.com.

David Dale Removals: Dale House, Forest Moor Road, Harrogate HG5 8LT; ☎ 01423-324 948; fax 01423-324 450; www.daviddale.co.uk. Takes part and full loads, has a regular weekly service, and storage available in Spain in Malaga and Alicante.

Edward Baden: Edward Baden House, Bellbrook Industrial Estate, Uckfield, East Sussex TN22 1QL; ☎ 01825-768 866; fax 01825-768 877; www.edwardbaden.co.uk.

Four Winds International Group: Georgian House, Wycombe End, Beaconsfield, Bucks HP9 7LX; ☎ 01494-675 588;www.fourwinds.co.uk.

Harrow Green Removals Group: Merganser House, Cooks Road, London E15 2PW; ☎ 020-8522 0101; fax 020-8522 0252; www.harrowgreen.com. Full removals service, and they can also make arrangements for pets.

Interpack Worldwide: Interpack House, Great Central Way, London NW10 0UX; ☎ 020-8324 2000; fax 020-8324 2096; www.interpack.co.uk. Services include pet shipping, full/part house contents, motor vehicles, air freight and storage.

Luker Bros (Removals & Storage) Ltd: Shelley Close, Headington, Oxford OX3 8HB; ☎ 01865-762 206.

Movers International (of Preston) Ltd: Unit A82 Red Scar Business Park, Longridge Road, Preston PR2 5NN; ☎ 01772-651 570; fax 01772-654 570; www.moversint.co.uk. A weekly trade service to Spain and Portugal.

Northover's Removals and Storage: Liphook, Surrey; ☎ 01428-751 554; fax

01428-751 564, and 04638 Mojácar Playa (Almería), Spain; ☎ 950 478 449; Has a regular service to Spain and storage available in Almería.

Richman-Ring Ltd: Eurolink Way, Sittingbourne, Kent ME10 3HH; ☎ 01795-427 151; fax 01795-428 804; www.richman-ring.com.

Robinsons International Moving and Storage: Nuffield Way, Abingdon, Oxon OX14 1TN; ☎ 01235-552 255; www.robinsons-intl.com. They can send a brochure on *International Moving*. Branches in London: ☎ 020-8208 8484; Basingstoke: ☎ 01256-465 533; fax 01256-324 959; Birmingham: ☎ 01527-830 860; fax 01527-526 812; Bristol: ☎ 0117-980 5800; fax 0117-980 5828; Manchester: ☎ 0161-766 8414; fax 0161-767 9057; and Southampton: ☎ 023-8022 0069; fax 023-800 31274; Darlington ☎ 01325-348 700; fax 01325-348 777; Glasgow: ☎ 0141-779 9477; fax 0141-779 9488.

Union Jack Logistics Limited: Unit 4 Hill Barton Business Park, Sidmouth Road, Clyst St Mary, Exeter, Devon EX5 1DR; ☎ 01395-233486; fax: 01395-233686; Spain tel/fax: 0034 965 704 740; Spain mobile: 0034 661 081 434; e-mail UK enquiries@unionjacklogistics.co.uk; e-mail Spain tommy.unionjack@terra.es; www.unionjacklogistics.co.uk. Specialists in removals between Britain and Spain.

IMPORTING PETS INTO SPAIN

Before deciding to take your pet to Spain think carefully about the implications for both yourself and the animal. Local authorities in the regions of Spain have different regulations regarding pets and it is a good idea to check what these are before importing your pet.

> In 2000, 'Passports' for pets were introduced. These allow people from the UK to take their animals abroad and to return with them without enduring the compulsory six-month quarantine that was formerly in force. Spain (including the Balearic and Canary Islands, though not the Spanish North African enclaves of Melilla and Ceuta) is one of the countries that the UK includes in its Pet Travel Scheme. The Pet Travel Scheme (PETS) allows dogs and cats to visit certain countries in mainland Europe and rabies free areas such as Australia and New Zealand provided that they are vaccinated against rabies. Additionally, they are required to have been treated against tapeworm (*echinococcus multilocularis*) – which can pass to humans – and the tick known as *Rhipicephalus sanguineus* – which also carries a disease transferable to humans.

The latest details of import conditions for taking your pets to Spain can be obtained by contacting the Pet Travel Scheme (Department for the Environment, Food and Rural Affairs, Area 201, 1a Page Street, London SW1P 4PQ; ☎ 0870 241 1710; fax 020-7904 6834; e-mail pets.helpline@defra.gov.uk; www.defra.gov.uk) and requesting the contact details of your nearest Animal Health Office. Although the 'Passports' scheme makes travelling with animals more straightforward, getting the necessary documentation can be a lengthy process. At the time of writing the *Department for the Environment, Food and Rural Affairs (DEFRA)* – the current name of the old Ministry of Agriculture, Food and Fisheries – was understood to be working to a six-month deadline, so you need to plan ahead.

Some but not all ferry companies and airlines will take accompanied pets, though the list of those that do is growing, so check with your carrier. Travelling by air from the UK to Spain a pet can travel as excess baggage, however, coming the other way the animal must travel as cargo. Once in the country the animal's documentation will be checked before being taken to the Animal Aircare Centre and then released to the owner. Quarantine is not usually necessary, although regulations may change and you should consult the Spanish consulate in your home country for up-to-date information well before your planned travel date. Note that in some cities in Spain dogs have to be registered and insured and a dog licence required or a tax levied. Information on the registration formalities once in Spain will be found at the local town hall (*ayuntamiento*).

TAKING PETS OUT OF THE UK

The procedures involved are:

- Vet inserts a tiny microchip just under the animal's skin (cost £20-£30).
- Vet administers a rabies shot, or two, given two weeks apart. (£50 x 2; second shot possibly cheaper).
- Vet takes a blood sample from animal and sends it to a DEFRA-approved laboratory. (£70-£80 including vet's handling charge). Note: If the blood test is negative, your pet must be vaccinated and tested again.
- Vet issues a PETS 1 Certificate, which you have to show to the transport company (e.g. airline, ferry, channel tunnel, etc).
- When taking pets from Britain to Spain you will need a PETS 5 certificate (this replaces a separate Export Health Certificate) which is issued at the same time as PETS 1 (see above).
- Total cost about £200.

Importing Pets Back into the UK

To get your pet back into the UK you will need a PETS Certificate to show the transport company when checking in your pet at the point of departure. A PETS Certificate is valid six months after the date of the blood test up to the date the animal's booster rabies shot is due (a dog has to be at least three months old before it can be vaccinated). You should obtain the PETS Certificate from a government-authorised vet and you can obtain a list of these from DEFRA's website (www.defra.gov.uk/animalh/quarantine/pets/contacts.shtml). Immediately (24-48 hours) prior to leaving Spain the animal must be treated against ticks and tapeworm by a vet. This has to be done *every* time your pet enters the UK. The vet will issue an official certificate bearing the vet's stamp with the microchip number, date and *time* of treatment, and the product used.

Pets Originating Outside Britain

If your pet originated from outside Britain where different systems for identifying dogs and cats are in force it will need a microchip insert for entry to the UK. Pets that have had other forms of registration (e.g. an ear tattoo) must be vaccinated; blood-tested and have a microchip insert. To enter the UK the animal must have the PETS Certificate showing that the vet has seen the registration document.

Pet Travel Insurance

Due to the introduction of the PETS scheme a niche market in pet travel insurance has opened up. *Pet Plan* (Allianz Cornhill Insurance plc, Computer House, Great West Road, Brentford, Middlesex TW8 9DX; ☎0800-072 7000; www.petplan.co.uk), a well-known British animal health insurance company, offers cover for pets taking trips abroad. The minimum 30-day cover costs about £16 for dogs and £10 for cats; 60 days and 90 days' cover is also available. *Petwise Insurance* (BDML Connect Ltd., Baltic House, Kingston Crescent, Northend, Portsmouth PO2 8QL; ☎08702-413 479; www.petwise-insurance.com), *RapidInsure* (Phoenix Park, Blakewater Road, Blackburn, Lancs. BB1 5SJ; ☎01254 266 266; www.rapidinsure.co.uk), *Pinnacle Pet Healthcare* (Pinnacle House, A1 Barnet Way, Borehamwood, Hertfordshire WD6 2XX; ☎020-8207 9000; fax 020-8953 6222; www.pinnacle.co.uk) and *MRL Insurance Direct* (☎0800-389 8505; www.mrlinsurance.co.uk) also offer travelling pet insurance.

Useful Contacts

Animal Airlines: 35 Beatrice Avenue, Manchester, Lancs. M18 7JU; ☎ 0160-223 4035.

Airpets Oceanic: Willowslea Farm Kennels, Spout Lane North, Stanwell Moor, Staines, Middlesex TW19 6BW; ☎ 01753-685 571; fax 01735-681 655; www.airpets.com. Pet exports, pet travel schemes, boarding, air kennels, transportation by road/air to and from all UK destinations.

Littleacre Quarantine Centre: 50 Dunscombes Road, Turves, Nr Whittlesey Cambs. PE7 2DS; ☎ 01733-840 291; fax 01733-840 348; www.quarantine1.co.uk. Pet collection and overland delivery service. Will collect from your home and arrange all the necessary documentation. Also return home service from Europe provided.

Independent Pet and Animal Transport Association: Route 5, Box 747, Highway 2869, 2-364 Winding Trail, Holly Lake Ranch, Big Sandy, Texas 75755 USA; ☎ 903-769-2267; fax 903-769-2867; www.ipata.com. An International Trade Association of animal handlers, pet moving providers, kennel operators, veterinarians and others who are dedicated to the care and welfare of pets and small animals during transport locally, nationwide and worldwide. Citizens of the USA can contact this address for a list of agents dealing in the transport of pets from the USA to Spain.

Par Air Services Livestock Ltd: Warren Lane, Stanway, Colchester, Essex C03 0LN; ☎ 01206-330 332; fax 01206-331 277; www.parair.co.uk. Handles international transportation and quarantine arrangements. Can arrange door-to-door delivery of pets by specially equipped vans.

Pet Travel Scheme: Department for the Environment, Food and Rural Affairs, Area 201, 1a Page Street, London SW1P 4PQ; ☎ 0870 241 1710; fax 020-7904 6834; e-mail pets.helpline@defra.gov.uk; www.defra.gov.uk.

Pets Will Travel: Unit 2A, 3 Newby Close, Norton, Stockton-On-Tees; www.petswilltravel.co.uk. Also have a good forum pages on their website.

Travelpets Ltd: 22 South Audley Street, London W1K 2NY; ☎ 020-7499 4979; www.travelpets.net.

Trans-Fur: 19, Dene Close, Sarisbury Green, Southampton, Hampshire SO31 7TT; tel/fax 01489-588 072.

Building or Renovating

CHAPTER SUMMARY

- **Running checks on property**. Once you have found a property you should have your lawyer run checks on it to find out if you will be permitted to carry out such building work as you have planned.
  - The town hall is where you will have to pay your annual property taxes and where you can discover what the *plus valia* tax is on the land you are hoping to buy.
  - The *Catastro* will give the assessed value (*valor catastral*) of the plot or property, which is used to value the property for tax purposes.
  - The Property Registry holds the title deeds (*escritura*) of any land or property and will be able to inform you who the registered owner is.
- **Licences**. If you are going to be carrying out major building work, either erecting a new building or renovating an existing property you will need to get a building permit (*licencia de obra*) from the town hall.
  - It is always advisable to discuss your ideas with your lawyer, a builder and an architect or surveyor before going ahead and buying a plot of land or a property in need of renovation.
- A registered architect, like a builder, must guarantee their plans and the instructions given to the builder for a period of ten years.
- **Builders**. When you sign a contract with the builder get your lawyer to check it to see whether there are any clauses included that may work to your detriment.
  - Arrange to pay builders by instalments, never in one lump sum.
- **Pools**. Even if you buy a property with an existing swimming pool you will need to consider the costs involved in its upkeep and maintenance.

- To keep a swimming pool in good condition, i.e. clean, warm and pure, it is necessary to remove the total body of water from the pool several times a day, pass it through filters and sanitise it.
- DIY superstores such as *Akí* and *Leroy Merlin* sell all the kit that you will need to knock up anything from a garden shed to a villa with pool.

LOCAL AUTHORITIES

There are several local authorities that will need to be visited when it comes to buying a property or a plot of land in Spain. In the first instance you will need to visit the foreigners department of the local police station, or *comisaría* in order to register for a residence permit *(tarjeta comunitaria)*. At the same time you also need to apply for an NIE (*Número de Identificatión de Extranjeros)* which is your Spanish tax identification number. This is an obligatory document to have if you are going to buy property in Spain and can be obtained from the foreigner's department of any local police station. You can either apply for these documents yourself or, if your Spanish is a little hazy, you can employ a *gestor* to arrange these for you. The *gestor* plays a large part of Spanish life and helps those who would rather not deal with red tape by dealing with officialdom for them. Because of their local knowledge you may find their service invaluable. *Gestors* are listed in the yellow pages (*las páginas amarillas*).

Once you have found a property you will want your lawyer to run checks on it to find out if you will be permitted to carry out such building work as you have planned. There are several local authorities that will need to be referred to.

The Town Hall (Ayuntamiento)

The local town hall is the place to go to seek out information about whether planning permissions and building permits will be granted. The town hall also houses the PGOU (*Plan General de Ordenación Urbana*) – the Town Plan. The Town Plan will tell you if the land is located on an existing and approved *urbanizatión* (in which case planning permission should not be a problem), and the nature of the restrictions on the land. For example, if the land or property is on land zoned as *Rustico* you will not be allowed to build. Also check the plots of land surrounding the one that you are hoping to buy. See what developments are in the pipeline, if any – these could be possible housing developments, planned roads or commercial enterprises. The town hall is where you will have to pay your annual property taxes and where you can discover what the *plus valia* tax is on the land you are hoping to buy.

The Land Registry (Catastro)

The land registry is where you will find a property's topographical description. The land registry holds details of a property's boundaries, its exact location, and a description of a property which will be invaluable when it comes to deciding whether all you have been told about a property or plot of land by the vendor is in fact true. The *Catastro* will also give the assessed value (*valor catastral*) of the plot or property which is used to value the property for tax purposes.

The Property Registry (Registro de la Propiedad)

If you discover at the town hall that you will be allowed to go ahead and build/renovate, and are clear on the exact borders and boundaries of your land, you will also need to find out if the vendor is in fact the owner (indeed the sole owner) of the land or property. The Property Registry holds the title deeds (*escritura*) of any land or property and will be able to inform you who the registered owner is. If you are buying from the developers of an *urbanizatión* you want to be sure that the developers are the registered owners of the land. Your lawyer will be able to obtain a *nota simple* from the Property Registry. Check the registry to find if there are any debts on the land or property as if there are, and if they are not cleared before you buy, then you will inherit these debts. All these checks are the same as those applying to any property purchase in Spain.

Permits

If you are going to be carrying out major building work, whether erecting a new building or renovating an existing property, you will need to get a building permit (*licencia de obra*) from the town hall. Before buying a property in need of renovation or a building plot make sure that the vendor and *notario* are aware that you will only buy subject to the planning permission and building licence being granted. Building permits (*licencia de obra*), if granted by the town hall will cost around 4% of the cost of the build.

Once everything has been checked out by your lawyer to your satisfaction you can go ahead, buy the land and sign for it at the office of the *notario.* The registration of the land or property can be left to your lawyer, together with the paying of taxes due.

THE SPANISH WAY

Buying land for building, or an old *cortijo* in need of a certain amount of renovation, should be approached with as much caution as when buying a resale property that is ready to move into. You will want to make sure that the land can actually be built on and that planning permission has been granted or will be granted without too much trouble. As is the Spanish way, in the past it was quite usual for properties to be built or alterations made to existing structures without first obtaining the necessary licences. In the old days, a fine would be imposed once the authorities found out, but there the matter would end. Today, things are tighter and fines are likely to be horrendously large plus, depending on the authority, a property could theoretically be pulled down if it has been erected without planning permission. You will want to ensure that the building plot is in fact large enough for the size of house you are planning to have built, and that the land is suitable for building, i.e. that it is easy enough to sink foundations, that subsidence is not going to be a problem and that the land is relatively easy to level off.

Depending on what you are aiming for, and how much time, money and patience you have, you might decide to hire an architect to design you a villa. In such a case you will be able to have complete control over the specifications of everything from the kitchen sink to the veranda's ironwork surround. Alternatively, you could hire a local builder and use one of their standard designs. Either way you will need planning permission and will need to jump through a few hoops wrapped in red tape.

If you are thinking about building your own home, during the planning stages you will need to take into account all the associated costs that will crop up during the building – e.g. the cost of extending services such as water, electricity and telecommunications lines to the property, road access and drainage, etc., and remember that most quotes can only really be estimates. The true cost of a building project will escalate due to modifications that may need to be made to overcome unforeseen hurdles, or the changing of minds about what is wanted in the way of interior fitted furniture, tiling, bathroom appliances etc.

> It is always advisable to discuss your ideas with your lawyer, a builder and an architect or surveyor before going ahead and buying a plot of land or a property in need of renovation. In Spain there are occasionally unexpected changes made to the categorisation of the different 'zones' under a town hall's jurisdiction. If this happens while you are in the middle of building on your plot of land you may find that you have built in the middle of a 'green zone' where building is prohibited, or in a rural area where no new construction is allowed. It may even be the case that building is only allowed on plots that are several times larger than the one you intend to buy. You or your lawyer will need to find out from the town hall about such things.

If you are looking to renovate rather than build from scratch, then ask yourself whether you have the know-how yourself to renovate a tumbledown property or if you have the necessary funds to hire builders who do. Depending on the amount of work involved in renovating a property, new build often tends to work out cheaper, by up to a third, than renovation. When you have found a property that you are interested in get a survey, or a local builder to come and look at it. Make sure that the external walls at least are sound. Before starting on any major renovation or building work, employ an architect. Shop around and get several quotes as these will vary a lot, and will depend on the size of the property, or the planned building work, and perhaps on how *au fait* you are with Spain and your ability to negotiate in Spanish. Employing an architect to design and oversee the building of a small villa may come to between £800-£1,600 for a small house, much more for a large villa. A registered architect, like a builder, must guarantee their plans and the instructions given to the builder for a period of ten years. Even though it may seem easier to deal with an architect from home, or someone who's mother tongue is English, a Spanish architect familiar with local building rules and regulations, and the local climate, is likely to more helpful to you in the long run.

An architect's fees will include plans (make sure that you are completely satisfied with them) and the supervision of the building project. The fee will also include the copies of the plans necessary for approval by the College of Architects before you can obtain the building permit and should also include the cost of preparing the *memoria*, or building specification. This states such things as the quantity and sizes of tiles, bricks, pipes etc, that are needed for the project, the type of concrete and cement needed, and the rest of the building materials to be used. It is likely that you will want to be involved in deciding on the type of electrical and bathroom fixtures and fittings, the colour and type of the tiles for the kitchen and bathroom, etc. Windows and doors and the kitchen units can all be discussed with the architect or builder while the *memoria* is being compiled.

Once the *memoria* is complete it is then given to the builder/s in order to get a quote for the cost of the building work involved. This quote will obviously be given after having taken into consideration all the materials listed in the *memoria*, and though it may change a bit as work proceeds, any alterations that you make to it later on will cost you extra – and you will need to amend the contract that you have with your builder accordingly. Sift through several quotes from builders who you have found through recommendation. Recommendation really is the only way to 'vet' a builder, though make sure that such praise comes from independent parties. Ask around among locals and expats and if a builder comes highly recommended then meet him and ask to be shown some of his work. Quotes that come in will vary and the highest quote will not necessarily guarantee the best results, just as a low quote doesn't necessarily mean that the work or materials will be second-rate. Also be advised that there are plenty of expats living in Spain who are looking for work without having registered with the Spanish tax authorities. If you employ such a person and the authorities find out you and your employee may both face heavy fines.

When you sign a contract with the builder get your lawyer to check it to see whether there are any clauses included that may work to your detriment. The contract should include the *memoria*, the total price for the job with payment schedule and work to be carried out. The cost of the job, at the end of the day, will need to be negotiated with the builder. Builders will often ask to be paid 50% before they start work with the balance payable in stages as the work progresses. Try and negotiate with them and if possible include a clause in the contract whereby you hold back say 10% of the total for a period to insure against possible building flaws or defects. Such things may not be evident until the house has managed to 'settle'.

BUILDERS

Any builder you employ should be covered by an insurance policy so that if they go bankrupt while in the middle of working on your house you will be able to claim compensation. By law, a builder in Spain must guarantee any work carried out for a period of ten years. Arrange to pay builders by instalments, never in one lump sum all in one go. It is also advisable to remain, if possible, *in situ* or nearby, while the builders are at your property. This isn't to say that you should be on hand to continually interfere and 'direct' operations, but to check that the builders are actually turning up for work and doing the hours that you are getting billed for. Also being aware of what is going on will ensure that the architect's original plans are being adhered to and that the fixtures and fittings are those that were originally agreed on.

Get references on your builders – Lindy Walsh

Our first builder was excellent. He retired before we'd finished phase one. Our second builder was good himself, but most of his team were poor. I've had a problem with a drain for NINE years because it was put in without the correct 'fall'. My third builder was a criminal who may or may not have been any good as a builder but took my 25% deposit and vanished. My fourth builder was a very poor builder with a very poor team. My fifth builder is a good builder and totally reliable. Most other (Spanish) tradesmen: electricians, plumbers, carpenters, decorators etc., seem very reliable in their standard of work as well as actually turning up to work when they should. Most British tradesmen in this area seem no better and most I gather are working illegally

There are good and bad, reliable and unreliable people all over the world, but if you are trusting someone with a hefty investment of your time and money you need to make sure that your investment is safe in their hands. Because of the amount of continued construction work going on in Spain, skilled tradesmen are in short supply. Builders often contract to take on several jobs at a time so that should interruptions occur on one project they can turn to the next. Be sure to get several quotes on any major job that you need doing. But there are many reliable and very professional builders in Spain who will build an individually designed house on your plot of land exactly as you wish, or will sell you a plot of land and build a house chosen from a range of standard designs.

SWIMMING POOLS

Most people thinking about buying property in Spain will also be dreaming about how great it will be to have their own swimming pool. With the amount of sunshine that Spain enjoys, owning a home without a pool seems a tragedy. Swimming is incredibly good for physical fitness and keeping the heart healthy and can be enjoyed by all ages: whether you are young or old, in the water we are almost all equal.

Unfortunately, swimming pools aren't cheap either to install or to maintain. The cost of installing an average sized pool of, say, 8 x 4 metres, is likely to come in at around €15,000. This price excludes the cost of heating. Even if you buy a property with an existing pool you will need to consider the costs involved in its upkeep and maintenance. A regular, rectangular pool is far easier to maintain than a freeform pool in the shape of a kidney or whatever, will be cheaper to build, and depending on the size will be better for actually swimming rather than 'lounging'. It will also be easier to find a pool cover to fit a rectangular pool.

There are several popular means of building a pool in Spain: using reinforced concrete, block construction; or an excavated hole, which is plastered and then PVC lined. The differences in design are reflected in a difference in cost. The cheapest option is to install an above ground, prefabricated pool. Obviously a pool needs a regular supply of clean water and this is something that you will need to plan for. Pools need regular maintenance and if you are buying to let, or only using a property for irregular holidays, you will need someone to take care of the pool.

The depth of pools in Spain is mostly around 1.4 metres – around shoulder height – and they are usually finished with either blue or green tiles, or the cheaper cement-based 'Grecite'. Filters, chlorine and heat pumps are expensive.

Sanitizing the Water. There are many ways to sanitize pool water. Chlorine is by far and away the most popular and the risk of overdosing or under-dosing is now greatly reduced by the use of automatic computerised dosing equipment. Other, non-chemical, forms of sanitation include ozone, ultra-violet light and ionisation. There are advantages and disadvantages to all of these systems but all of them require a chlorine backup to cover the possibility of a sudden contamination of the tank of pool water. When used in conjunction with a non-chemical system, however, chlorine levels can be reduced. Sanitizing pools once a week with chlorine will prevent water-born viruses and bacteria.

To keep a swimming pool in good condition, i.e. clean, warm and pure, it is necessary to remove the total body of water from the pool several times a day, pass it through filters and sanitize it by one means or another. Filters remove the dirt, drowned wasps, crumbs etc., from the water, while a sanitizer kills any bacteria that may lurk. In a skimmer or freeboard pool, the water is removed through floor sumps and skimmers located at water level (to remove surface floating matter). The water is then passed through filters by means of circulating pumps and is then sanitized (and, if there is the equipment, heated) before returning to the pool via return water inlets located in the walls or floor. The time required for all the pool water to pass through the filters etc. is called the 'pool turnover' time. In the case of a domestic pool a turnover time of 6-8 hours is quite sufficient, because usage is generally very low.

Because electricity in Spain is relatively expensive (and about three times the price of gas or oil) should you want to heat your swimming pool it may be an option to go for a heater that is fired by gas or oil or, even better, through solar panelling. If you do decide on solar panelling you will need to consider stainless steel for most of the installation, as swimming pool water and copper don't react too well.

A swimming pool cover can also effectively cut a pool's running costs by about 50%. Check out several quotes before going with a particular pool construction company. Your pool should have at least a five-year guarantee.

DIY

For basics such as nuts and bolts and screws, wire, nails, etc., the local *ferretería* (hardware store/ironmongers') is going to be a useful resource, and you will find shops that specialise in electrics and others specialising in plumbing. Additionally, on the outskirts of towns and cities are large industrial estates where you will find workshops and wholesalers who will often be in the building trade. There are also DIY superstores such as *Akí* and *Leroy Merlin* which sell all the kit that you will need to knock up anything from a garden shed to a villa with pool.

For projects that need a professional touch plumbers (*fontaneros*), carpenters (*carpinteros*), bricklayers (albañiles) etc., will be listed in the local yellow pages (*las páginas amarillas*) or found through talking to neighbours. As with when choosing builders the best way to find tradesmen is by recommendation. If you live in a rural area there may only be a few specialists around and you might need to tread carefully when choosing the one to carry out work on your property. If you live in a more urban environment then it won't hurt to get several quotes on a job before hiring.

If you are intent on carrying out much of the electrical, plumbing and brickwork on your renovation or building project yourself it is as well to remember that in Spain individual, sheathed cables for Live, Neutral and Earth, run through plastic conduit are used, rather than the standard 'twin and earth' that electricians use in the UK. House wiring for sockets is done on radial circuits, not ring circuits as in the UK. And it isn't unheard of for the authorities inspecting property to condemn new wiring installations based upon ring circuits. Remember to fit Spanish two-pin sockets (which will be all you will be able to buy in Spain anyway). Doing otherwise may seem a good idea so that you can run your electrical equipment from the UK, but will be a minus point if and when you decide to sell. Spanish plumbing uses similar sizes to those in the UK (i.e. 15, 18 and 22mm) and the water in properties is often heated by an immersion heater, which is invariably unvented and wall mounted, with a two-kilowatt element. Spanish homes also use 'Valient' style boilers powered by bottled gas; rarely do they have cylinders unless they are headed by solar panels. The heating of houses tends to vary throughout the country but in southern Spain it tends to be electric, as it is rarely needed. New builds in the north of Spain where it does get chilly in the winter is often under-floor electric or radiators.

Spanish houses in the south tend not to use much, if any, guttering, basically because it rarely rains. However, when it does rain it pours and therefore it is a good idea to make sure that you incorporate a roof that has a good size overhang from the walls. This will stop any rain from running down the walls. Any major work carried out on external walls should be done using good quality ceramic blocks. Although these are a lot more expensive than solid concrete blocks they offer good thermal insulation. Solid concrete blocks let the heat in during summer and out during the winter. Remember that Spanish houses are built with solid walls, i.e. no cavity to provide the necessary insulation. And if you are redesigning an older property you will want to look into increasing the insulation qualities of the property.

Making Money From Your Property

CHAPTER SUMMARY

- **Licences**. Anyone intending to set up their own business must apply to the local town hall for a business licence (*licencia de apertura*).
  - If you plan to practise your own trade or profession in Spain you will have to become a member of the appropriate professional association in Spain.
- Letting property is often a good way of accruing income on an investment, or simply helping to repay the monthly mortgage.
- Placing an advert in supermarkets, marinas and golf clubs and even in shop windows back home is a cheap or even free form of advertising your property and can often bring in clients.
- **Location.** The amount of rental income that can be expected from a property will depend to a large degree on the property concerned.
  - Many golf courses in Spain are surrounded by residential developments; although villas or apartments on these are expensive to buy they can provide a healthy return on your investment.
- **Rental Contracts**. It is standard practice when letting out any property to charge prospective tenants rent in advance for their stay and to ask for a deposit against possible damage.
  - In Spain there are two types of rental contract: short-term, known as *alquiler de temporada*; and long-term known as *alquiler de vivienda*.
  - If a tenant fails to fulfil any of his obligations, the landlord has the right to begin eviction proceedings.

In the first instance the tenant should be notified in writing.

- Non-residents renting out property are liable for income tax at the rate of 25% from rental income.
- **Management Agencies.** Agencies offer a comprehensive range of services including cleaning, maintenance, and payment of utility bills.
  - Agents' Commission varies but most charge around 15% of the gross rental.
- There is a thriving market for resale properties in Spain and the procedure may be carried out privately or by engaging the services of a registered property agent.

RUNNING A BUSINESS FROM YOUR PROPERTY

Anyone intending to set up their own business must first of all follow a few basic but essential procedures. Depending on your level of fluency in Spanish you may find the services of a *gestor* invaluable when going about the bureaucratic procedures involved. You will need to apply to the local town hall for a business licence (*licencia de apertura*), which will be granted once the authorities are sure that the premises are suitable for the proposed business, that they comply with planning permission and are safe and hygienic. If you are going to employ staff you will be required by law to have at least one Spaniard on the staff, and comply with Spanish labour laws in connection with minimum wages, social security payments etc. It is possible to register as a self-employed person (*autonomo*) if running a one-person operation. In this case, it is necessary to pay a monthly contribution to the social security system (health plus pension). You will have to register with the Spanish Social Security Service for income tax and IVA (VAT) and you will require an NIE (tax identification number). You should also register with the Spanish National Health Service.

If you plan to practise your own trade or profession in Spain, whether you are a doctor or an accountant, a lawyer or a qualified electrician, you will have to become a member of the appropriate professional association and to have the right, agreed qualifications. Your own trade or professional association at home will be able to give you advice about whom to contact in such circumstances, and local business advice centres, as well as Euro Advisers in your local job centre, can provide the relevant leaflet.

Since 17 April 1991 there has been a mutual recognition of professional qualifications of citizens of EU member states. Around 200 professions and trades are included in the terms of the EU directive, which effectively allows the free movement within the European Union of professionals from a wide range of occupations. Fully qualified members of a profession or trade in an EU member state are entitled to membership of the equivalent profession in Spain without having to requalify. For more information on the equivalence of qualification in the EU you can contact the *National Academic Recognition Information Centre*, (ECCTIS Ltd, Oriel House, Oriel Road, Cheltenham, Glos GL50 1XP; ☎ 01242-260 010; fax 01242-258 611; www.naric.org.uk).

The EU directive has, however, incorporated some safeguards into the ruling allowing the regulating authorities to require the individual in question to undertake an adaptation period or to take an aptitude test. Some professions such as teaching may be difficult to enter in Spain, where teachers are considered to be civil servants working for the state; and where the individual's professional qualification period is shorter than that in the host country, evidence of professional experience can be required.

Despite the implementation of the directive throughout the EU, UK nationals moving to Spain with the intention of continuing in their own profession may encounter some animosity from the equivalent professional body. This will largely be the result of an understandable lack of enthusiasm on the part of the Spanish body to admit foreign competition within its ranks. However, with the law on your side, any such attitudes should not prove to be a deterrent to enthusiasm and determination. Some of the main professional bodies in Spain are listed here.

Professional Bodies in Spain.

Architects: Consejo Superior de los Colegios de Arquitectos de España, Paseo de la Castellana 12, 28046 Madrid; ☎ 914 352 200; www.cscae.com.

Commercial Agents: Consejo General de Colegios de Agentes Comerciales de España, Goya 55, 28001 Madrid; ☎ 914 363 650; fax 915 770 084; www.cgac.es.

Estate Agents: Consejo General de los Colegios Oficiales de Agentes de la Propiedad Inmobiliaria, Gran Vía 66, 2a Planta, 28013 Madrid; ☎ 915 470 741; www.consejocoapis.org.

Lawyers: Consejo General de la Abogacía España, C/Paseo de Recoletos, 13, 28004 Madrid; ☎ 915 232 593; www.cgae.es.

Pharmacists: Consejo General de Colegios Oficiales de Farmacéuticos de España, Villanueva 11, Planta 6, 28001 Madrid; ☎ 914 312 560; www.cof.es.

RENTING OUT PROPERTY

Letting property is often a good way of accruing income on an investment, or simply helping to repay the monthly mortgage. Buying to let is a boom area at the moment with many people buying properties to rent. When renting out your property it is advisable to, as one estate agent has put it, 'lock away the emotion and look at the maximum return available'. The requirements of the rental and residence markets are very different and it is worth remembering if you intend to buy in the north of Spain that the holiday rental period really only runs between July and August. Hotter weather in the south means of course that the season can extend into spring and autumn – and even through the winter – so the potential income you may earn from property there is much higher.

Because of the amount of property out there looking for short-term tenants, there is a lot of competition in the rental market, with hundreds of companies renting out villas and offering a similar service. A good head for business and the right choice of property will be of great importance if you want to make money from your property in Spain. Word-of-mouth may bring some custom (let neighbours, local shop owners and businesses know that you have property to let), as will advertising or asking friendly shop owners to advertise your holiday home in the window of their premises. Placing an advert in supermarkets, marinas and golf clubs and even in shop windows back home is a cheap or even free form of advertising your property and can often bring in clients. Many properties are now advertised for rent on the Internet, and placing ads in local and national newspapers is another option. If you can design your own page, or hire someone to do so, sign up with as many Internet sites as possible, get regional sites to provide Internet links to your home page, and register with search engines. Dependent on the budget available include the location, size and price of the property and talk up the main selling points. Local estate agents may keep properties for rent on their books and it will be a good idea to register with those that do, as well placing an advert in the local yellow pages. The more time and energy you spend on advertising, the more people will be aware of what you have to offer.

The amount of rental income that can be expected from a property will depend to a large degree on the property concerned. Buying a property in a pleasant, out-of-the-way location will often have an advantage over many other properties for those looking to rent on a long-term basis. Villas, especially those with pools, attract well-heeled families, and can often command rents in excess of £1,000 per week at the height of the summer season depending on location. If you are buying specifically to rent you should find out about neighbouring properties and their letting potential if you can. For holiday rentals, a good position within sight and sound of the sea will also obviously be an advantage. Seafront apartments also generally have easy access to shops and leisure facilities which is an added attractive for prospective tenants. If your property is in a major tourist area – the Costa del Sol, the Balearic Islands, Tenerife, the Costa Blanca, etc., then demand is likely to be high. Demand is likely to be much lower for properties in some of the lesser known resorts, or tucked away inland. Grouped houses or apartments in low-rise complexes also tend to do better than individual villas; and there are very high occupancy rates in places like Alicante during the summer where there is a rising demand for long-term leases and quality residences to rent.

Many golf courses in Spain are surrounded by residential developments, which can provide a healthy return on your investment although villas or apartments on these are expensive to buy. Golfers flock to Spain to improve their handicap on these courses, especially during the northern European winter. In addition, the golfing fraternity tend to be fairly well off and will pay a good price for the convenience of staying in course-side properties rather than having to travel too far to a course. For those looking to rent property out as an investment only, and not looking to make use of the property themselves, buying an apartment in one of the larger cities, especially Madrid and Barcelona, though expensive, will guarantee a regular source of tenants.

It is standard practice when letting out any property to charge prospective tenants rent in advance for their stay and to ask for a deposit against possible damage. Telephone and electricity bills can often cause friction between tenant and landlord and it may be as well to remove or lock the phone, or install a payphone while renting out property and to include electricity, water and gas charges – whether this be for two weeks, two months, or longer – in the advance payment to avoid misunderstandings later on. To avoid disputes, it is also a good idea to make a fairly exhaustive inventory of the contents of the property, including a description of their condition. Before you sign a contract, make sure that the details on the inventory correspond exactly with what is in the property at the time. If something is missing, broken or not as stated on the inventory you should agree with the tenant to change the inventory. At the end of the lease, check the inventory and, if items are missing or broken, you have the right to use the deposit (*fianza*) to replace or repair. For short-term rentals the price charged should also include cleaning and linen provision.

A landlord is entitled to evict a tenant for the following reasons: failure to pay rent (although courts have a frustrating – for landlords – habit of ruling that the arrears must exceed six months before any action can be taken); wilful damage to a property; the use of a property for immoral purposes; sub-letting of a property where no such provision has been made in the contract, and for causing a social nuisance to neighbours. As non-payment of rent can be as much as six months in arrears before a court will rule in the landlord's favour, an efficient approach to managing your property will be your best protection; and the legal approach only a last (and often unsatisfactory) resort.

Apart from advertising for tenants for your property in the local newspapers, it is also worth contacting local letting agencies if they exist, but be sure to check their credentials. Make sure that you are dealing with people who are competent and whom you can trust. All too often you can find that extra fees and charges from the agency begin to mount up, or that maintenance of the property is not attended to properly in your absence. Additionally, some estate agents dealing in Spanish property will arrange lets for Spanish property in the areas in which they specialise (and advertise in expatriate newspapers and elsewhere). Remember that VAT (at 16%) for short-term lets, and income tax, will have to be paid on earnings from rental.

It is a legal requirement for those letting out property on short-term lets to be registered with the tourist authorities. Subject to the property being deemed suitable for letting by the tourist authorities you will be issued with a permit. Although many owners are not registered there are fines imposed for non-registration.

RENTAL CONTRACTS

In Spain there are two types of rental contract: short-term, known as *alquiler de temporada*; and long-term known as *alquiler de vivienda*. A short-term contract covers any period under a year, long-term covers tenancies of least five years. Both types of contract are strictly binding for both parties and before you sign any contract as a landlord you should carefully check all the clauses; better still have the contract checked by a lawyer. Pre-printed contracts can be bought from tobacconists (*estancos*) and kiosks. A contract will include the tenant's details (name, address and passport or residence card number), the landlord's details, information about the property (location, size, furnishings, fittings etc.), the terms of the lease and information relating to payment and expenses.

If you decide to hand over the running of your property to a management company (which if you are not resident in Spain may be a good idea), take a copy of the contract between yourself and the management company to a lawyer and have it checked for legality before you sign anything.

Also ask your lawyer to check the rental contract between the tenant and management company that the company will sign on your behalf. If possible, ask that the management company asks for rent to be paid in advance and that they always collect a deposit before a tenant moves in to the property. If you intend to still use the property occasionally for holidays etc, make sure that the management company is aware of this as soon in advance as possible.

Short-term Rentals

Rental returns on short-term holiday lets are high and this kind of contract is probably the best option for foreign property owners since your property can be available for personal use during the year and it is likely to be less difficult to evict problematic tenants. However, it may also mean that during the low season your property will remain empty and you are receiving no income from it.

> Short-term lets require a lot of management time spent on them, as tenants may be coming and going every week or fortnight, especially during the high season. Obviously, if you are resident in Spain and live near the property then this may not cause much of a problem and the cheapest option will be to manage the property yourself. You will need to be on hand to clean the property before new visitors arrive, welcome the visitors and hand over the keys, troubleshoot and provide information about the area such as where to hire a car, find a bank, the best bars, restaurants, beaches, leisure parks etc. If you also have other work or run other businesses then managing your own rental business on top of this may become onerous.

Bookings for short-term rentals tend to vary according to the season and the highest rates, both of booking and rents are during the months of July and August. Some owners often also charge peak rates at Christmas and Easter. If you decide to let your property through a management company then they will be able to tell you what the going rates are. If not, you can always check adverts in the local newspapers or ask other landlords.

Bear in mind that short-term rentals usually mean a lot of wear and tear on fittings and furnishings, and items will have to be replaced on a regular basis. Because short-term tenants are very often on holiday and in a holiday spirit they will probably take less care of the property than a long-term tenant would, so don't furnish your property with anything valuable or irreplaceable. However, this statement may be qualified if you are looking to attract very wealthy tenants with sumptuous décor.

Long-term Rentals

Tenancies lasting from a couple of months to a year or more will bring in a lower rent than those on a short-term tenancy agreement, but tenants holding them are normally responsible for paying their own utility bills, cleaning costs etc. Most management companies ask long-term tenants for two months' rent as a returnable deposit plus one month's rent in advance and if you are renting privately you would do well to ask for the same.

Long-term rentals, regardless of what the contract may state, are for a minimum period of five years. Even if the contract states that the rental period is for one year, a tenant is well within their rights to renew the tenancy annually for up to five years. Spanish legislation regarding rentals still tends to favour the tenant rather than the landlord and should you need to evict a tenant you are likely to find the process a lengthy one. If a tenant doesn't give the landlord one month's notice before the end of the year, the contract continues. A tenant must inform the landlord in advance, in writing, at least a month before vacating the property.

Recovering a property before the five-year term is up can be problematical. You will need to prove that you own no other properties in the same locality and that you require the property for yourself, for your children or for your work purposes. In practice, it is fairly unusual for a landlord to recover a property from a long-term tenant before the five-year period is up unless, of course, the tenant doesn't pay the rent.

> Long-term rentals are really only a good idea if you are not looking to make personal use of your property for several years at least. Think very carefully before going into long-term lets and seek legal advice before committing yourself. Ready-printed rental contracts can be bought from tobacconists (*estancos*). Make sure you understand all the clauses in the rental agreement, have the contract checked by a lawyer, and ensure that you are totally happy with any contract you sign with a tenant. Any contract should state who is responsible for the payment of rates, the property tax (IBI) and community charges (imposed by the *comunidad de propietarios*). Usual practice is for the landlord to pay the rates and for the tenant to pay the community charges. Long-term tenants should pay utility bills.

Tenants are expected to pay the rent on time, maintain the property in a good state of repair and may not sublet the property without the permission of the landlord or use the premises for immoral purposes. Failure to fulfil any of these obligations can lead to eviction. As a landlord you will have the right to inspect the property at any time providing you inform the tenant in good time of your proposed visit. Inspect your property every few months to check the general state of repair. The landlord is also obliged to carry out any necessary repair work and general maintenance to the property, and replace any fixtures and fittings that have broken or worn out through general wear and tear. Additional obligations may also be included in the rental contract. Failure to comply with your obligations as a landlord could lead to a tenant demanding compensation.

EVICTION, COURT ORDERS AND THE TENANT'S RIGHTS

If a tenant fails to fulfil any of his obligations, the landlord has the right to begin eviction proceedings. In the first instance the tenant should be notified in writing. If this has no affect the landlord will need to consult a lawyer and start legal proceedings. Note that many courts may rule that arrears in rental payments should be over six months late before action may be taken. A tenant may agree to leave after receiving a letter from the landlord's lawyer or a tenant will wait until a court order arrives. Once the court has ordered an eviction, the landlord will have to wait for a court official to carry out the eviction. The process of eviction can be very slow and could take several months to reach its inevitable conclusion, therefore the sooner you start legal action should the worst come to the worst, the sooner the eviction will take place.

It is important to be aware that tenants have a certain amount of rights after signing a rental agreement:

- A tenant has the right to pass on the tenancy to a spouse or child.
- If a landlord puts a property up for sale and does not offer the tenant the opportunity to buy then the tenant has the right to annul the sale of the property.
- Should the landlord decided to sell the property a tenant has the right to buy the property if he or she can match (or improve upon) the offer of another interested party. There will be no obligation to sell to a tenant if they offer a lower bid than another party.

TAXES

It is perfectly legal for owners of private houses, villas or flats to rent out their property without paying any advance taxes or making any business declarations. However, owners are liable for Spanish income tax if the yearly income from the rent exceeds a certain sum (€7,800), as this is then regarded as taxable income arising in Spain. For more information about this and other tax matters you can contact one of the Spanish consulates or the local tax office (*hacienda*) when in Spain. You can also write to the *Ministerio de Hacienda* about tax matters (c/ Alcalá 9, 28014 Madrid; ☎901

335 533); or from Spain to the *Direccion General de Tributos* (c/ Alcalá 5, 28014 Madrid; ☎915 221 000).

Although the non-taxable limit, or threshold, for earned income is similar to that in Britain, this limit is much less when the income originates from investments or real estate and will depend also on whether you are resident in Spain. Non-residents renting out property are liable for income tax at the rate of 25% from the very first euro of rental income. Even if a tenant pays you rent in a non-euro currency in a bank account outside Spain, legally this income arises in Spain because the property itself is situated there. Although many owners undoubtedly do let their property out on the quiet taking this risk is really not recommended; and it is advisable to keep records of all income generated through renting.

Anyone intending to make it a full-time business letting property, who provides hotel-type services such as Bed & Breakfast, or deals with a lot of visitors on a short-term basis is moving away into a whole new area with regards to the tax situation. Such activities will be deemed to be a business; and therefore all income received will need to be declared, with 25% of the rent set aside as a witholding tax paid to the Spanish government; and an extra 16% VAT (IVA) added to the rent, which must be paid to the Spanish Finance Ministry. This tax is declared on Form 210, available from *haciendas*. The positive side of declaring new business status is that maintenance expenses from rental income can be deducted before tax is calculated.

PROPERTY MANAGEMENT COMPANIES

Spanish-based rental and property management agencies abound along the Spanish *costas* and many estate agents will also offer some kind of property management service. Agencies offer a comprehensive range of services – cleaning, maintenance, and payment of utility bills. Management companies may also advertise your property and find and vet tenants for you, but there may be an extra charge for this. Monthly statements are often forwarded on to non-resident owners detailing the income and expenditure pertaining to a property. Rental income may be deposited in the owner's Spanish bank account, sent to owners wherever they may be, or held for collection.

If you are buying solely to let, rather than buying for your own holiday or permanent use, then it is a good idea to contact property management agencies to get an idea of the areas in Spain where there is most need for holiday properties. Obviously, the *costas*, the Canaries and the Balearics require rental properties but within these large areas there will be some parts more heavily touristed than others. What about the northern coasts where property is cheaper but tourist traffic less dense? Sounding out management companies is always a good idea.

Choosing a Management Company.

If you don't know an area well then choosing a management company can be difficult. Visit several agencies and ask for a complete breakdown of their services and charges. Look at how much they charge per month to act on your behalf (there is usually a monthly charge regardless of whether there are any tenants in your property), what commission they charge on rentals and what penalties there are if you decide to terminate your contract with them. Find out their charges for cleaning the property (the going rate is around €7 an hour) and for laundry service.

Additionally, ask for their references, a copy of the contract you would sign with them should you decide to use their services and if possible ask to speak to other customers that they have on there books. Visit a few management agencies and compare services and prices carefully. Another option is to ask the locals for recommendations. All these precautions may smack of paranoia, but you will want to be sure that you have left your valuable property in the care of a trustworthy company, especially if you are a non resident.

Agents' commission varies but most charge around 15% of the gross rental. Any repairs, cleaning and maintenance costs incurred by the agent will be billed to you and listed on your monthly statement. Management companies are likely to have contacts with the local council, banks and other offices and know about Spanish bureaucracy, which will be to your advantage.

SERVICES OFFERED BY MANAGEMENT AGENCIES

- Paying all routine bills – electricity, water, community charges, insurance, local rates etc., from their own bank account, billing you at the end of each month.
- Monitoring your local bank account every month and converting your Spanish bank statements to UK-style bank statements, which you will be sent every month.
- Looking after the general maintenance of the property: routine and emergency, painting, plumbing, etc.
- Pool cleaning.
- Gardening – routine or one-off service.
- Security.
- All year round supervision of property.

- Spring-cleaning and laundry service.
- Providing maid service during holiday-let tenancies.
- Welcoming holiday-let tenants.
- Being on hand to offer tenants advice, or in case of emergencies.
- Finding and vetting tenants for your property.

Useful Addresses

AWS Realty: Urb. Carolina Park, Edificio Aries No 37, Crta. de Cádiz, km 178,5 Marbella, 29600, Málaga; ☎ 952 827 705; www.aws-realty.com. Rental and maintenance management, bill paying services on the Costa del Sol.

Calida Management: ☎ 650 811 841 (Spain); 01273-305 415 (UK); email celabd@aol.co.uk. Property management agency for Costa Blanca South, Mar Menor and La Manga.

Home Iberia: Unit 1, St. Peter's Road, Maidenhead, Berks S16 7QU; ☎ 01628 631 999; fax 01628 638 666; www.homeiberia.com. English property management company dealing with properties on the Costa Blanca and the Costa del Sol.

Menorca Home Care: Apartado 524, 07700 Mahón, Menorca; tel/fax 971 377 090; www.menorcahomecare.com.

SELLING ON

There is a thriving market for resale properties in Spain and the procedure is quite simple. It may be carried out privately or by engaging the services of a registered property agent who deals with all matters including advertising the property, accompanying prospective buyers and dealing with the legal technicalities of the sale (contracts, signing before the notary, paying necessary taxes on the property etc.). This ensures the smooth progress of the sale and relieves the client of much of the usual worry and concern relating to the sale of a property. As was the case when you bought the property, the vendor (you in this case) does not necessarily need to hire a lawyer, though the purchaser should. Make sure that if you have paid the *plus valia* tax on the property when you bought it, it is paid by the purchaser when you come to sell, otherwise you will have paid the tax twice.

Note that Capital Gains Tax is charged on the profit from the sale of property and depending on how long you have owned a property before selling on, this tax could be as high as 35% for non-residents and 18% for residents, though there are exceptions to the rules (see the Finance chapter). It is better to hang on to a property as Capital Gains Tax lessens the longer you own a property, and your property will increase in value the longer you own it. If you can afford to it is often better to hold on to property and rent it out, rather than go for a quick sale, for example a villa bought on the Costa del Sol for £200,000 in 1997 would now be worth around £450,000 in 2003, which is far above rates of inflation.

You can advertise your property for sale through several estate agencies, and negotiate your own contract with them individually – commission rates charged vary. If you bought the property though local estate agents it could be useful to ask them to deal with the vending process as they will know the property and you and, having had dealings with them in the past, you will know them.

As always when planning to sell a home, presentation is the key to the process. A lick of paint here and there, the replacement of old or faded interior decorations and fixtures and fittings will create the best impression and move the home faster than if it is put on the market without being spruced up. Price, of course is also important, and if you ask for too much, then the property will be difficult to shift. However, if the property is individual enough, or the location spectacular then it is only a matter of waiting for the right customer to come along. Your cast-offs could be another's dream.

There are a number of documents that you will need to gather together when it comes to selling on your property. These are:

- The *escritura*: You will have received a copy of the title deeds to your property after the original was filed with the *Registro de la Propiedad* (the property registry office) by the notary when you originally bought the property. This details any charges, mortgages etc. that there are listed as being against the property.
- Receipt of payment of the *Impuesto sobre Bienes Inmeubles – IBI*: This indicates that the Real Estate Tax has been paid on the property to date and that the property is registered with the local authorities for taxes. The IBI receipt will also show the *valor catastral* – the value of the property as assessed by the local authorities (though this may well be lower than the market rate).
- The *Referencia Catastral*: This is the file number of the property as kept by the *Catastro* (Land Registry). The Catastro has a record of the physical characteristics of the property – boundaries, size of plot, outhouses, pools, etc.
- Copies of all utility bills – preferably going back over a period of five to give the purchaser an idea of what to expect bills-wise.
- Copies of any community charges imposed by the *comunidad de propietarios* should your property be part of an *urbanización* or

apartment block – preferably going back over a period of five to give the purchaser an idea of what to expect bills-wise.

- Copies of the transfer tax, stamp duty and *plus valia* tax that you paid on the property when you originally bought it.
- Declaration of income tax: Depending on whether you are resident or non-resident in Spain your tax liabilities through the sale of property will differ. If you are a non-resident the purchaser will retain a 5% tax deposit from the purchase price and pay it on your behalf to the tax authorities. If you are a resident you will want to make sure that your tax status is known by the notary and purchaser.

Personal Case Histories

LINDY WALSH

Lindy and her husband Bill were approaching fifty. Free of debt, they were bored with their jobs and their children had left home. Bill also had a bad back and wanted to escape the English winters. They had inherited a house in London and worked out that with the income from the rental of the London house, plus working during the summer months in the UK, they could afford about six months a year living in a small house abroad that they would gradually renovate themselves (having had experience of such a project in the UK). They were planning to look for a property in Italy, Portugal, Spain or southern France. In the Autumn of 1987 they explored France and Spain, discovered Almería and found 'The House'. This was a massive *cortijo* with 250 acres of land and it was for sale for far more than they were looking to pay. However, with the sale of the London house they were able to afford the *cortijo* and moved to Spain permanently in the autumn of 1988.

What type of property do you have – new, old, villa, flat, etc., and with hindsight would you now change the choice that you made of the type of property you bought?

The house, the equivalent of a manor house in the UK, was abandoned and falling into ruin. There was another, larger and even more ruinous farmhouse 100 metres or so up the hill. We decided to convert this into youth hostel type accommodation for 40 people. The manor house (*cortijo*) was finally completed at the end of 2002 (12 years after we first bought the property). If I had known how long a project it would be I would never have begun it, though now it is completed I love the house and wouldn't change a thing, except perhaps the standard of workmanship.

What were the factors that influenced you on your choice of location?

Location! We didn't want to be on the coast in an English ghetto. We needed minimal support from other English speakers while we learned Spanish. We loved the scenery; we liked the attitude of the Spanish locals towards us. There were a few (very few) English and Dutch living nearby whom we could call on. The property is ten minutes drive from the town, which has a police station, a petrol station and mechanic, a 24-hour health centre, a bank and shops. It covers our basic needs.

How traumatic or otherwise is dealing with bureaucracy in Spain? Did you use the services of a *gestor*?

We used an *abogado* for the purchase, but it was still fairly traumatic as he was a city lawyer (there weren't any local *gestors* who spoke English) and didn't know much about laws affecting property such as ours and what licences we needed. For example we got 'denounced' [the Spanish word is *denuncia* and refers to being reported to the police by a neighbour for – generally – a minor infraction such as having a dog that barks all night long, or putting up an unsightly satellite dish that 'lowers the tone' of a neighbourhood, etc] to the river police for having a well dug without their permission. We'd got four licences (local town hall, local ministry of the environment, mines, water authority) and he didn't know that within half a kilometre of a dried up riverbed we needed another permit too. He got the hunting laws wrong which led to lots of trouble and he didn't bother to find out about the Andalucian Tourist laws, which affected us greatly, telling us we only had to keep inside the building regulations. For nearly ten years our business was 'illegal' and I am still unable to develop certain aspects that we had planned for back in 1988 and which he had told us would be 'no problem'.

How traumatic or otherwise was the process of moving your life to Spain – getting things shipped over, getting settled in etc.?

Moving our lives to Spain wasn't traumatic at all. It was exciting and lots of fun. We started out camping in a ruin with rats, and I didn't like that, but we quickly made at least one rat-proof room. We shipped our stuff very gradually over 12 years, using family and friends to bring over a bit at a time as we had space for it. Some things we had crated up in 1988 intending to bring over 'one day' got irrelevant as time passed and got given away or just abandoned.

How have you found dealing with local builders and other tradesmen? Have you found them trying and unreliable, much the same as back home, or better on the whole?

Local builders: Our first builder was excellent. He retired before we'd finished phase one. Our second builder was good himself, but most of his team were poor. I've had a problem with a drain for NINE years because it was put in without the correct 'fall'. My third builder was a criminal who may or may not have been any good as a builder but took my 25% deposit and vanished. My fourth builder was a very poor builder with a very poor team. My fifth builder is a good builder and totally reliable. Most other (Spanish) tradesmen: electricians, plumbers, carpenters, decorators etc., seem very reliable in their standard of work as well as actually turning up to work when they should. Most British tradesmen in this area seem no better and most, I gather, are working illegally.

What do you miss about 'home' – if anything? What are the best things about living in Spain?

After 14 years 'home' is here in Spain. I don't miss anything at all about England but still have a few friends I'd like to see more often than I actually do. I don't pretend to know about Spain. I know why I love my little bit of it. Firstly, because it has the most beautiful scenery of anywhere I've ever been and secondly, because the people here are so friendly. Let's be honest the climate is pretty good, but that's a definite third in importance.

What advice would you give first time buyers?

Buying 'inland' is totally different from buying on the coast. Buying rural is as different again from buying inside a town or village boundary. Don't take anything for granted. I know awful cases of people buying land with water running through it, but not being allowed to use one drop; of buying land with trees and finding out too late that they hadn't bought the trees (or their harvest); of buying a 'house' (it looked like a house) and finding that it was registered as a chicken shed and not able to be registered as habitable because it didn't conform to the newest building standards. Check and check again and don't part with any money until you have a copy of a registered *escritura* that has been looked over by a local (but perhaps not too local as he may be the vendor's brother) *gestor* or *abogado*. Better a local *gestor* who doesn't speak English, and pay the extra to a translator, than an English speaker who doesn't know the area.

I would also advise a potential first time buyer to spend the extra money and take the extra time to visit the chosen area for at least a week in the height of summer and the depth of winter. Find out if the water supply goes down to two or three hours a day in temperatures in the high 30s when even at night it's too hot to sleep without artificial cooling. Find out if your area floods – it may only flood every few years but then leave you totally marooned for a couple of days. How cold does it get at night in February? Who are your neighbours, and are they permanent residents? It isn't only foreigners who have second homes. Are you assuming you'll be able to get mains water and electricity (I waited nine years for electricity) and if they are already connected how reliable is the supply? I know someone who bought a house with a barn, which he intended to use as a workshop. He found out too late that he could only get half a kilowatt of power – not enough for a fridge or a TV as well as lighting; and forget the welding equipment!

Perhaps the most important consideration of all for anyone considering buying an old property in the interior to 'do up' is: What are you going to do when it is done? It's not just a question of money, but how to pass the days. On the coast the expats either have a business (usually a bar or shop catering to other expats) or they take to golf and/or alcohol. Inland what? We have a desperate shortage of genuinely skilled, legally registered, plumbers and electricians. A good one will find work with the native Spaniards as well as any Brits etc. No one wants anymore the 'turn my hand to most things', unqualified, unregistered jack-of-all-trades. If I employed one of these, my nosey Spanish neighbours would know at once and they would be perfectly justified in reporting me to the authorities. Then I, as well as the employee, would be fined.

I know several people who bought property out here expecting to be able to scratch an income in one way or another, and who have finished up going back to Britain for months at a time to earn enough money to return. It's what my husband and I expected we'd have to do, knowing we'd got skills that would ensure us work back there. But there are people out here who left Britain because they couldn't get decent jobs there and hoped to work here. Quite honestly, not a hope!

J. STUART ANDERSON

Stuart Anderson lived in Cumbria for 33 years. After retirement he became far more aware of and affected by the often inclement weather. The high rainfall made him feel imprisoned in his house when all he wanted to do was enjoy a walk with his dogs out on the Pennine Fells. Walking in the rain was no fun. He began taking classes in Spanish with a view to travelling in South America and started visiting Spain (Catalunya and Andalucía) for holidays – using charter flights offered by the cheap no frills airlines. Once in Spain he travelled around by public transport 'off the beaten track', meeting locals and working to become fluent in Castillian Spanish. In February 1999, he and a friend travelled to Spain by car with a view to finding a permanent home there. They spent three weeks searching for 'the ideal location' and managed to find both the location and the house. They moved permanently to Spain six months later in August 1999.

What type of property do you have – new, old, villa, flat etc., and with

hindsight would you now change the choice that you made of the type of property you bought?

The house is of concrete and stone construction built in 1984 and resembles a mountain chalet. It has an expansive south-facing porch, which serves as a living room for six months of the year. There is a large terraced garden. With hindsight the only other kind of house we would have purchased would have been an older house, slightly larger and even more isolated that the house that we own now. However, these houses very often need a good deal of restoration work, which can mean expense. Also, in many cases the water supply can be inadequate. We are perfectly happy with our choice, although sometime in the future when 'old age' begins to tell, we might need to find another place less isolated.

What were the factors that influenced you on your choice of location?

First and foremost, the climate. Whilst still in the UK I obtained, via the Internet, climatic details of all the regions of Spain and soon reached the conclusion that Catalunya offered the best climate for me. Other factors were access to airports (for the occasional trip 'back home' and also for visitors), mountains, proximity to a village community, and also to not be too distant from the coast, which, apart from July and August, can be very pleasant for day trips. Good maps proved their worth in finding this place 'from a distance'.

How traumatic or otherwise is dealing with bureaucracy in Spain? Did you use the services of a *gestor*?

To try and cope with all the bureaucracy on one's own in a foreign country is never worth it. With the purchase of the house, which was a private deal with the previous owners (i.e. no estate agents involved), we sought out an English-speaking *abogada* (using the helpful services of the local Colegio de Abogadas). Her work was thorough and she made all the necessary arrangements right through to the completion of signing in the presence of the *notario* and the processing of the *escrituras* (which duly arrived some three months later). For other purposes we have used a *gestor*, again extremely valuable and well worth a little extra expense. He led us through the steps required for obtaining residencia permits; arranging car insurance; private health insurance; property and contents insurance; and kindly reminding me before my 62nd birthday that I needed to arrange a medical test for myself in order to update my driving licence. A good *gestor* is worth his weight in gold and we found ours by recommendation.

How traumatic or otherwise was the process of moving your life to

Spain – getting things shipped over, getting settled in etc.?

The move to Spain was well planned and ran smoothly. Thanks to friends who volunteered to drive the furniture van here in a self-drive hired van (the largest that one can drive with an ordinary UK driving licence) from Cumbria to Portsmouth and then via the St. Malo ferry, through France and finally here, a journey of three days. Simultaneously, our two cars and three dogs travelled via the Channel Tunnel. We met up at Angoulême and travelled the rest of the journey in convoy. I booked overnight accommodation in advance, staying at inexpensive 'Premiere Classe' hotels in France where dogs were made quite welcome.

Settling-in was fairly traumatic as everything was new and the previous owners had left, taking all the lights with them! It was also August when many shops are closed for the month. However, by October, and after some hard work, all was up and running.

How have you found dealing with local builders and other tradesmen? Have you found them trying and unreliable, much the same as back home, or better on the whole?

As in the UK standards vary. After three years we know which firms are dependable. Before we were known here the *facturas* (invoices) were presented within days. Now, quite the reverse!

What do you miss about 'home' – if anything? What are the best things about living in Spain?

Nothing is really missed, apart from the closer proximity of friends and family. The best thing about living in Spain is the sense of freedom and the fact that nobody appears the least bit interested in social status – former jobs, the school you attended, the number/kind of cars you own, etc. A breath of fresh air!

What advice would you give first time buyers?

Firstly, and most important: learn Spanish to a reasonable degree of fluency before even venturing on the housing front. Otherwise you will be beholden to other people who have the linguistic skills – and perhaps forever dependent. Being able to converse with the local people pays great dividends and establishes new friends.

- Beware of visitors. True friends are great and to be valued. Once you move here, however, everyone finds you, particularly 'freeloaders' who are always keen to have a free holiday. Visitors can be like fish – they tend to go off after three days!
- Beware of the black economy when buying property [under declaring

the value of the property on the *escritura*]. Whilst it might be to your advantage when buying, it will be the reverse when selling.

- Once living here on a permanent basis, it is essential to make a Spanish will. Again, we employed an *abogada* who, after our last wishes were made known, drew up the final document and accompanied us to the *notario* for the reading, signature and deposit.
- Beware of British/German estate agents.
- There are plenty of free newspapers with property advertisements. They are published weekly and readily available.

INDEX

Vacation Work Publications

	Paperback	Hardback
Summer Jobs Abroad	£9.99	£15.95
Summer Jobs in Britain	£9.99	£15.95
Supplement to Summer Jobs Britain and Abroad *published in May*	£6.00	-
Work Your Way Around the World	£12.95	-
Taking a Gap Year	£11.95	-
Taking a Career Break	£11.95	-
Working in Tourism – The UK, Europe & Beyond	£11.95	-
Kibbutz Volunteer	£10.99	-
Working on Yachts and Superyachts	£10.99	-
Working on Cruise Ships	£10.99	-
Teaching English Abroad	£12.95	-
The Au Pair & Nanny's Guide to Working Abroad	£12.95	-
The Good Cook's Guide to Working Worldwide	£11.95	-
Working in Ski Resorts – Europe & North America	£11.95	-
Working with Animals – The UK, Europe & Worldwide	£11.95	-
Live & Work Abroad – A Guide for Modern Nomads	£11.95	-
Working with the Environment	£11.95	-
The Directory of Jobs & Careers Abroad	£12.95	-
The International Directory of Voluntary Work	£11.95	-
Buying a House in France	£11.95	-
Buying a House in Spain	£11.95	-
Buying a House in Italy	£11.95	-
Live & Work in Australia & New Zealand	£10.99	-
Live & Work in Belgium, The Netherlands & Luxembourg	£10.99	-
Live & Work in France	£10.99	-
Live & Work in Germany	£10.99	-
Live & Work in Italy	£10.99	-
Live & Work in Japan	£10.99	-
Live & Work in Russia & Eastern Europe	£10.99	-
Live & Work in Saudi & the Gulf	£10.99	-
Live & Work in Scandinavia	£10.99	-
Live & Work in Scotland	£10.99	-
Live &Work in Spain & Portugal	£10.99	-
Live & Work in the USA & Canada	£10.99	-
Drive USA	£10.99	-
Hand Made in Britain – The Visitors Guide	£10.99	-
Scottish Islands – The Western Isles	£12.95	-
Scottish Islands – Orkney & Shetland	£11.95	-
The Panamericana: On the Road through Mexico and Central America	£12.95	-
Travellers Survival Kit Australia & New Zealand	£11.95	-
Travellers Survival Kit Cuba	£10.99	-
Travellers Survival Kit Lebanon	£10.99	-
Travellers Survival Kit Madagascar, Mayotte & Comoros	£10.99	-
Travellers Survival Kit Mauritius, Seychelles & Réunion	£10.99	-
Travellers Survival Kit Mozambique	£10.99	-
Travellers Survival Kit Oman & The Arabian Gulf	£11.95	-
Travellers Survival Kit South America	£15.95	-
Travellers Survival Kit Sri Lanka	£10.99	-

Distributors of:

	Paperback	Hardback
Summer Jobs in the USA	£10.99	-
Internships	£19.99	-
World Volunteers	£10.99	-
Green Volunteers	£10.99	-
Archaeo-Volunteers	£10.99	-

Vacation Work Publications, 9 Park End Street, Oxford OX1 1HJ
Tel 01865-241978 Fax 01865-790885

Visit us online for more information on our unrivalled range of titles for work, travel and gap years, readers' feedback and regular updates:

www.vacationwork.co.uk

MS